Fundamentals of Successful Newsletters

EVERYTHING YOU NEED TO WRITE, DESIGN AND PUBLISH
MORE EFFECTIVE NEWSLETTERS

Fundamentals of Successful Newsletters

EVERYTHING YOU NEED TO WRITE, DESIGN AND PUBLISH MORE EFFECTIVE NEWSLETTERS

Thomas H. Bivins

University of Oregon

Printed on recyclable paper

NTC Business Books

NTC a division of *NTC Publishing Group* • Lincolnwood, Illinois USA

Bivins, Thomas.
    Fundamentals of successful newsletters : how to write, design and
publish more effective newsletters / Thomas H. Bivins.
        p. cm.
    Includes index.
        1. Newsletters--Publishing.   I. Title.
Z286.N46B58   1991
070.1'75--dc20   91-23013
                                                                 CIP

1994 Printing

Published by NTC Business Books, a division of NTC Publishing Group
4255 West Touhy Avenue
Lincolnwood (Chicago), Illinois 60646-1975, U.S.A.

    4 5 6 7 8 9 0 VP 9 8 7 6 5 4

Contents

Foreword

The majority of journalists and public relations professionals still consider their work to be a form of mass communication—communication to a heterogeneous mass of people—even though mass communication seldom takes place today. Audiences, issues, and interests all have become specialized. Newsletters, therefore, have become a primary medium of communication in our segmented society.

As a teacher both of public relations and science communication, I am aware especially of the value of newsletters. Specialized newsletters have become the primary medium for much communication about science, health, and technology—both commercial newsletters and newsletters produced by the public relations departments of organizations dealing with these issues. In the broader field of public relations, newsletters provide a channel for communication with employees, stockholders, donors, volunteers, consumers and users of services, community residents, activists, and many other strategic constituencies that support or affect an organization.

With desktop publishing, newsletters also have become a flexible medium that can be customized for each public. Desktop publishing also makes the newsletter a feasible publication for volunteer organizations as well as more formalized ones.

In his introduction to this new book, Tom Bivins points out that he would liked to have had a book on newsletters when he edited one. I echo that sentiment. I also would have liked to have had a book on newsletters to help teach students and to recommend to professionals who have taken on the editorship of a newsletter without any formal training. *Fundamentals of Successful Newsletters* fills this gap admirably. It provides the technical fundamentals of writing, designing, and laying out newsletters. It also describes how to use the principles of management by objectives, segmentation of audiences, research, and evaluation to decide whether a newsletter is an appropriate vehicle for communicating with a public, to identify what messages to put in the newsletter, and to determine if the newsletter achieves the editor's communication objectives.

Fundamentals of Successful Newsletters, therefore, is a book that fits the needs of professional communicators in the 1990s. It will help them become more effective *public communicators*, professionals who are replacing the now obsolete *mass communicators* of only a few years ago.

James E. Grunig
Professor of Journalism
University of Maryland
College Park

Introduction

Producing a newsletter is among the most rewarding and the most frustrating of all editorial experiences. The one-person nature of the job has both advantages and disadvantages, and a number of pitfalls for the unwary.

This book is dedicated to all those who have fallen into the role of newsletter editor/designer/writer/lay-out artist/distributor. Although some are published by small editorial staffs, it's probably not an exaggeration to say that most newsletters are one-person operations. They are put together from scratch by one lonely individual, slaving away, often without recognition. It can be a rewarding, although frequently frustrating, job—or it can be a nightmare. The choice is usually yours and usually depends on whether you look at it as a chore or a challenge.

Newsletters are a particular love of mine—mostly *because* they allow me to take on so many creative tasks at once. In other words, the newsletter is one of those rare projects on which you get to work without supervision (or meddling) from others. It is really your baby and lives or dies because of you. And because it is typically a one-person operation, there is no one else to blame for your mistakes.

This places a responsibility on you to pool all your available skills, develop a few others, and learn to beg for those you either don't have or can't learn. And that's what this book is all about.

I have designed this book using a management-by-objectives (MBO) approach. I have found this method of organization among the best I have ever used. It allows you to set goals and objectives, and then measure everything you do by referring back to them. Newsletter publishing on a regular basis can be a logistical labyrinth. MBO helps you get organized and stay organized.

In addition to the traditional techniques for producing a newsletter as explained here, I have included healthy doses of desktop publishing methods. I have found that nearly everyone I know is either practicing desktop publishing or trying desperately to learn it. I have been using it almost exclusively to produce dozens of different publications for more than six years. In fact, this book has been written, designed, and laid out completely on a desktop publishing system. Even the artwork, for the most part, was created on computer.

Yet, despite the advances in technology, nothing substitutes for a basic understanding of design, writing, editing, and layout. A computer is merely another tool. In the hands of the inexperienced or careless user, it will only serve to magnify shortcomings. But in the hands of a practiced, professional editor, a computer becomes the ultimate helpmate—one that will gain for your newsletter the respect it deserves.

I've tried to pull together everything I have learned through 20 years of producing newsletters in order that you might gain from that experience. I wish I'd had a book on newsletters when I first began. It would have saved me countless hours of frustration and a good deal of embarrassment.

As a teacher, nothing is quite as humbling as to turn up a newsletter you produced 15 years ago, only to realize that my students are *already* doing a better job in class than I did for a living. That's part of what teaching is all about—preventing others from encountering the kinds of problems that you had to cope with on your own. I hope this book helps you in the same way.

Before You Start: A Glossary of Terms

Before you begin working on your newsletter, there are some very basic terms you have to become familiar with. These are standard publishing terms and are useful not only for newsletter production, but also for working on magazines, newspapers, and a number of other print formats.

- **Alley**. The space between columns. A one-pica space is traditional; however, width depends on a number of factors, such as the decision to justify text or not, size of text type, and width of columns.

- **Banner**. This is the name of your newsletter. It is as often called a *nameplate* as a banner, so don't be confused. In this book I call the subhead information beneath the banner the nameplate. Banners are normally designed— not just typeset—and the best ones show a definite artistic flair.

- **Deck head**. An introductory line of text run below a headline, usually italicized and run in a larger size than the body copy that follows. Often a rule separates a deck head from the body copy of the article it precedes.

- **Folio**. The page numbers. The front page of a newsletter is usually unnumbered.

- **Gutter**. The space between the pages of a two-page spread. It is usually, but not always, twice the width of the outside margins.

- **Headline**. A primary head is usually reserved for the cover story and any other articles of close-to-equal importance inside. Secondary heads are reserved for articles of less than front-page importance. Of course, headlines can be typeset in an almost infinite variety of sizes, weights, and widths—each imparting a slightly different emphasis.

- **Indicia**. Postage-paid franking for bulk mailing.

- **Jump line**. A brief statement that a story is continued on another page or continued from another page.

- **Kicker**. An introductory line run above a headline, usually italic and underlined.

- **Mailer**. The portion of newsletter reserved for the mailing label, return address, and indicia or stamp.

- **Masthead**. Publication information usually containing the name of the publication, publisher and editor, editorial statement, and the address.

- **Nameplate.** The subhead beneath a banner indicating who the newsletter is published for.

- **Pull quote**. Sometimes called a *blurb*, a pull quote is a section of copy taken out of an article, enlarged or set in a different type, and inserted back into your article. Pull quotes are used for emphasis and attention-getting or simply to take up space when articles run short.

- **Rule**. A solid line used to separate editorial matter. Rules can be used either vertically or horizontally, and in various thicknesses.

- **Sidebar**. A block of copy, often boxed, that gives a unique or different perspective on the feature article it accompanies.

- **Table of contents**. This appears on the front page and may or may not include page numbers. In most cases, it is a stylistic device, since newsletters are usually too short to need a detailed table of contents.

On the following page, you will find a sample layout with these terms illustrated.

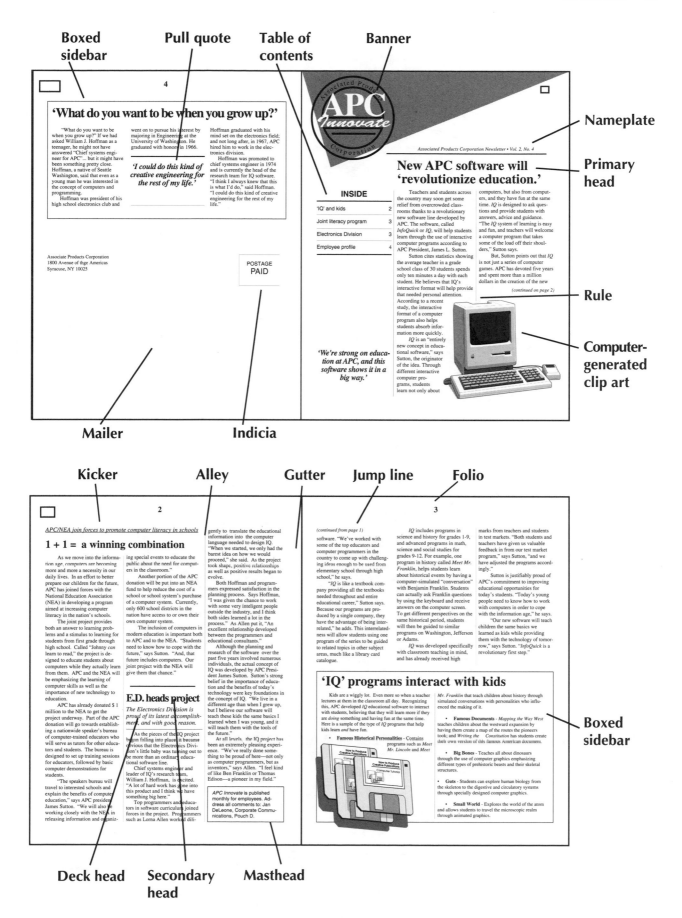

What Is a Newsletter?

The newsletter is one of the most versatile of all print media. However, planning for its production takes more than just a good idea. It requires an organized approach based on audience-centered objectives that govern every step of the process.

Every day in the United States thousands of newsletters are published and distributed to hundreds of thousands of readers. It is estimated that some 50,000 corporate newsletters alone are published each year. Most newsletters are internal publications in the sense that they reach a highly unified public—employees, shareholders, members, volunteers, voting constituencies, and others with a common interest. In fact, if you ask any experienced communications professional for the most effective means of reaching a primarily internal audience, the response will most likely be the newsletter.

The newsletter is probably the most versatile of all print media. It can be a daily digest of events and news of interest distributed as photocopies to a small, in-house constituency, a weekly flyer distributed to customers or patrons, a monthly compendium of news about the organization it serves distributed through interoffice mail or special non-profit bulk mail to members and volunteers, a quarterly journal outlining industry news to busy executives, or literally anything between or beyond these categories.

The newsletter's versatility and popularity stem from two sources—the relative ease with which it can be produced and its ability to be targeted easily to either a small or large audience. Ease of design and layout derive from its standard format, an 8½" x 11" page. Its targetability stems from its relatively small print run and the timeliness and relevance of its contents.

With the advent of desktop publishing, the newsletter has become even more popular, since it can now be produced with even more ease. Desktop publishing gives the editor of a newsletter more control than ever before—control over content, design, typesetting, layout, and, to a certain degree, printing. It remains to be seen, however, whether this increased control will benefit all equally or will result in a proliferation of unfocused and thus unread newsletters.

A newsletter, then, can be said to be any typically small-format, print publication that purports to deliver timely news and information to a limited target audience in a fairly perishable format, quickly, inexpensively, and with little effort. The name *newsletter* comes from its earliest format—a single-page news digest delivered to a limited audience in a rather informal, almost personal letter style.

The Newsletter Defined by Purpose

Newsletters are as varied as the audiences who read them; however, defining a newsletter by purpose is one of the easiest methods for determining the nature of the publication. Newsletters defined by purpose break down into two primary categories, each based on the *demographic* distribution of the reading audience. The reason why your target audience is reading your newsletter is based on common interest, a *psychographic* consideration, and is assumed. Newsletters break down broadly into four categories.

- **Constituency newsletters.** This is the broadest of the categories in that it covers any newsletter published to reach a special-interest audience for the purposes of keeping in touch. Examples of newsletters in this category might be a healthcare newsletter sent out by a local hospital, an update newsletter from an elected official to his or her voting constituency, an association newsletter sent out to members, a social service agency newsletter to members, volunteers, donors and potential donors, and university or college newsletters sent out to alumni. Clearly, there are many other examples, but what they all have in common is a need to communicate with a common-interest group in order to foster a sense of community.

• **Employee or member newsletters.** This is probably the second most common type of newsletter. As the name implies, it is usually distributed among employees or members and any other constituency considered to be primarily an internal audience, including shareholders, retirees, and the families of these primary audiences. This type of newsletter is used by both profit and non-profit organizations and is designed to give readers a feeling of belonging. Newsletters in this category frequently include a balanced mix of employee- or member-related information and news about the organization.

• **For-profit newsletters.** This type of newsletter often creates its own audience by appealing to a rather small special-interest group. Newsletters in this category are developed to make a profit for the publisher. The individuals or groups who develop them typically offer advice or present solutions to problems held in common by their target readers. These often come in the form of a sort of "digest" of topics of interest to a certain profession. This category also includes newsletters produced by marketing departments as public relations or sales activities. In addition, many attorneys and physicians use this type of newsletter as client-building tools. Literally thousands of these newsletters exist covering almost every occupation and industry.

• **Advocacy newsletters.** These newsletters are usually produced in addition to other types of newsletters already being published by an organization, but the focus is extremely narrow.

Audiences are targeted by their importance to the issue being examined by the newsletter. For example, a newsletter advocating recycling might be targeted to legislators, business executives, environmental groups, association executives, and other opinion leaders for whom this topic is of concern. Advocacy newsletters usually make no bones about being biased; however, they often use a fairly balanced approach in discussing an issue while, at the same time, presenting a definite point of view.

Naturally, there will be overlap among these categories and their target publics. One newsletter may accomplish the goals of several of these categories. For example, a special issue of an employee newsletter might be distributed more broadly to community opinion leaders in order to advance a company-wide position. There is no reason why a newsletter shouldn't occasionally attempt to kill more than one bird with a single stone.

The Newsletter Defined by Distribution

Newsletters that are distributed *within* an organization are usually considered **vertical** publications because they are intended for everyone from the mailroom clerk to the CEO. This may also apply to newsletters produced to reach any constituency in which the audience is distributed up and down the readership scale. That is, the readers are likely to range in terms of demographic descriptors, such as age, education, income, gender, etc. This implies a broad presentation of writing and design styles in order that the newsletter include something for each of the demographic groupings. The typical presentation of such a newsletter is based on a demographic *mean* rather than an *average*. For example, to make the newsletter accessible by all readers, the use of language might be based on the midpoint readability level of the audience.

Newsletters that are distributed to a more narrowly defined group with a common interest are called **horizontal** publications. Industry-specific newsletters, professional newsletters, or certain hobbyist newsletters, for example, can be considered horizontal publications. A horizontal publication assumes certain average demographic characteristics, such as age, income, education, etc. Editorial and design styles are set according to an average rather

than a mean. For example, since demographic characteristics will be similar, the reading level should reflect the average readability level of the group.

Exhibit 1.1

(Clockwise from top left) A constituency newsletter targeted to community users of a health-care facility (Sacred Heart General Hospital); a for-profit newsletter targeted to those interested in the wood-products industry (Random Lengths, Inc.); an employee newsletter for a single division within a larger corporation (Weyerheauser Corporation); an advocacy newsletter dealing with a single issue (Dow Chemical Company).

The Newsletter Defined by Format

Format plays an equally important part in defining a newsletter. Format, like function, should be suited to the purpose of the newsletter. Here, again, the versatility of the newsletter as a communication tool allows incredible flexibility.

For our discussion, format refers loosely to two elements—size, and cover design. The most commonly used format size for newsletters is the 8½" x 11" page. This is usually accomplished in an 11" x 17" original, folded in half, thus giving you a four-page newsletter. Additional pages can be added in increments of two or four. If an extra page is needed, a loose insert or an attached page in an 11" x 25½" format folded twice can be used. Pages are 8½" x 11", usually stapled. (See **Exhibit 1.2**.)

Part of the confusion of defining a newsletter by format alone has to do with the other, more non-traditional size options. Many newsletters come in hybrid formats, borrowing either from newspaper or magazine formats. For example, newsletters of more than eight pages become almost magazine-like in length. The key difference between the two has to do with the cover design. By definition, a newsletter, like its cousin the newspaper, has a self-contained cover, usually of the same paper as the interior pages. A self-contained cover implies that the articles begin on the cover, usually immediately beneath the banner or nameplate. So, regardless of length, a publication with a self-contained cover could rightly be called a newsletter.

Another standard size for newsletters is the tabloid format—11" x 17", laid out vertically. The tabloid-format newsletter is much more difficult to distinguish from the tabloid newspaper than the magazine-format newsletter is from the magazine. Both tabloid newsletters and tabloid newspapers have similar cover characteristics, that is, banners followed by articles. The key difference, in many but not all cases, may be the use of *magazine-style layout* versus *newspaper-style layout* elements.

For example, while most tabloid newspapers follow a strict newspaper style, tabloid newsletters may use many magazine-style elements, such as pull-quotes, deck heads, large graphics, a lot of white space, unjustified text columns, and uneven bottom column margins. These design elements will be discussed in more detail in a later chapter.

The key point to remember here is that no matter what format you elect to use for your newsletter, it will still be a newsletter if *you* call it a newsletter. In other words, its function is decided by you.

Exhibit 1.2

A one-page addition (printed both sides) can be inserted as a loose page into a standard four-page newsletter; however, many of these loose pages fall out or become lost during distribution or reading. If you opt for an attached page as part of a two-fold format, the last page should fold inward.

The Newsletter Defined by Frequency

A final element of definition is frequency of publication. A newsletter is generally published on a regular basis because its content is highly perishable—that is, it is timely information not usually of interest after a certain date. Choosing a newsletter as a communication medium implies that you have information that will regularly need to reach your target audience in a timely fashion and that does not usually need to be saved.

Because of this, newsletters are generally published weekly, monthly, or quarterly. The frequency of publication doesn't necessarily determine length. For instance, a monthly newsletter may not be any longer than a weekly. You may have decided to publish monthly or quarterly because you simply don't have enough information to warrant publishing weekly. On the other hand, weekly publication normally implies a shorter format. Daily publication is rare; however, some single-page, flyer-type newsletters are published daily in the form of news notes or memo-type announcements.

Whatever frequency you choose, remember that the primary reason for a newsletter is to keep in touch with your constituency. Publish on a basis frequent enough to accomplish this goal. Too infrequent, and you might lose your audience. Too frequent and you run the risk of inundating your audience with trivia.

A Management-by-Objectives Approach to Newsletter Publishing

There are basically three reasons for a publication to be produced: entertainment, information, or persuasion. For most newsletters, the last two are the most important. Entertainment should be used sparingly, usually as a method of winning the readers' attention so that you can better inform or persuade them. What you ultimately say in your newsletter depends to a great extent on the purpose to which the publication is to be put. But, before you even put pen to paper (or text to screen), you have to begin the whole process from an organizational perspective. This means planning.

Almost all writing goes through, or should go through, several stages before it reaches completion. Before you start writing, you have to develop a plan by which your message will ultimately reach its intended audience and accomplish its intended purpose.

One of the most useful techniques for planning a publication is *management by objectives* (MBO). MBO is a method of organization that allows you to set objectives in advance for your publication and provides you with the criteria you need to measure its effectiveness all along the way. MBO requires that you think before you act. It forces you to consider why you are producing a newsletter, who your target audiences are, what you hope to achieve by communicating with them, exactly what you should say to them, and how you should measure the effectiveness of your presentation.

An MBO approach to publication includes four stages or processes—research, planning, implementation, and evaluation.

Research: Asking the Right Questions

MBO requires research, both before and following your activity—in this case, the development of a newsletter. Any communication has to compete with thousands of other messages for attention. Research has shown that each of us is subjected to thousands of informational messages a day, ranging from interpersonal conversations to billboards, radio, television, and newspapers. What we don't need (what doesn't fit into our current information seeking framework), we reject automatically by simply tuning it out. Researchers call this unwanted information, *noise.* The best way to insure that your communication will not become noise— that is, that it will reach its intended audience with the least amount of resistance—is to target very carefully. And the best way to target is through a thorough understanding of who you are speaking to. This requires research.

The steps of the research process include:

- Asking yourself whether a newsletter is the proper medium for your message,
- Defining target audiences,
- Defining a goal,
- Setting objectives and evaluative techniques to insure that your messages do what you intend them to,
- Developing an editorial statement.

Planning: Making the Right Choices

Once you have set the direction of your newsletter, the next step is to plan the details of your publication. The planning process includes:

- Determining quality,
- Determining format,
- Determining frequency,
- Budgeting for production,
- Developing a message strategy,
- Selecting content,
- Deciding on a design,
- Selecting an effective name.

Implementation: Doing the Right Things

Once planning is complete—really complete—you can begin to produce your newsletter. A word of warning: Don't begin to work on your newsletter without sufficient planning. The result will invariably be a misdirected effort and the results will be less than you had hoped for. The implementation stage includes:

- Gathering information for stories,
- Writing the stories,
- Editing the stories,
- Writing headlines,
- Arranging for or taking photographs,
- Obtaining any additional artwork,
- Copyfitting stories,
- Typesetting stories,
- Having any pre-press work done (such as photo halftones),
- Pasting up a camera-ready mechanical,
- Printing the newsletter,
- Distributing the newsletter.

Evaluation: Keeping It on the Right Track

Your work is not over once your first issue is in the hands of your readers. You must now research the effectiveness of your publication. Did it accomplish what you had hoped? This is where the evaluative techniques you set up when establishing your objectives come into play. Without measuring the effectiveness of your newsletter, you will never know whether you are really reaching your intended target audience. Nor will you know if your readers understand or act on your messages. The evaluation process includes:

- Testing your messages in advance of distribution,
- Evaluating the messages during and following the program.

Without a planned approach to publishing a newsletter, results will be minimal or nonexistent—and results are what it's all about. No one publishes a newsletter without some goal in mind, whether it's to make money, inform employees, keep in touch with a scattered constituency, or persuade a selected audience of a certain point of view. A management-by-objectives approach to planning your publication will formalize the process through which your goals and the needs of your readers can be fully realized.

The chapters that follow will lead you through each of the steps itemized here. Remember, no MBO plan is complete until you have covered each of the steps in the proper order. Leaving out any step may jeopardize your chances of a successful publication.

Research

Without research, a publication may look good and even read well. However, a newsletter not carefully researched will seldom reach its intended audience with the kind of information they want, nor will it get you the kind of results you want.

Research is the most vital component of modern communications. Without it, you will never know where you are going, how to get there, or even if you have arrived. Research implies thinking, and often can be accomplished solely by doing just that. Don't get the mistaken idea that research means having to hire a marketing firm to do random-sample surveys in order to determine how your proposed target audience feels about you. You may already know, or you may be able to find out by simply asking a few questions yourself. The problem with many communicators is that they don't think before they speak or write. If you want your communication to reach the right audience, at the right time, with just the right message, you had better give the process some thought.

Why a Newsletter?

The first step is to decide whether you actually need a newsletter or not. Newsletters address an audience with a common interest—usually either an internal audience or special-interest groups, such as professionals and executives outside a formal organizational structure. But why a newsletter instead of a magazine, booklets, bulletin boards, or—heaven forbid—more meetings? There are several questions you can ask yourself when deciding whether a newsletter is the publication that best suits your purpose.

- What *is* the purpose of the publication? Is it to entertain? Inform? Solicit? This will be important later when you set your goals and objectives.

- What is the nature and scope of the information you wish to present? Longer information is probably better suited to a longer publication such as a magazine; shorter, to brochures or folders. If your information is strictly entertainment or human interest, it may also be better received within a magazine format.

- Who, exactly, are you trying to reach? For instance, with a corporate newsletter, are you speaking to all members of the organization from the top down, or only a select few— executives, engineers, secretaries?

- How often do you need to publish in order to realize the aims or objectives you set in answering the previous questions? Newsletters are best suited to situations requiring a short editorial and design lead time.

Keep in mind that newsletters are best for small print runs and information that needs a quick turnover. They handle information that is considered necessary but disposable (much like a newspaper, which in a sense the newsletter mimics). However, this is *generally*, but not *universally* true. Many fine newsletters are designed to be kept. Health and financial newsletters, for instance, are often hole-punched so that the reader can save them in ring binders. For the most part, though, newsletters are considered disposable.

Once you have decided that a newsletter is the proper vehicle for your communication, you must approach the development of your publication with a clarity of purpose, specific goals, and achievable results in mind.

Defining the Target Audience

Imagine holding a complex conversation with someone you don't know at all. If you are trying to persuade that person towards your point of view, you will have a better chance if you know his or her predispositions in advance. The same holds true for written communication. In order to write for an audience, you have to know that audience intimately.

In the world of modern communications research, a number of methods of identifying target audiences have been suggested. In their simplest forms, they allow you to categorize audiences by whether they know about or need your information. These methods of categorization allow a newsletter publisher to gauge what type of information to provide an audience and are applicable to both informational and persuasive messages. Among the most useful for our purposes are the following.

Defining Audiences by Level of Awareness

What newsletter editors and publishers normally refer to as *audiences* are called by various names, depending on who's doing the talking. Marketing and advertising people typically refer to them as *markets*. Public relations people call them *publics*. The terms are fairly interchangeable and shouldn't confuse you if you are forewarned.

In 1927, John Dewey proposed that people coalesce into groups (or—as he referred to them—publics) based on whether or not they were affected by a situation, recognized that they were affected by it, and organized to do something about it.[1] This definition limited a target audience only to those who fit all three of Dewey's criteria.

More recently, researcher James Grunig took Dewey's definition and expanded on it. Grunig, through years of surveying various corporate publics, found that, for most issues, target groups typically fall into three categories.

- **Latent public**. A group of people who are affected by an issue but don't know it yet.

- **Aware public.** A group of people who are affected by an issue and recognize that it exists.

- **Active public**. A group of people, who, recognizing that they are affected by an issue, organize to do something about it.[2]

For anyone trying to identify and respond to a target audience's need for information, these categories provide a general starting point. The question is, what do these categories mean to you as a newsletter editor/publisher?

First, if part of your audience is latent—that is, they don't know anything about your newsletter or the issues it covers, yet they are affected by these issues, and you want them to become subscribers—you will have to inform them. This implies that you will have to reach these people with a pitch that, at once, reveals the issues, shows them how the issues relate to them, and convinces them that your newsletter can help them deal with these issues.

If part of your target audience is aware—that is, they know these issues exist and that they are affected by them, but haven't decided yet if they should or can do anything about them—not only will you have to inform them, you will also have to persuade them to your point of view. This means that the information you provide will have to be in addition to what they already know. These readers will want details beyond a mere description of the basic issues your newsletter deals with.

Finally, if part of your target audience is active—they have already formed opinions on these issues, either pro or con, and are actively engaged in or considering action—you will need to supply them with even more detailed information, based on your point of view, in order to bring them to your way of thinking or to support their position if they already agree with you.

Latent audiences are the easiest to inform and to persuade since you may be the first to reach them with a message. Aware audiences may be on the verge of forming opinions and your information may be what decides them. Active audiences, depending on which side of an issue they are on, may simply need to be maintained as allies or persuaded of your point of view. Most publishers won't waste newsletters on those not already at least partially allied to their cause.

This doesn't mean that all newsletters have vital issues that polarize audiences to one side or the other. However, most newsletters do have a point of view. For example, employee publications obviously state the company position and assume that their employees will support that position. It may be true, however, that some employees aren't even aware of certain issues affecting the company, and, by association, them. These constitute a latent audience that needs to be informed. Other employees may be aware of the issues affecting your company and need further information to solidify their opinions on your side. Still others may be active on behalf of your position and need to be maintained as allies; while others may have been swayed by counter arguments and need to be won over again.

Defining Audiences by Level of Interest

Grunig, expanding even more on his definition of audiences by level of awareness, also suggested that how you craft your message (both in your writing and the way you package or design it) depends on whether your target audience is seeking the information or simply processing it as part of the normal informational clutter we are all subjected to daily. He suggested, again based on years of thorough research, that most people either seek out information based on their current interests or they simply process information as it comes to them—randomly, taking what appeals to them and discarding the rest. This kind of "junk mail" approach implies that if the message (or the way it's packaged) doesn't catch your eye immediately, it gets thrown away.[3]

Grunig calls the first group *information seekers*. These are members of your proposed target audience who are aware, or even active, in relation to the issues or topics you typically cover in your newsletter and who are interested in reading about them. Obviously, these readers will *actively* look for your information and won't be hard sells.

Information processors, on the other hand, will typically be audiences in the latent stage. These people may not be aware of an issue or topic, or realize its importance to them. Information processors will simply process information randomly as it comes to them, ignoring that which doesn't fit with anything they are currently interested in. In order to attract these potential readers, you must first make them aware that your information is of importance to them.

This lesson, only formalized recently by communications researchers, actually has its roots in common sense. It is best expressed through the old joke about a farmer trying to sell a plow mule. The farmer claimed that the mule would go straight ahead, turn left and right, and back up on command. However, when the prospective buyer asked for a demonstration, the farmer responded by smacking the mule in the head with a large piece of wood. Alarmed, the buyer asked why the farmer had to hit the mule. "Oh, he'll do what you want him too, all right," replied the farmer, "but, you have to get his attention first."

Knowing that a particular audience is seeking your information will allow you to spend less effort in attracting their attention. Many newsletters targeted to information-seeking audiences are fairly plain in presentation (one-color, typed rather than typeset, quick printed rather than offset printed, etc.). The publishers of these newsletters know that, for this audience, it's the information that counts, not the packaging.

If, however, you are trying to attract a broader audience—one that is now only processing information on your topic—you will first need to attract their attention. Before you can even begin to make an audience aware of the importance of an issue, you need to get them interested. In other words, you have to smack them in the head.

Defining Audiences by the Order in Which They Are Addressed

One of the easiest ways to define target audiences is by deciding which you want to receive your message first, which second, and so on. The focus of your message and presentation will thus be based on this order. The simplest method is to group your target audiences as primary, secondary and tertiary; however, there are other versions of this approach that take into account additional audiences who can aid you in getting your information to your primary audience.

For example, let's assume you are working on a newsletter designed specifically to support a drug and alcohol anti-abuse campaign. Clearly, the people you would most like to reach are the abusers. They would become your *primary* audience. A primary audience is the group to whom you ultimately target your message. This is the group you wish to affect in some way through your information. However, this doesn't mean you will automatically target them. Let's suppose that your research has shown this is the audience *least likely* to be listening. Directing your message to them would be a waste of time.

One option is to reach those others who have some control over abusers, or to whom abusers might look for advice. These might be relatives, clergy, counselors, peers, etc. They would be classified as a *moderating* audience. A moderating audience is a group that is usually related in some way to your primary audience. They might share the same position on issues and topics of interest, or belong to the same social groups, or simply be someone your primary audience admires or wants to emulate. Since this group can take your information, translate it into action or terms more palatable to your primary audience, you might decide to target them first.

Using any of these methods for defining your audiences forces you to think in nonstandard terms about who you are trying to reach, and the best method of reaching them. The value of doing so is that you may find that the most obvious audience for your newsletter isn't really the most appropriate.

In summary, these methods of categorizing audiences force you to ask *why* people need or want your information, or even if they are aware of their need. Once you have taken this kind of broad look at your potential readership, it is time to develop a clear reader profile.

Developing a Reader Profile

Knowing *exactly* for whom you are writing is probably the most important factor in setting message strategy. The success of your writing will be determined, to a great extent, on how well you've aimed your message. The best way to write is to write for an imagined reader, an individual to whom you are speaking directly. In order to understand this individual, you need to know him or her intimately. To do this, you will have to develop a *profile* of this "typical" reader. And this means gathering information in three categories: demographics, psychographics, and geographics.

Demographics

Demographic information is easily quantifiable, such as information on age, gender, income, education, etc. All of these characteristics say something general about your audience and imply levels of commonality. For example, your readers may all be in the 25–40 age group with average incomes of $25,000 a year, evenly split between male and female, and with college degrees. Implications for your newsletter might include the level of language style you choose or the balance of articles addressed to

men or women. Demographics help you to develop a cross-section of your target audience.

Psychographics

Psychographic information is that which tells you something about a target audience's attitudinal and behavior patterns. For example, a psychographic survey may indicate that most of your readers regularly attend conferences, or feel strongly about tax reform, or use certain media for entertainment and others for information. Psychographic information tells you *why* readers do what they do and believe what they believe. You can use this information to plan editorial content, to decide whether to advocate a certain point of view, to plan future stories on tax reform or to include a regular column on conference schedules.

Geographics

Geographic information tells you where your readers are and is one of the simplest types of information to gather. It may not be important for an employee publication distributed in-house, but it may be crucial to a national publication whose readership is scattered all over the country with large concentrations in certain areas. Knowing where your reading audience lives will tell you what language or dialect they are familiar with. (For example, in the east, soft drinks are called sodas, while in the west, they are pops.) Knowing where your readers are may alert you to regional issues of concern to large portions of your reading audience. While demographic and psychographic information is almost always necessary, geographic information is either important to you or it's not.

Collecting Audience Information

There are a number of methods for collecting information on your target audiences, ranging from fairly expensive formal research to secondary research gathered from such sources as the library or your own organization.

Many newsletter editors are put off by the notion of having to gather hard-core information about their readers. Unfortunately, many a newsletter has totally missed its audience because it was not built around this information.

If you can't afford the luxury of a formal survey, try gathering demographic information from other departments within your own organization. For example, if your organization has a marketing department and your publication is external, you might be able to extract some solid audience demographics from existing marketing research. And, don't discount the value of a visit to the library. Government documents such as the *American Statistics Index* (*ASI*) can be invaluable sources. *ASI* is a compendium of statistical material including the US Census and hundreds of periodicals that can be obtained directly from the sponsoring agencies or, often, from the library itself. *ASI* also publishes an alphabetical index arranged by subject, name, category, and title. Other sources of market information include the Simmons Market Research Bureau's annual *Study of Media and Markets*. This publication includes information on audiences for over a hundred magazines, with readership delineated by demographic and psychographic characteristics. When using secondary research such as this, be aware that you will find much information that is not directly applicable to your target audience. You not only have to know where to look, but you also have to know how to decipher what you read and apply it to your needs.

Finally, you can always ask members of your target audience in person. Don't discount the value of talking directly to them. If you are producing an employee publication, talk to a few employees to ascertain their attitudes about the company. Try a focus group, for instance. This is a marketing technique that has been used successfully for years. For example, magazine publishers regularly use this approach to test the market for new publications. All you need is a set of questions you need answered and a person who knows how to ask them properly, how to lead the respondents through the process of talking openly, and how to analyze the answers. You normally don't need more than eight to ten people in a focus group as long as they're a true representative sample of your larger audience.

Focus group surveys are inexpensive to conduct (marketers usually pay their respondents a small fee for their time), and informal enough to be comfortable for everyone concerned. This type of information may be all you need to get you going.

Using Audience Information

Once you have gathered the information you need to construct a profile, you should have answered the questions listed on the worksheet in **Exhibit 2.1**.

Once you have completed the worksheet, you should have a pretty good idea of who you are writing

for and whether they are going to be receptive to your newsletter. Remember, without an audience profile constructed through careful research, you will be talking to strangers—and they may not be listening.

Defining the Goal of Your Newsletter

As we have seen, using management by objectives means developing an overall goal for your newsletter. A goal can be expressed in general terms and doesn't always need to be specific. In fact, a goal merely suggests a destination, while objectives explain how you are going to get there. Like most everything else that has to do with planning your newsletter, your goal should be audience centered. In other words, a goal should describe what your readers will be getting out of your newsletter, not just what your newsletter will contain.

An example of a goal for an employee newsletter designed specifically for benefits information might be:

> To explain the various elements of the company benefits package to employees so that they will have fewer questions concerning these benefits and be able to use them to full advantage.

The trick to setting a goal is to think in terms of what the ultimate outcome will be. In this case, you want employees to become aware enough of their company benefits so that they will use them properly and have fewer questions about them.

A goal for a newsletter servicing the telecommunications industry, targeted to industry executives might be:

> To keep telecommunications executives abreast of the latest industry news in a manner that is pertinent and useful enough to them so that they will continue to subscribe to our newsletter.

Since this is a for-profit newsletter, part of the goal naturally pertains to continued subscription.

Remember, a goal needn't be specific. While both of the preceding goals are fairly specific, others might be less so.

> To contribute to the overall success of our latest fundraising campaign.

> To impart a sense of community between our target audiences and St. Vincent's Hospital.

Reader Profile Worksheet

1. Who are your readers? (Include any appropriate demographic information here.)

2. Where are your readers? (Include any pertinent geographic information here.)

3. What do your readers know about the topics or issues you plan to cover in your newsletter? (This will allow you to categorize them by level of awareness and tell you whether you need to introduce them to your issues or merely add to existing information.)

4. What media do your readers already use to obtain information about the issues or topics you plan to cover? If there is already a wealth of information, do you need a newsletter at all? If you do, is it for some reason other than coverage of certain issues or topics? (For example, maybe the primary reason is simply to keep in touch with your constituency, announce events, or increase membership.)

5. If you are attempting to persuade or advocate a particular point of view, how do your readers currently feel about your subject?

6. What is your audience's attitude toward you? (Without formal research, often the best you can do is make an educated guess. It is much easier to reach others when you know that you already have credibility with them.)

7. How do you hope to affect your target audience through your newsletter? (The answer to this question will lay the groundwork for setting objectives later on.)

Exhibit 2.1

To keep our membership informed as to how their money is being spent and to attract new members.

Once your goal has been established, it is time to set objectives.

Setting Objectives and Evaluation Criteria

Objectives tell how you are going to reach the destination described in your goal. If, for example, your goal were to keep your membership informed as to how their money is being spent, an objective stemming from this goal might be:

To notify members of the Dinner for Dollars event scheduled for March in time for them to plan their participation.

or

To inform members of the new Meals on Wheels program and how their contributions helped make it a reality.

Notice that each of these objectives relates to a specific article or message and are both realistic and measurable. Although you may not need to write one down for each article, objectives help keep your article on track according to what you want it to accomplish. And remember, every article should contribute to the overall goal of your newsletter. If it doesn't, either it shouldn't be included or you should rethink your goal.

Types of Objectives

An objective should contain at least three basic elements: *who* it is targeted to, *what* you want the target audience to do (or what you are going to do for them), and *when* you want them to respond to your message (or when you need to reach them with your message). There are three basic types of objectives: informational, attitudinal, and behavioral.

Informational objectives are used most often to present balanced information on a topic of interest to your target audience. For instance, if you are simply attempting to let your employees know that your organization has developed a new healthcare package, your objective might read something like this:

To inform all employees of the newest options available in their health care benefits package by the end of the October open enrollment period.

Notice that the objective begins with an infinitive phrase. Objectives should always be written this way. Notice, too, that the number of employees is addressed (all), and a specific time period for the completion of the objective is also included. To be complete this objective would be followed by the proposed method by which its success could be measured. For example:

To inform all employees of the newest options available in their health care benefits package by the end of the October open enrollment period. Personnel will keep a record of all employees requesting information on the new health care plan during the open enrollment period.

If your objective is **attitudinal** or **behavioral** rather than informational, your message is probably going to be persuasive. There are three ways you can attempt to influence attitude and behavior.

- You can create an attitude or behavior where none exists. This is the easiest to accomplish because, if no attitude exists, there is usually no predisposition on the part of your target audience.

- You can reinforce an attitude or behavior. This is also relatively easy to do because your target audience already believes or behaves in the way you desire.

- You can attempt to change or alter an attitude. This last is the most difficult to accomplish and, realistically, shouldn't be attempted unless you are willing to expend a lot of time and energy on an, at best, dubious outcome.

At one time or another, we have all received information propounding points of view opposite of ours. Once we realize what the message is, what do we usually do with it? That's right—we throw it away. Research tells us that reaching the hard-core oppostition is both extremely difficult and usually a waste of resources. This may be the hardest lesson to learn for those of us with a cause to support or a philosophy to impart. However, if you want to make the most of your newsletter, be realistic and resist the urge to preach to the unconvertible. Instead, try to reach those who haven't made up their minds yet. By convincing them, you will neutralize those opposed to you.

So, an example of a realistic attitudinal objective might be:

Northwest Media Update

Northwest Media Update is published for professionals in the communications industry by the Northwest Media Center. Its purpose is to keep media professionals abreast of the latest research techniques and findings in the mass communication industry.

Subscription rates are $45 a year for 12 issues.

Send subscription inquiries, address changes, and all correspondence to:

Northwest Media Center
P.O. Box 156
Seattle, WA 94811

© 1991 Northwest Media Center. All rights reserved. Permission to reprint articles must be obtained in writing from the Northwest Media Center.

ONLINE

Online is published quarterly by the

Public Relations Student Society of America
University of Oregon Chapter
Allen Hall
University of Oregon
Eugene, Oregon, 97403

Editor: Corrie Peterson

Mental Health BRIGHTS

Mental Health Brights is published quarterly by the Mental Health Association of Eugene. Its purpose is to acquaint the community with issues related to mental health care.

Executive Editor, Marion Allen
Writer, Walter Elliotson
Design & Layout, Barbara Miller

Address all correspondence to:

Editor, *Mental Health Brights*
P.O. Box 6523
Eugene, OR 97405

Exhibit 2.2

You will sometimes find people using the term *masthead* to mean *banner*. The masthead is where you place editorial information such as your editorial statement, address of your publication, names of the people who put it together, ordering and subscription information, and copyright notices. Mastheads need contain only the information absolutely necessary for *your* newsletter. It usually appears either on the second page near the bottom, or on the back page.

To create a favorable attitude among the undecided segment of Lane County voters concerning the development of the closed portion of the downtown mall into a more open, vehicle-centered shopping area.

Methods for measuring this type of objective range from informal feedback to formal surveys of attitudes leading up to and following the voting.

An example of a realistic behavioral objective might be:

To increase the number of employees in attendance at the annual company picnic by 25 percent.

Obviously, measuring the effectiveness of this objective is easier; however, if you don't see an increase in attendance, you will have to do some serious research into the reasons why. And, be aware that these reasons might not involve your message or its presentation at all. You might simply have picked the Sunday of the big state fair to hold your picnic. The lesson here is, don't ever conclude that your message is automatically the problem without exploring all variables affecting its desired results.

Developing an Editorial Statement

An editorial statement is nothing more than an explanation of who your newsletter is for and/or why it is being published. Editorial statements should be based loosely on your overall goal and usually appear on the masthead.

> *Centerline* is published for Dow U.S.A. employees in the headquarters unit in Midland.
> *Centerline*, Dow U.S.A.

> Produced for employees and retirees of Pacific Power by the Communications Department.
> *Bulletin*, Pacific Power

> The *Sentinel Quarterly* is published by the marketing division of the *Orlando Sentinel* for the Central Florida community and the newspaper industry.
> *Sentinel Quarterly*, *Orlando Sentinel*

In many cases, an organization publishes more than one newsletter. An editorial statement becomes even more important to these publications.

> Published especially for the Friends of Sacred Heart General Hospital.
> *Prime Time*, Sacred Heart General Hospital

> A newsletter of community health education and services.
> *House Call*, Sacred Heart General Hospital

> A health business update for the friends of Sacred Heart.
> *Health Trends*, Sacred Heart General Hospital

Newsletters whose purposes aren't immediately apparent often rely on lengthy editorial statements.

> First Capital Connection is a quarterly newsletter published for investors in First Capital limited partnerships. Its purpose is to deliver the latest information about those partnerships and to comment on significant issues affecting the real estate and investment industries.
> *First Capital Connection*, First Capital Financial Corporation

> Purpose: To help those who are very busy with their careers handle their personal lives more effectively. To bring to them the best information from the most knowledgable sources. To select and generate that information free from the influence of advertising. And to give them access to the information they need quickly, accurately, and efficiently.
> *Bottom Line*, Boardroom Reports, Inc.

> Cawood Communications publishes this newsletter to present current perspectives and offer useful tips on how to communicate effectively.
> *Cawood Communicates,* Cawood Communications

If you are publishing a newsletter that is easily recognized, such as an employee publication distributed strictly in-house, or an association publication for a fairly narrow audience, distributed through the mail, you may not need an editorial statement. However, an editorial statement does help if you are regularly seeking new readers or if you distribute copies of your newsletter to others outside your primary target audience. Simply remember, anything that aids clarity is useful, and editorial statements certainly aid clarity.

NOTES

[1] John Dewey, *The Public and Its Problems* (Chicago: Swallow, 1927).

[2] James E. Grunig, "A New Measure of Public Opinions on Corporate Social Responsibility," *Academy of Management Journal* 22 (December 1979): 740–41.

[3] James E. Grunig and Todd Hunt, *Managing Public Relations* (New York: Holt, Rinehart and Winston, 1984).

Planning

There are several larger decisions you must make before you can begin to work on the details of publication. You must develop a general description of your newsletter to serve as a guideline until the realities of publication can be determined after the first issue is printed.

Once the general direction of your newsletter has been set, you must then begin to determine some of the details of publication. These details involve working with the less concrete, but nonetheless vital, non-verbal look of your publication and setting up the more practical aspects of frequency and budget.

Determining Quality

The look of any publication says a great deal about its content. We know that, for many people, the quality of the books they purchase for their home libraries is often as important as the contents. A number of book clubs base their sales pitches on the look of the book as much as on the authors and titles they carry. Special editions of famous classics bring premium prices if they are leather bound and beautifully illustrated and type set. The contents may be identical to the paperback version you bought for your college English class, but the look is substantially different enough to attract your attention and your consideration for purchase.

The same is true of any publication. Think of the differences among magazines. The very look of a magazine tells you whether it's to be read, passed on, and discarded; or read, savored, and kept for reference. *National Geographic* has become part of millions of readers' libraries. Why? Because its liberal use of expensive-looking photography, timeless in-

formation, and exquisite cover illustrations all say "keep me." *TV Guide*, by the nature of its content, is perishable; however, its look also says "use me, then throw me away." The size is convenient, the paper stock is inexpensive—almost newspaper-like in quality. Other than content, then, a publication derives its theme from non-verbal messages designed into its look. "Keep me" isn't the only non-verbal message a publication can impart.

Newspapers have spent millions of dollars in the past few years updating their looks in the wake of the success of that visual feast, *USA Today*. *USA Today* was born of reader preference. It was the most carefully researched newspaper ever published. Newspaper readers were surveyed as to their reading tastes, graphic preferences, color preferences, page size and layout, order of story preference, and numerous other wants and needs. Not surprisingly, when *USA Today* premiered, it was an immediate success. Among the innovative non-verbal techniques it used to attract readers and satisfy their stated preferences were the use of bright blue on its banner, full-color graphics sprinkled liberally throughout, strict compartmentalization of topics (sports and weather getting the most prominent play), and the actual layout of its stories. For example, no story jumps except the lead story in each section, front page—and it jumps only to the back page of that section, thus saving the reader from having to open the paper to look for a continued article. The paper stock is bright, less flimsy than most newspapers, and the ink doesn't rub off on your hands. Even the look of the boxes in which the paper is sold was carefully researched. You have probably noticed that the boxes look very much like a TV set. That's no accident.

Editorially, *USA Today* sticks strictly to short articles—preferably those that can be finished on one page. They know busy commuters don't have time to read through lengthy analyses or struggle with unwieldy pages, folding and unfolding them to search for jumped stories. They know that morning readers want instant weather information (a full-color weather map is on the back of section A). They know that their readers are primarily male and interested in sports—that's the biggest section of the paper. In short, the publishers of *USA Today* did their homework *before* ever putting a single word on paper.

Elements Determining Quality

The lesson here is that the look of your publication is linked to its theme. Leather-bound, gold-embossed books say "quality." They say, "This is a classic." The look of *USA Today* says, "Pick me up, read me quickly, I'm like an evening newscast—colorful, succinct, interesting." There are several non-verbal characteristics of newsletter that are subtly, and sometimes not so subtly, linked to theme or message.

Paper Stock

The quality of the paper you choose says something about your newsletter. Weight, texture and color all combine to give your newsletter a "look" that says something to your readers. Heavy, textured papers usually impart higher quality. Thin, plain paper says "I'm disposable." The color of the paper you choose will also impart a message. Various shades of white,

Exhibit 3.1
This award-winning *USA Today* cover shows several of the design features that have made this daily so popular: a colorful banner, full-color photographs, short articles, inviting table of contents, and a generally easy-to-follow page design.

from pure white to softer ivory hues, impart a business-like appearance or, at least, a clean, organized feel. Very light grays in heavier weights also add a business-like look to your newsletter. Light browns are "natural" looking and, thus, less formal. Add some texture and you've got the perfect stock for an environmental message. Use recycled paper and your message is further strengthened. Never use extremely dark paper or colored paper without texture. Both smack of amateurishness. Never use bright colors such as pink, green, purple or some iridescent paper you find on special at the local print shop. Light blue should be avoided; however, some shades of blue to which black have been added, such as slate blue, can be used.

Ink Color

Most newsletters are printed in one or two colors, depending on budget. If your budget allows, print in two color. It always imparts a sense of quality. Blanks (newsletter pages pre-printed in one color and used for subsequent print runs of another color) can be made up in advance with your banner, for instance, printed in the second color. Black is the most common color ink for most publications; however, other colors can be used in conjunction with colored paper to impart a two-color look to your newsletter. For example, dark-blue ink can be used on light-gray or slate-blue paper for a sophisticated look. Very dark brown can be used on a light-brown stock for a warm look. Remember, columns of text will pick up the color you are using and intensify it on the page. Stick with black, dark blue, or dark brown for most uses.

Picking the appropriate second color is more difficult. If you are pre-printing blanks, you will have to decide, for each issue, where you want your second color to appear every issue. This limits you to a few choices, because, if you pre-print 1,000 blanks and print only 200 copies per issue, you won't be able to change where the second color appears for five issues.

If you intend to run both colors each time you print your newsletter, you have a great deal more flexibility. You can run the banner, headlines, rules, tint blocks, and practically any other element in the second color whenever you want.

Exhibit 3.2

Running second-color blanks is a good way to save money if you print enough to last you through several issues. Printing two colors each issue means having to set up the press for each color, each time—thus, increased cost. Printing on pre-printed blanks allows the printer to work in a single color— usually black— for each subsequent issue, and thus save you money. (See below.) The second color is on the left, while the black plate is on the right.

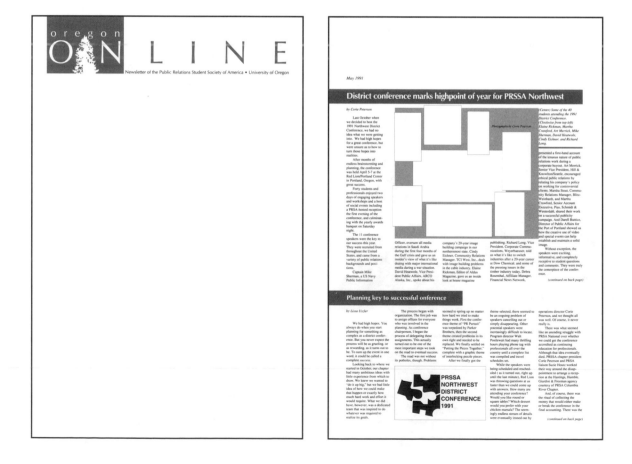

Of course, this greatly complicates the layout process, and it means you have to pick a second color that is completely compatible with your primary color and the paper you have chosen. For example, if you choose red as your second color, make it a deep red, not a bright, candy-apple red. You're going to be using it for a number of things, including headlines. Will candy-apple red work for headlines, or will it make them literally jump off the page? Second colors should also be picked for their ability to be screened. Using a 20 percent screen behind a block of text looks great, but if your second color is red, your screen will be pink. Do you want a pink screen? Blue screens nicely, as do green and brown. Be careful with pastels and off-colors. It is usually best to stick to primary colors if possible. If you're pre-printing blanks or not using screens, the choices are greater. Just remember not to mix incompatible colors. If in doubt, ask your printer.

Layout

Layout will be covered in more detail in a later chapter. However, as an element of quality, it needs to be discussed briefly here. The way in which you literally put the elements of your newsletter on the page also imparts a non-verbal message. For instance, justified columns are fairly formal. A number of business newsletters use justified type. Type set flush left (unjustified) is less formal. Wider columns tend to be less formal. Some typefaces are less formal than others. The design of your banner will also speak to your newsletter's level of formality. A script face usually indicates a less formal newsletter, while a sans serif face is more formal. The actual name of a newsletter also says a great deal about its message; however, this will be covered later. Using rules makes a newsletter appear more formal. Heavy lines of any kind add a formal, structured look to your publication. Types of graphics, from business-like charts and graphs to cartoon clip art, all impart different levels of formality.

Exhibit 3.3

A formal, business newsletter (top) displays justified columns, but uses no rules. A slightly less formal newsletter (bottom) uses unjustified columns, yet uses rules to set columns apart visually. Both are standard business formats.

Format

Size and other elements of format impart very subtle messages about your newsletter. For example, an alumni newsletter for a journalism school might be a tabloid newspaper format. This format practically *says* "journalism." An alumni newsletter for a law school chooses a magazine-style layout instead. This is more formal, more business-like. Hole-punching your newsletter says "keep me, put me in a binder." Many newsletters are hole-punched for just this reason. The message is non-verbal, yet unmistakably clear. Do you use a big format or a small format? Will it have one page or many pages? Will it be folded, or folded and stapled?

Most of these questions have a lot to do with the expected length of your publication. If you are going to publish weekly, chances are it will be a short newsletter, thus requiring a small format—a one-page flyer printed both sides or a standard 11" x 17" four-page newsletter folded in half. If you are publishing less frequently, you may want to go to a larger format, such as a tabloid, or an expanded number of pages folded and stapled. Perhaps you are designing a small newsletter to go out in a monthly billing, or one to be sent out in a standard business envelope (see **Exhibit 3.4**). All of these considerations and more have to be made in advance of other editorial decisions.

Cost as the Controlling Factor

All of the considerations discussed above are moot if you don't have the budget to upgrade the quality of your newsletter. You will have to balance carefully what you can afford versus what you need to spend to accomplish what you want. Too many newsletter publishers assume that it's the editorial content that carries the message load. This is basically true; however, if you are trying to reach an information processing audience (those not yet convinced they need your information) you must dress up your presentation.

On the other hand, nearly everyone reacts positively to a good-looking publication. It is unfortunately true that we live in a visual age in which readers often buy the look before even considering the contents. You must play to that inclination as much as possible. I am convinced that the look of your publication will do a great deal toward convincing your target audience of your message, whatever it is.

To that end, you must consider matters of cost versus quality. Keep in mind, however, that quality is also a matter of skill. Even a newsletter printed on a shoestring budget can impart quality if executed skillfully. If you can expand your newsletter budget, do so in order to expand on the quality of your publication. This might mean hiring an artist to redesign your banner, upgrading your paper stock, adding a second color, or changing the format. Remember, the quality of your newsletter reflects the way you see your readers. Aren't they important enough to deserve the highest quality you can afford to give them? Throughout this book, you will find ways to improve quality with a minimal amount of cost. The real cost is in time and effort, and, to a great extent, the development of your skills.

Determining Frequency

How often should you publish? This depends on several factors: the perishability of your information, the amount of information you have to publish, and how often you need to reach your readers in order to maintain their interest in what you have to say.

The "news" in newsletter means that most of what you have to say is fairly perishable. That is, it will only be news for a short time, then it will be old news. You need to reach your readers with information while it is still fresh and interesting. Publishing any less than quarterly defeats the primary purpose of a newsletter. You might as well be publishing a magazine or a journal. Publishing too frequently may overwhelm your readers. They may begin to tune out your information the same way they do with the thousands of other unwanted messages they receive every day.

Obviously, you have to strike a balance. Daily tidbits of information might be okay for a school district newsletter that goes each morning to the thousands of teachers who work in the various schools. A one-page digest may serve as a memorandum set up on a standard format to resemble a newsletter. Weekly digests might also work if you have enough of interest to present to your readers, or if you think you might have at least one feature to run weekly. It is difficult to publish weekly unless you anticipate enough information to fill the format you have decided on.

For-profit newsletters, typically published to provide information to a narrow spectrum of readers, are generally composed of short industry-related articles. For example, *Random Lengths*, a

Exhibit 3.4

Shown here (top to bottom) are a tabloid-size newsletter, standard format flyer-type newsletter, an unusual 6½" x 12½" format designed to be folded twice and used as a bill stuffer, and a more standard small format 8½" x 11" horizontal layout, folded down to 5½" x 8½".

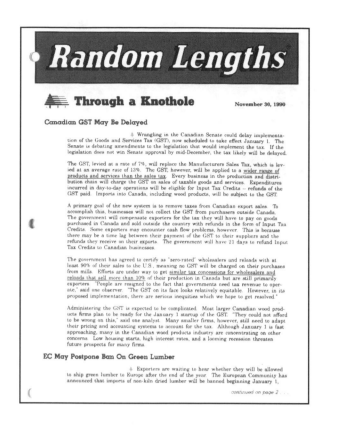

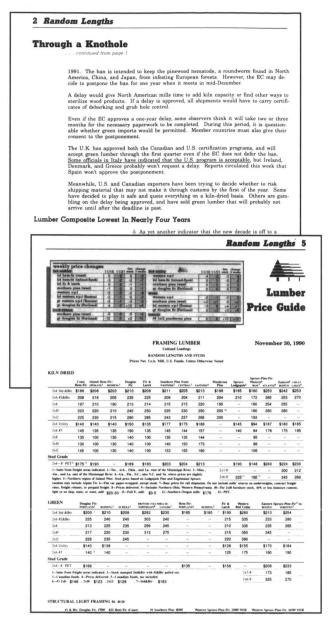

Exhibit 3.5
The pages from *Random Lengths* show (clockwise from top left) the cover, editorial page, and market information section. Courtesy, *Random Lengths*, Inc.

newsletter published for the timber industry, bills itself as "the weekly report on North American forest products markets." It runs to twelve pages. The first four are editorial matter—primarily brief features and straight news including several standing columns. A center insert, printed on a second color paper, features tables of current lumber market prices, while the final four pages are in-depth articles on various market issues. The entire twelve-page newsletter is put together weekly by a small staff and is in the hands of its national and international readers on the following Monday.

A weekly may be too much work for those publishing a newsletter without a staff; however, a dedicated editor whose sole responsibility is the newsletter may be able to gather and write up enough information for a weekly. When we discuss formats in more detail later, you will begin to see how easy it actually is to fill up four pages with narrow columns and a fair number of graphic elements.

In deciding on frequency, there are several questions you must answer.

1. Will you have enough "news" to publish as frequently as you wish and fill the number of pages you have decided to print?

2. Is the nature of your news highly perishable? If it is, publishing more frequently may be a necessity.

3. In the same light, do your readers need to have your newsletter information with the frequency you have chosen? Be careful not to overload your readers with trivia just so you can publish weekly. Monthly contact is usually enough for most readers, unless—as in the case of *Random Lengths*—the news is highly perishable and

the source of your information provides it weekly as well.

4. Can you *afford* to publish as frequently as you wish? See the following section on budgeting before making this determination.

5. Can you physically handle a stepped-up publishing schedule? If you have a staff—perhaps. If not, you must consider how much a single person can accomplish in the time frame you have allotted yourself.

Determining Quantity

Obviously you need to print enough of your newsletter for each reader to have a copy. Beyond that, do you want to entice broader readership? If you do, you will have to print extra copies each month to distribute to specially targeted readers not currently on your primary list. If you rely on pick-up points for part of your distribution—that is, people simply pick them up from a counter or rack—you may have to print extras until you determine how many are distributed this way each issue. If your newsletter carries information that is worth saving, you may

want to print extra copies each time so that readers may order back issues they've missed or misplaced.

Printing a few more copies now will save you money later. For instance, increasing your print run from 1000 to 1500 should only cost you a few dollars more since the press is already set up for your print job. If you have to reprint an issue later, it will cost you the full amount for press setup. In addition, you should always keep back issues for your own files to check for consistency, compare design changes over a number of issues, and monitor quality.

Budgeting for Production

Setting a preliminary budget now is essential, even though your costs may be only estimates until you have ironed out the details of design and production. With that in mind, here are a few things you have to consider.

Exhibit 3.6

A weekly digest-type newsletter layout (left) shows a full-page column width consisting of very short articles. The monthly (right) shows a more standard page layout with a feature article and a secondary article on the cover.

- **Staff expenditures.** If you are part of an in-house department and only part of your time is devoted to newsletter publishing, you will have to determine how much of your time it takes up. You will need to perform this calculation for each person involved in any part of the newsletter production for whom you or another department is paying. This calculation should include salaries and benefits. Outside help for production purposes is covered below.

- **Office space**. Do you lease an office, or work from your home? You must calculate the cost of rent or space allocation, including utilities, telephones, FAX, and other office equipment such as photocopiers.

- **Production**. This is the greatest cost you will incur. Include the costs of on-site equipment such as computers and typewriters. Also include any outside help you pay for, such as typesetting, graphic designers, photographers, paste-up artists, etc. Make sure that any outside services you pay for are worth your money. For example, if you are running less than 1,000 copies of a newsletter each issue, expensive design costs may be extravagant. On the other hand, if a good-looking newsletter will help you raise more money or increase membership, the costs may be worth it. In other words, don't spend money where it isn't needed.

  Printing should be calculated based on design needs, frequency and quantity. Shop around for the best deal at the most acceptable quality. There will be more on selecting a printer in a later chapter.

- **Distribution**. Cost of mailing or other methods of distribution, such as hand delivery, should be calculated based on quantity, format, etc. Postal regulations have recently changed, causing large-scale newsletter publishers to incur increased costs in the thousands of dollars. Bulk mailing is a tricky and sometimes costly endeavor. Make sure that bulk mail is the way you want to go before you begin. A lot depends on the number of newsletters you have to mail and whether there are alternative delivery possibilities. This will be discussed in more detail in a later chapter.

- **Supplies**. Include all on-site supplies exclusive of printing supplies, such as paper for computers, typewriters and copiers; ribbons and toner cartridges; and all miscellaneous supplies no matter how small, such as pencils, pens, writing pads, and paper clips.

Overestimate in all areas. Your actual outlay will invariably be much greater than you calculate otherwise. Assume that whatever you estimate will be low. You'll know for sure after you run your first issue. (See sample budget on **page 25**.)

Scheduling

Finally, you need to set up a ballpark schedule for production. As with budget, this is a preliminary estimate until you have run your first issue. The best way to schedule is to back-time your production based on when you need to have your newsletter in your readers' hands. For example, *Random Lengths* needs its readers to receive each issue on Monday. Their production schedule begins roughly mid-week with information gathering and writing. Production takes place on predesigned templates on Thursday, and the newsletter is delivered for printing on Friday. They know from experience that it can be printed, sorted for bulk mailing, and mailed in one day, allowing the weekend for transit through the mail.

Again, when you are starting out, overestimate the amount of time it will take you to gather information, write and edit your stories, lay out your camera-ready copy, get it printed, and distribute your finished newsletter to your readers. Once you have experienced the frustrations of a tight publishing schedule, you will begin to allow more time where you need it the most. Remember, in newsletter production, the operative rule is Murphy's law—if anything can go wrong, it will, and at the most inopportune time. Plan as if Mr. Murphy were your production coordinator. (See sample production schedule on **page 26**.)

Preliminary Budget: 6 Months

Frequency	January	February	March	April	May	June
Staff expenditures:						
Salaries						
Benefits						
Office Space:						
Rent/Lease						
Utilities						
Telephone/FAX						
Copier						
Other						
Production/on-site:						
Computers						
Printer						
Typewriters						
Production/contracted:						
Writing						
Design						
Photography						
Typesetting						
Paste-up						
Printing						
Distribution:						
Bulk-mail services						
Postage						
Other delivery						
Supplies:						
Computer/typewriter/ copier paper						
Ribbons/toner						
Misc.						

Notes:

Sample Production Schedule

(The basic work of determining target audiences, basic design and format, paper and ink, budget, printing process, and frequency and distribution is assumed to have been accomplished prior to beginning the actual production process. What remains is the sequence of events common to the physical production of each issue.)

Activity	Responsibility	Date Accomplished
Decide on basic content for current issue		
Determine number and type and approximate length of stories		
Make up dummy layout for current issue		
Gather information and/or interview appropriate sources		
Write first draft		
Obtain critiques and edit first draft		
Create graphics for each story (photos taken, illustrations created or obtained, charts/graphs created, etc.)		
Write final draft		
Obtain critiques, edit final draft and copyfit to dummy		
Write headlines, captions, pull quotes, etc., and copyfit to dummy		
Send all copy out for typesetting if needed		
Select graphics (photos sized, cropped and printed, artwork sized) and fit to dummy		
Send all graphics out for screening or PMTs		
Create mechanical		
Proof mechanical		
Send to printer		
Check proofs		

Content

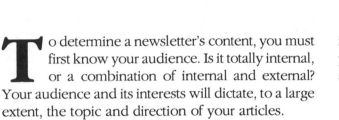

Choices of content depend on audience needs, space requirements, and a balance of consistency and flexibility. Research has shown definite reader preferences for in-house newsletters, while constituency newsletter preferences are based on industry or service orientation.

To determine a newsletter's content, you must first know your audience. Is it totally internal, or a combination of internal and external? Your audience and its interests will dictate, to a large extent, the topic and direction of your articles.

Setting Message Strategy

Before deciding on detailed content, you should decide on an overall theme. This is often called *message strategy*. Message strategy has to do with what you want your newsletter to accomplish—the desired effect you want it to have on your targeted audiences. Following the MBO method of organization, your message strategies should logically follow your objectives and contribute either directly or indirectly to them. You will need to develop individual message strategies for each of your target publics, based on what you have learned about them through your research. Remember, the strategy or strategies you employ will be determined, to a great extent, by your audience's makeup, predispositions and perceived needs.

For most newsletters, there are three basic strategies: *entertainment*, *information*, or *persuasion*. Entertainment, as mentioned earlier, is normally used as a packaging device for the other two strategies. For example, if you want to present an article on using a new dental plan to your employees, you might develop an entertaining feature story about participating dentists, full of humorous anecdotes about frightened patients and so on. The strategy is a little

information, a little persuasion, in a colorful wrapping of entertainment. Most strategies overlap quite a bit. Even so, there are some basic differences.

- **Entertainment**. Entertainment strategy is commonly used in all types of writing, including advertising. Remember, entertainment can be an excellent strategy for "selling" your ideas, philosophies, or whatever, regardless of the medium or format. The entertainment value of a message helps it gain and maintain attention. Entertainment alone is not often used in newsletter writing without a complementary strategy such as information or persuasion.

- **Information**. An information strategy is usually a straightforward statement of fact best used on audiences interested enough to seek out the information you can provide. This strategy is frequently employed for such messages as new product announcements, consumer awareness campaigns, and public information programs. It is also used for supplemental messages (such as position statements) to persuasive campaigns.

- **Persuasion**. A persuasion strategy assumes that there are at least two sides to the issue you are addressing. Persuasive messages usually require an audience that is already interested in the issue and able to process information fairly well. Persuasive strategy makes frequent appeals to reasoning and logic and is best structured to reach either those who are already convinced or those who are neutral and open to reasoning.

In addition to these primary strategies, there are two secondary strategies that, like entertainment, can be used in conjunction with other approaches.

- **Image strategy**. Image strategy is used to develop or maintain a strong, memorable identity for a person, idea, product, or organization. Image can be portrayed through use of the other strategies, but it has attributes of its own not normally found in the other approaches. For example, image strategy attempts to alter or develop predispositions about its subject. This can be accomplished through a number of methods, such as repeating a slogan or logo throughout your newsletter, showing through other strategies a certain consistent picture of your organization or program, or simply explaining your position in increasing detail from issue to issue. The effect of image strategy is cumulative.

- **Emotional strategy**. Emotional strategy is generally intended to persuade. It is best used for messages aimed at those who are either neutral or already on your side, and will rarely convince the hard-core opposition. Emotional strategy depends on the use of emotionally laden words, images, or style elements, such as the structure of a speech or the use of certain "hot buttons" in a message. Most of us think of emotional strategy as useful only in the context of emotionally charged issues; however, everything from political candidates to soft drinks can be sold through emotional appeal, or through association of the "product" with emotions, such as patriotism or romance. Even humor can be seen as an emotional strategy because typically it makes us *feel* good about the message.

Newsletter Content

Depending on the type of newsletter you are publishing, the focus will be broad or narrow. For example, when you write for an internal, employee public, you must carefully balance information with entertainment. You must please management by providing information it wants to see in print and you must please the employees by providing information they want to read. Otis Baskin & Craig Aronoff, in their book *Public Relations: The Profession and the Practice*, present a rule of thumb for an appropriate mix

in an internal publication (not necessarily a newsletter) aimed primarily at an employee audience.

- 50 percent information about the organization—local, national and international
- 20 percent employee information—benefits, quality of working life, etc.
- 20 percent relevant noncompany information—competitors, community, etc.
- 10 percent small talk and personals

Given that most newsletters are fairly short, such a complete mix may be impractical; however, a close approximation will probably work. Remember, though, that this mix is only appropriate for vertical publications such as institutional newsletters.

By comparison, most horizontal publications tend to focus on items of interest to a more narrowly defined target public. For example, a newsletter for telecommunications executives may concentrate on news about that industry, omitting human interest items, small talk, or industry gossip. In fact, almost every newsletter targeted to executives contains only short, no-nonsense articles. The reason, of course, is that busy executives simply don't have the time to read the type of article that interests the average employee.

Consistency vs. Flexibility

One of the decisions you're going to have to make early on is whether to include standing columns or not. A *standing column* is a recurring column, normally covering a single theme and holding the same physical position in each issue. Typical standing columns include:

- **Table of contents/news briefs**: Usually run on the first page. Can be used for teasers—short blurbs of articles on inside pages.

- **Announcements**: Usually as boxed information, but sometimes run as regular columns for job placement, promotions, etc.

- **Letters:** If the publication is designed for two-way communication, a letters column is a common addition.

- **Editorial**: Can be in the form of a "President's Column," a signed editorial from management or the publication's editor.

- **News notes**: A quick (and brief) look at what's happening—often a boxed item or sometimes run in very narrow columns as *marginalia*.

- **Calendar**: Upcoming events of interest to readers.

Although there are variations on these elements, most newsletters include at least some of them. The question is, how much flexibility do you surrender by having standing columns? The answer is—a lot. Even if you don't pre-print standing column heads in a second color, for instance, you still lock yourself into filling that space each issue for consistency's sake, if nothing else. The whole purpose of a standing column is to add consistency to a publication so that readers know where to look each issue for their favorite information tidbits. It provides a sort of comfort to readers to know where things are. Standing columns can be useful and many newsletters follow the exact format in each issue for years without a complaint or problem.

However, if you want the maximum flexibility to put your articles where you want them each time, or play with the layout (without altering the basic design, of course), you'll want to give the inclusion of standing columns a good deal of thought. What you lose in consistency (or comfort) you may gain in your ability to adapt to special needs each issue. Of course, you also have the flexibility to keep your articles in pretty much the same order each issue as well, without locking yourself into a confining format. The trick here is not to have the same name for these topics each time. Once you have decided on a standing head, you have a standing column.

Selecting Topics

No one can tell you what to put in your newsletter. Content depends entirely on reader interest; however, there are some basic choices derived from research and just plain common sense. For example, a survey conducted under the auspices of the International Association of Business Communicators (IABC) showed the topics employees were most interested in. Following is a partial list in order of importance.

- The organization's plans for the future
- Personnel policies and practices
- Productivity improvement
- Job-related information
- The organization's competitive position
- News of other departments/divisions
- The organization's stand on current issues
- The organization's community involvement

- Personnel changes/promotions
- Financial information
- Stories about other employees
- Personal news (birthdays, anniversaries, etc.)

As you can see, what many editors and managers used to think of as the most interesting type of employee news (human interest news) is at the bottom of the list. This is very much in line with other research that shows employees seeking hard information about the organization, its plans, its current market position, and how all this affects employee jobs. What a surprise! For years, managers believed that if you produced warm, fuzzy copy designed to make employees feel like part of one big, happy family, they wouldn't want anything substantive. Wrong. Now we know they are as interested in their organization's well being as any executive.

Topics for constituent newsletters vary widely according to the needs of the readers. There is no sure-fire list of topics or order of importance of information since the range of constituency newsletters is infinite. However, you can bet that most readers, regardless of the focus of the newsletter, want hard facts, no-frills reporting, attention to detail, and a quick read. At the top of everyone's list will undoubtedly be information about the organization, the industry, or the cause—whether it is a non-profit charity, a trade or professional association, or a special interest group. If you stick to information related to your primary subject, you can't go wrong.

How Much Is Enough?

How many articles to run depends on the focus and length of your publication. Fortunately, newsletters are extremely flexible. If you run a four-page newsletter but you always have more information than room, you can expand to six or eight pages. A one-page insert (loose, or run on a larger sheet with a folder-type fold) will give you enough room for two or three more stories—more if your articles are short. (See **Exhibit 4.1** for an example of how typed copy translates into typeset copy.)

There is truly no set number for how much is enough; however, here are some contents from a variety of newsletters showing what is typical for them.

- *Oregon Columbia IABC Ampersand*: A regional monthly association newsletter of the

International Association of Business Communicators.

> **Number of Pages:** 4
> **Number of Articles:** 4
> **Average Length:** 500 words
> **Other Editorial Matter:** table of contents, announcements, masthead, help wanted.

- *Action Connection*: A monthly institutional newsletter for employees of the Weyerhaeuser Paper Company Packaging Division.

> **Number of Pages:** 8
> **Number of Articles:** 7
> **Average Length:** 447 words
> **Other Editorial Matter:** recognition by plant site, employee recognition, masthead.

- *Resource:* A monthly institutional newsletter for employees of the Western Wood Products manufacturing Division of Georgia Pacific.

> **Number of Pages:** 4
> **Number of Articles:** 5
> **Average Length:** 650 words
> **Other Editorial Matter:** table of contents, a news notes column, employee recognition, masthead information on mailer.

- *The Sampler from Response Analysis*: A digest newsletter for clients and prospective clients featuring articles on research findings from Response Analysis Corporation of Princeton, New Jersey.

> **Number of Pages:** 4
> **Number of Articles:** 10
> **Average Length:** 252 words
> **Other Editorial Matter:** table of contents, editorial, masthead.

- *Northwest Business Barometer.* A quarterly economic review for customers from the Department of Economics, U.S. Bancorp.

> **Number of Pages:** 8
> **Number of Articles:** 6 (Divided geographically and topically)
> **Average Length:** 850 words
> **Other Editorial Matter:** a news notes called "Random Thoughts." Masthead information is included as part of the nameplate or banner.

- *N.E.T.M.A. (Nobody Ever Tells Me Anything)*: An employee/public newsbriefs newsletter from Eugene, Oregon, Development Department/ Business Development Division.

> **Number of Pages:** 4
> **Number of Articles:** 14 (not articles in the true sense, but digested news)
> **Average Length:** 90 words
> **Other Editorial Matter:** a list of publications of interest to the business community, business community recognition column, calendar of events, trivia column.

Making Your Articles Fit

Most newsletters lead off with the most topical or interesting story on the front page—much like a newspaper. Your choice of lead article will be based on management dictates or your assessment of reader interest.

Before you begin to lay out your newsletter, you should list all your potential articles, their lengths, and approximate placement by importance/interest in the newsletter. This way, if space gets tight, you can edit from the bottom up. A secondary choice is to carry over articles that aren't "time bound"—that is, articles that could just as well wait for the next issue. And, finally, you can edit each story until *all* of them fit in the space you have. This assumes that some information in each article is superfluous which, under ideal editorial circumstances, shouldn't happen. But, as any experienced editor can tell you, there is always something you can cut.

Standing columns—articles such as editorials or employee recognition that recur from issue to issue—should already have a reserved space in your layout. It is in your best interest to allot a certain amount of space to these recurring articles and stick to it. That way, your other articles will have the space they need and deserve.

If you run out of space and can afford it, consider adding two pages (a single page run on both sides) either as an insert or an extra fold. If you only have enough copy to add literally one page (a single sheet printed only on one side), don't do it. Nothing is as unattractive as a publication page printed only on one side. The sole exception might be a calendar designed to be pulled out and posted.

Lorem ipsum dolor sit amet, consectetuer adipiscing elit, sed diam nonummy nibh euismod tincidunt ut laoreet dolore magna aliquam erat volutpat. Ut wisi enim ad minim veniam, quis nostrud exerci tation ullamcorper suscipit lobortis nisl ut aliquip ex ea commodo consequat. Duis autem vel eum iriure dolor in hendrerit in vulputate velit esse molestie consequat, vel illum dolore eu feugiat nulla facilisis at vero eros et accumsan et iusto odio dignissim qui blandit praesent luptatum zzril delenit augue duis dolore te feugait nulla facilisi. Lorem ipsum dolor sit amet, consectetuer adipiscing elit, sed diam nonummy nibh euismod tincidunt ut laoreet dolore magna aliquam erat volutpat. Ut wisi enim ad minim veniam, quis nostrud exerci tation ullamcorper suscipit lobortis nisl ut aliquip ex ea commodo consequat.

Duis autem vel eum iriure dolor in hendrerit in vulputate velit esse molestie consequat, vel illum dolore eu feugiat nulla facilisis at vero eros et accumsan et iusto odio dignissim qui blandit praesent luptatum zzril delenit augue duis dolore te feugait nulla facilisi. Nam liber tempor cum soluta nobis eleifend option congue nihil imperdiet doming id quod mazim placerat facer possim assum.

Lorem ipsum dolor sit amet, consectetuer adipiscing elit, sed diam nonummy nibh euismod tincidunt ut laoreet dolore magna aliquam erat volutpat. Ut wisi enim ad minim veniam, quis nostrud exerci tation ullamcorper suscipit lobortis nisl ut aliquip ex ea commodo consequat. Duis autem vel eum iriure dolor in hendrerit in vulputate velit esse molestie consequat, vel illum dolore eu feugiat nulla facilisis at vero eros et accumsan et iusto odio dignissim qui blandit praesent luptatum zzril delenit augue duis dolore te feugait nulla facilisi. Lorem ipsum dolor sit amet, consectetuer adipiscing elit, sed diam nonummy nibh euismod tincidunt ut laoreet dolore magna aliquam erat volutpat.

Story of the week

Lorem ipsum dolor sit amet, consectetuer adipiscing elit, sed diam nonummy nibh euismod tincidunt ut laoreet dolore magna aliquam erat volutpat. Ut wisi enim ad minim veniam, quis nostrud exerci tation ullamcorper suscipit lobortis nisl ut aliquip ex ea commodo consequat.

Duis autem vel eum iriure dolor in hendrerit in vulputate velit esse molestie consequat, vel illum dolore eu feugiat nulla facilisis at vero eros et accumsan et iusto odio dignissim qui blandit praesent luptatum zzril delenit augue duis dolore te feugait nulla facilisi. Lorem ipsum dolor sit amet, consectetuer adipiscing elit, sed diam nonummy nibh euismod tincidunt ut laoreet dolore magna aliquam erat volutpat.

Ut wisi enim ad minim veniam, quis nostrud exerci tation ullamcorper suscipit lobortis nisl ut aliquip ex ea commodo consequat.

Duis autem vel eum iriure dolor in hendrerit in vulputate velit esse molestie consequat, vel illum dolore eu feugiat nulla facilisis at vero eros et accumsan et iusto odio dignissim qui blandit praesent luptatum zzril delenit augue duis dolore te feugait nulla facilisi.

Nam liber tempor cum soluta nobis eleifend option congue nihil imperdiet doming id quod mazim placerat facer possim assum.

Lorem ipsum dolor sit amet, consectetuer adipiscing elit, sed diam nonummy nibh euismod tincidunt ut laoreet dolore magna aliquam erat volutpat. Ut wisi enim ad minim veniam, quis nostrud exerci tation ullamcorper suscipit lobortis nisl ut aliquip ex ea commodo consequat.

Duis autem vel eum iriure dolor in hendrerit in vulputate velit esse molestie consequat, vel illum dolore eu feugiat nulla facilisis at vero eros et accumsan et iusto odio dignissim qui blandit praesent luptatum zzril delenit augue duis dolore te feugait nulla facilisi. Lorem ipsum dolor sit amet, consectetuer adipiscing elit,

sed diam nonummy nibh euismod tincidunt ut laoreet dolore magna aliquam erat volutpat.

Ut wisi enim ad minim veniam, quis nostrud exerci tation ullamcorper suscipit lobortis nisl ut aliquip ex ea commodo consequat. Duis autem vel eum iriure dolor in hendrerit in vulputate velit esse molestie consequat, vel illum dolore eu feugiat nulla facilisis at vero eros et accumsan et iusto odio dignissim qui blandit praesent luptatum zzril delenit augue duis dolore te feugait nulla facilisi.

Lorem ipsum dolor sit amet, consectetuer adipiscing elit, sed diam

Lorem ipsum dolor sit amet, consectetuer adipiscing elit, sed diam nonummy nibh euismod tincidunt ut laoreet dolore magna aliquam erat volutpat. Ut wisi enim ad minim

nonummy nibh euismod tincidunt ut laoreet dolore magna aliquam erat volutpat.

Ut wisi enim ad minim veniam, quis nostrud exerci tation ullamcorper suscipit lobortis nisl ut aliquip ex ea commodo consequat. Duis autem vel eum iriure dolor in hendrerit in vulputate velit esse

molestie consequat, vel illum dolore eu feugiat nulla facilisis at vero eros et accumsan et iusto odio dignissim qui blandit praesent luptatum zzril delenit augue duis dolore te feugait nulla facilisi.

Lorem ipsum dolor sit amet, consectetuer adipiscing elit, sed diam nonummy nibh euismod tincidunt ut laoreet dolore magna aliquam erat volutpat. Ut wisi enim ad minim veniam, quis nostrud exerci tation ullamcorper suscipit lobortis nisl ut aliquip ex ea commodo consequat. Duis autem vel eum iriure dolor in hendrerit in vulputate velit esse molestie consequat, vel illum dolore eu feugiat nulla facilisis at.

Vero eros et accumsan et iusto odio dignissim qui blandit praesent luptatum zzril delenit augue duis dolore te feugait nulla facilisi. Lorem ipsum dolor sit amet, consectetuer adipiscing elit, sed diam nonummy nibh euismod tincidunt ut laoreet dolore magna aliquam erat volutpat. Ut wisi enim ad minim veniam, quis nostrud exerci tation ullamcorper suscipit lobortis nisl ut aliquip ex ea commodo consequat.

Autem vel eum iriure dolor in hendrerit in vulputate velit esse molestie consequat, vel illum dolore eu feugiat nulla facilisis at vero eros et accumsan et iusto odio dignissim qui blandit praesent luptatum zzril delenit augue duis dolore te feugait nulla facilisi.

Exhibit 4.1

Calculating by eye how much space typed copy will take up on a typeset layout can be risky. As you can see, two pages of double-spaced, typewritten copy almost fills a three-column page (with the addition of a graphic and pull quote). See the section on copyfitting in **Chapter 6** for details on how to fit prewritten copy to your layout and vice versa.

Design

Versatility is the operative word for newsletter design. A solid understanding of the basic principles of design combined with a working knowledge of the flexibility of modular layout can result in a format that is, at once, eye-catching and memorable.

What most designers love the most about newsletters is the wide variety of available formats. Just picking one can be a challenge. As mentioned in **Chapter 1**, a newsletter can take on any number of disguises, ranging from the standard 11" x 17" format folded down to a four-page 8½" x 11" size, to a lengthy magazine-like format folded and stapled, to a tabloid newspaper, to a tabloid-sized magazine-type format known as a *magapaper*. Audience needs and cost are the most important deciding factors in picking a format for your newsletter.

The thing to remember is that no matter what format you ultimately decide on, you will be stuck with it for quite some time. If you are going to have enough information to fill a twelve-page magazine format four times a year—good, use a magazine format. If not, try something smaller. If you need to insert your newsletter in a monthly billing envelope, try something even smaller. If size is what attracts your audience (and you usually don't have to mail your newsletter) try a magapaper or a tabloid; although, even these can be mailed—they just cost a lot more.

Whatever you decide on, remember, your design elements must fit your format. Large formats call for larger artwork. Small formats call for shorter articles. White space is an extravagance in a bill stuffer, but not in a tabloid. Folding and mailing differs immensely among the various sizes. In other words, suit your format to your needs. Once you *have* decided on a basic format, the job of design begins in earnest, and requires a good deal of practice.

Exhibit 5.1
Weyerhaeuser Today is an 11" x 17", 16-page magapaper. It doesn't use a self-cover like most standard newsletters, yet it runs copy and a mailer on the back page.

The Elements of Design

The single most exciting element of newsletter publication, for most of us, is design. If you were to pick up, at random, a dozen well-produced newsletters, you would notice at once the similarities. What you might not notice, however, is the thoughtful attention to design detail that is so much a part of newsletter production.

The well-designed newsletter won't shout "look at my look." Instead, it will simply say, "pick me up and read me." More than anything else, the design you choose and the skill you use in implementing that design will be nearly subliminal to the message you impart. As mentioned earlier, the non–verbal message imparted through choices of paper, color and format is as important as anything you have to say; because if you fail to entice your readers through these subtle nuances, you may not have any readers.

Most of us don't pay much attention to a design if it's a good one. In fact, we only tend to notice a design when it is either badly executed or when it is so overdone that it shouts down the content. Designing a newsletter, like designing anything else, is a matter of understatement, not overstatement.

In order to get the most out of a newsletter, you must design it with your target audience always in mind. Are they a conservative, business executive group? Shouldn't your newsletter reflect that conservatism? Are they an artistic, easygoing audience? Shouldn't your newsletter appeal to their sense of freedom of expression? In fact, your newsletter has to appeal to your readers' sense of what is correct for them—both in the information you provide, and in the packaging in which you provide that information.

Before we can begin to discuss the specifics of designing a newsletter, you should become familiar with a few basic design principles that are relevant to all publications. Those principles are: *balance, proportion, sequence, emphasis,* and *unity.*

Balance

Most of us intuitively understand balance—at least to the extent that we notice immediately if something is out of balance. As children, we seemed to just *know* that if the person on the other end of the teeter-totter were bigger than we were, we had to sit closer to the end to counter-balance their weight. In a way, we might say that balance is natural to human beings. We seek it in our lives, our budgets, and in the way we view the world. The very fact that we walk upright (at least most of the time) suggests that we understand balance somewhere deep in our genetic programming.

In its simplest form, balance means that what is put on one side of a page should "weigh" as much as what is on the other side. All the elements you place on the page have weight, even the white space you leave by not placing elements. Size, color, degree of darkness—all play a part in balance. Weight will be discussed more thoroughly below under *contrast/ emphasis.*

There are two ways to achieve balance. The easiest is the symmetrical approach. To balance symmetrically means to place exactly the same amount of weight in exactly the same positions on either side of the page (or two-page spread). Symmetrically balanced pages tend to appear more formal and can be used to impart a non-verbal conservatism to your layout. Since symmetrical bal-

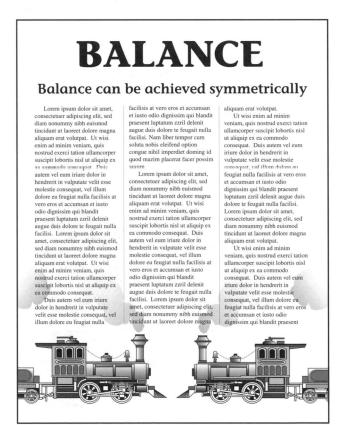

Exhibit 5.2

The easiest way to achieve balance is through pure symmetry. Place identically weighted elements on either side of the center axis of the page. In this example, even the headline and subhead are centered to enhance the symmetrical effect. Although this type of layout is the easiest to deal with, it is aesthetically boring.

ance is relatively easy to achieve, beginning newsletter designers should stick to a balanced layout until they are secure enough in their skills to experiment with asymmetry.

The asymmetrical approach is generally more interesting. The technique involves the teeter-totter example above of shifting weight on one side of a page or spread to balance the opposite side. For example, if a two-page spread has a big photo near the gutter on one side of the layout, you can achieve balance by placing a smaller picture closer to the outside edge of the opposite page. Remember, this arrangement works with all elements of varying weight, including white space. An asymmetric layout appears less formal than its symmetric counterpart.

When you increase the number of elements on a page or spread, you increase the difficulty of working with symmetrical balance. It is difficult, for instance,

to insure that all your photos will be the same size, or all your headlines (especially if you want to emphasize a story over others on the page), or that your illustrations will be roughly all the same shape. In fact, we are almost forced into asymmetry on most layouts unless we plan carefully for the opposite effect.

For the beginner, there are several ways to check whether your layout is balanced, all based on looking at it from an altered perspective. You can squint at your layout. The blurring attained through narrowing your eyes tends to block out the light areas and bring the darker areas of your layout to the forefront. You can turn your layout upside down or look at it in a mirror. Both of these methods provide you with an opposite view, and, thus, a new look at your layout. Balance, or lack of it, will jump out at you almost immediately.

Exhibit 5.3

Asymmetric balance requires more patience and a great deal more practice to achieve. The fundamental rule in asymmetric balance requires visualizing your layout as a teeter-totter. Balance the objects on either of your vertical axis (in this case, the gutter between the two pages) according to weight and distance from the fulcrum.

Proportion

We tend to think of proportion in terms of comparison. For instance, a picture on a page is bigger or smaller than another picture on the page, or it is the largest element on the page (in comparison to the other elements). Thus, proportion is a measure of relationship. It helps to show one object's relation-

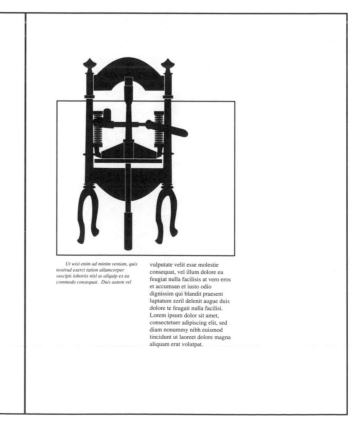

ship to other objects in your layout. For example, articles and their accompanying pictures, cutlines, and pull quotes will typically form a proportional whole in relationship to the rest of the page. The space that separates articles from one another may be greater than that which separates the elements within an article. We use proportion to tell us what belongs with what on a page.

Our sense of proportion has, or should have, a parallel in nature. Pythagorus, the Greek mathematician and philosopher, noticed this over 2,000 years ago when he suggested that the most pleasing proportion is based on a roughly 2 to 3 ratio. That is (in Pythagorian terms), the lesser dimension in a plane figure is to the greater as the greater is to the sum of both. Using the 2:3 ratio, 2 is to 3 what 3 is to 5. Get it?

Fortunately, there is a much simpler method of explaining this Golden Section, or *Golden Mean* as Aristotle later called it. Think of a page of typing paper. It is 8½" x 11"—roughly, a 2:3 ratio. In other words, an asymmetric proportion rather than a 1 to 1, symmetric proportion. For designers, this means avoiding dividing a page into halves, or any increment of a 1:1 ratio, such as 4 to 2 or 6 to 3. Not that this rule has to be religiously followed, but it does add visual interest to your layout.

A more practical, and easier, method of working with a page layout is the rule of *ground thirds*. This method requires that you divide a page into thirds,

Exhibit 5.4

In these two examples, proportion is achieved by utilizing the *Golden Mean* or *ground thirds*. In the top example, the ratio of total white space to other design elements on both pages taken together is roughly 2 to 3, or the Golden Mean. In the bottom example, each of the pages is laid out according to the rule of ground thirds. Notice that neither of the pages is split equally in half horizontally. Rather, both rely on a roughly two-thirds/one-third split. Our eyes are more comfortable with this type display and it reduces the static look that accompanies halved layouts. Notice, also, how balance is achieved in both layouts.

and that you balance the page using a two-thirds to one-third ratio. You've probably already noticed that two-thirds is roughly equivalent to three-fifths, the Golden Mean. This two-thirds:one-third ratio is commonly used in newsletter layout, but is most often apparent in print advertisements in which a large graphic image takes up two-thirds of the page, while the copy takes up the other third.

Don't get the idea that you have to group two-thirds of your elements into two-thirds of every page. This ration can be achieved in a number of ways. For instance, you can have a page two-thirds full and one-third empty. Or you can have a page that is two-thirds empty and one–third full (although your boss might think this a little wasteful).

The non-verbal message imparted by the use of ground thirds is decidedly informal. A layout based on halving the page is more formal, more constrained.

Sequence and Emphasis

Since sequence and emphasis work together toward the same end, we will cover them both here. Readers, at least occidental readers, read left to right, top to bottom. Sequence refers to how you place the elements on your page to aid this natural tendency, or, in some cases, to overcome it.

In addition to affecting a particular reading order, we tend to move from big elements to smaller elements, dark areas to lighter areas, colored elements to black and white elements, bright colors to muted colors, and unusual shape to usual shape. Properly sequencing the elements on your layout will literally lead your readers through your page.

Emphasis has to do with focusing your readers' attention on a single element on a page. This is what you want them to see first, and is usually where you want them to start interpreting your page. We emphasize elements by assigning them more optical weight than other items on the page. These emphasized elements are larger, darker, more colorful, oddly shaped. They draw the readers' attention first among all the other items on the page.

Exhibit 5.5

In this example, the headline in the upper left corner draws your eye naturally to the starting point (helped by our natural inclination to look there anyway). The ragged column ends and the pull quote helps direct the eye to the right, and the artwork and final pull quote indicate an exit point.

Sequence
Means leading your reader through your pages

Lorem ipsum dolor sit amet, consectetuer adipiscing elit, sed diam nonummy nibh euismod tincidunt ut laoreet dolore magna aliquam erat volutpat. Ut wisi enim ad minim veniam, quis nostrud exerci tation ullamcorper suscipit lobortis nisl ut aliquip ex ea commodo consequat. Duis autem vel eum iriure dolor in hendrerit in vulputate velit esse molestie consequat, vel illum dolore eu feugiat nulla facilisis at vero eros et accumsan et iusto odio dignissim qui blandit praesent luptatum zzril delenit augue duis dolore te feugait nulla facilisi. Lorem ipsum dolor sit amet, consectetuer adipiscing elit, sed diam nonummy nibh euismod tincidunt ut laoreet dolore magna aliquam erat volutpat. Ut wisi enim ad minim veniam, quis nostrud exerci tation ullamcorper suscipit lobortis nisl ut aliquip ex ea commodo consequat.

Duis autem vel eum iriure dolor in hendrerit in vulputate velit esse molestie consequat, vel illum dolore eu feugiat nulla facilisis at vero eros et accumsan et iusto odio dignissim qui blandit praesent luptatum zzril delenit augue duis dolore te feugait nulla

Make a roadmap out of your design elements

facilisi. Nam liber tempor cum soluta nobis eleifend option congue nihil imperdiet doming id quod mazim placerat facer possim assum.

Lorem ipsum dolor sit amet, consectetuer adipiscing elit, sed diam nonummy nibh euismod tincidunt ut laoreet dolore magna aliquam erat volutpat. Ut wisi enim ad minim veniam, quis nostrud exerci tation ullamcorper suscipit lobortis nisl ut aliquip ex

Lorem ipsum dolor sit amet, consectetuer adipiscing elit, sed diam nonummy nibh euismod tincidunt ut laoreet dolore magna aliquam erat volutpat. Ut wisi enim ad minim veniam, quis nostrud exerci tation ullamcorper suscipit lobortis nisl ut aliquip ex ea commodo consequat. Duis autem vel eum iriure dolor in hendrerit in vulputate velit esse molestie consequat, vel illum dolore eu feugiat nulla facilisis at vero eros et accumsan et iusto odio dignissim qui blandit praesent luptatum zzril delenit augue duis dolore te feugait nulla facilisi. Lorem ipsum dolor sit amet, consectetuer adipiscing elit, sed diam nonummy nibh euismod tincidunt ut laoreet dolore magna aliquam erat volutpat. Ut wisi enim ad minim veniam, quis nostrud exerci tation ullamcorper suscipit lobortis nisl ut aliquip ex ea commodo consequat.

Duis autem vel eum iriure dolor in hendrerit in vulputate

velit esse molestie consequat, vel illum dolore eu feugiat nulla facilisis at vero eros et accumsan et iusto odio dignissim qui blandit praesent luptatum zzril delenit augue duis dolore te feugait nulla facilisi. Nam liber tempor cum soluta nobis eleifend option congue nihil imperdiet doming id quod mazim placerat facer possim assum.

Lorem ipsum dolor sit amet, consectetuer adipiscing elit, sed diam nonummy nibh euismod tincidunt ut laoreet dolore magna aliquam erat volutpat. Ut wisi enim ad minim veniam, quis nostrud exerci tation ullamcorper suscipit lobortis nisl ut aliquip ex ea commodo consequat. Duis autem vel eum iriure dolor in hendrerit in vulputate velit esse molestie consequat, vel illum

dolore eu feugiat nulla facilisis at vero eros et accumsan et iusto odio dignissim qui blandit praesent luptatum zzril delenit augue duis dolore te feugait nulla facilisi. Lorem ipsum dolor sit amet, consectetuer adipiscing elit, sed diam nonummy nibh euismod tincidunt ut laoreet dolore magna aliquam erat volutpat.

Lorem ipsum dolor sit amet, consectetuer adipiscing elit, sed diam nonummy nibh euismod tincidunt ut laoreet dolore magna aliquam erat volutpat. Ut wisi enim ad minim veniam, quis nostrud exerci tation ullamcorper suscipit lobortis nisl ut aliquip ex ea commodo consequat. Duis autem vel eum iriure dolor in hendrerit in vulputate velit esse molestie consequat, vel illum dolore eu feugiat nulla facilisis at vero eros et accumsan et iusto

Don't gamble with your readers' attention

As a newsletter designer, there are a number of simple techniques that, if used properly, will show your readers exactly where to look first, and where to go from there.

- **All elements.** Placement high on the page will gain emphasis. Elements placed at or near the bottom will have less emphasis. Placement near or at the center of the page will also gain emphasis, especially if used in conjunction with another form of emphasis such as color or size. The left side of a page or the left page of a two-page spread has priority over the right. On the other hand, the outside margins of a two-page spread (the left margin of the left page and the right margin of the right page) are focal points as well.

- **Headlines**. For heavier emphasis, place headlines at the top or near the center of the page. The eye naturally falls in these areas. Additional emphasis can be gained by using a larger point size or stretching the headline over more than one column width. Typical options, then, are one-column heads in a smaller point size, more than one-column heads in a smaller point size, one-column heads in a larger point size, and more than one-column heads in a larger point size.

Depending on the number of columns you are working with and the range of point sizes you choose, the degrees of emphasis are many. Keep in mind, however, that you should vary headline size by no more than a few basic increments. For example, if minor heads are set at 18 points, major heads should not be larger than 24 or 30 points. The rare exception might be the major headline on the front page of your newsletter. You might go all the way to 36 points; however, be sure that your headline doesn't then conflict with and lessen the impact of your banner or nameplate.

Exhibit 5.6

Using strong graphics, color, unusual shapes or large type will all indicate to your readers where you want them to look first; however, this may not mean you want them to start reading there. Don't confuse emphasis with sequence. Although emphasis can be used to establish sequence, it can be used simply to draw attention to something, with the understanding that the reader should then know where to look to begin reading.

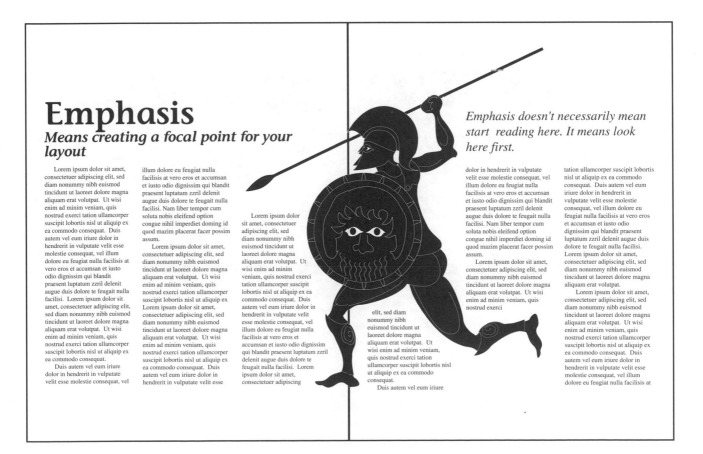

- **Articles**. Place lead articles at or near the top of the page. Also place jumped articles at or near the top. Since jump lines are usually small, you can still emphasize another article on the same page as a jumped article by working with the headline. By using boxes and tint blocks, you can emphasize an article by setting it off from other elements on the page. Also, dividing your page into ground thirds and placing an emphasized article in either portion by itself will get it attention.

- **Graphics**. Larger photographs and other graphic devices impart greater emphasis, no matter where they are placed. Smaller elements placed at the top or bottom of the page can also gain emphasis. A small photo, for example, placed at or near the bottom of a page might help balance a large headline placed at the top of the page.

    Again, graphic elements should follow the general restrictions of your grid. Thus, a three-column grid will allow photos of one, two, or three columns in width. Remember, too, that the darker the graphic element, the more emphasis it will have. This applies to boxed articles and tint blocks as well.

- **White space**. Remember, white space is weighted just like any other design element; however, using it effectively requires a lot of practice. White space is not usually thought of as an element of emphasis. Rather it is usually an element of contrast. That is, it is used to emphasize something else, not draw attention to itself. The one rule to remember when using white space is, don't trap it. Don't surround it with other elements. White space should be pushed to the outside of your pages, not the inside. And on a two-page spread, the only white space between the two pages should be the gutter. Wide side margins, heavy drops (the amount of white space at the top of a page), or uneven bottoms all add contrast. The creative use of white space will add an air of affluence to your publication, make it look more sophisticated. Too much white space, on the other hand, will make a newsletter look like its editor ran out of stories.

Unity

Unity might be thought of as synonymous with consistency. It refers to the entire publication and implies that each element will be linked in some way to the whole. As human beings, we need unity just like we need balance. In fact, one element of unity—closure—is so psychologically necessary that if we don't get it, we try to construct it for ourselves. This is known as *gestalt*, and refers to our natural tendency to organize or make sense out of chaos. For example, when we view a newscaster on TV, we don't see anything but his or her upper torso. We don't assume that the person is cut in half. We automatically fill in the other parts. In other words, we see a person, not just the parts that make up that person.

Unity is one way of providing readers with a whole by drawing relationships among its various parts. This means that body type and headline type should be compatible. Photos should be either all black and white or all color. The layout should be all formal or all informal. In other words, we need to create a recognizable pattern. However, what we've looked at so far in this section are the separate parts that make up the whole we call unity. Perhaps the best way to gain overall unity of design has more to do with an overall look, a unifying design. In publication design, this unifying element is called a grid.

Working with Grids

Grids are guides around which you build your publication. Their importance to layout can't be overstressed. Grids are not, as some graphic artists will tell you, confining. They do not stifle creativity or limit your imagination. They do aid you in balancing your publication page by page or from spread to spread. For longer or regularly produced publications such as a weekly newsletter, grids are indispensable.

Grids set up a typical page as a series of rectangular elements or, more commonly, columns of two, three, four, or five. Layout sheets are designed as multi-purpose grids that offer you a wide variety of rectangular options, both vertical and horizontal. These sheets come in sizes suited to nearly any format and frequently contain registration marks, margin lines, and vertical and horizontal rules marked in picas as well as inches.

For the editor laying out a newsletter using traditional methods (cut and paste), these sheets are printed in a nonphoto blue that can't be picked up by a printer's camera. If you use a nonphoto blue pencil or pen, you can mark up your layout with instructions to yourself and the printer without worrying about them being reproduced; however, most printers would prefer that you don't write on your layout at all.

A good grid offers you an infinite possibility of choices for placement of elements. For example, a three-column grid (the most popular for newsletters) allows you to use one-, two-, or three-column photos; vary type size for articles running two-columns in width; run headlines in varying sizes in one-, two-, or three-column widths; and an infinite number of other options.

On the following pages are the most basic grids for newsletter layout as well as various options for each basic model.

←――――――――――――――――→

Exhibit 5.7
Unity is the most difficult design principle to explain. In its simplest terms, it means using compatible type faces, artwork, and photographs all the way through your newsletter. In its more complex form, unity includes the other elements, such as balance, proportion, sequence and emphasis. To use these elements in a consistent way throughout a publication also aids unity of design. The best way to lose unity is to combine too many disparate elements in your publication, especially if they conflict with one another. In this layout, unity is provided by a relaxed, informal style, including cartoon art, a large italic headline, unjustified columns, and plenty of white space.

Two-column Grids

The simplest newsletter grid is the two-column. This is a classic in newsletter design and is useful if you need simplicity and speed. If, for example, you know in advance that you won't have much time to put a newsletter together each week, this grid will provide you with a good-looking format with a minimum of layout time.

The key to the simplicity of this design is that the articles flow one after the other until the pages are filled up. No particular emphasis is sought for any one article and both long and short articles fit with equal ease. No jumps are necessary since each article is completely finished before the next is started.

In **Exhibit 5.8**, a minimum of graphic elements are used: the banner and the news briefs column, "High Notes." The purpose of this column (on page 2) is to handle several small articles that do not require major headlines. You can adapt this column to almost any need—People in the News, Calendar of Events, or announcements of some kind.

A simplified version of page 2, **Exhibit 5.9**, would omit the newsbriefs column and merely continue with the articles.

A more sophisticated version of the two-column newsletter (**Exhibit 5.10**) adds additional elements—photos, captions, and some graphic design elements in the news notes column head. In a simple newsletter, a caption is usually run immediately beneath the photo to which it refers. Captions are frequently one point size less than text type and italicized.

Notice that the photos are restricted to a near-square, horizontal shape due to the width of the columns. If they were much larger, the photos would overwhelm the page, much smaller and you would have to wrap the text around the photo, and, thus, reduce the simplicity and speed of laying out your newsletter—the primary reasons for using a two-column grid in the first place. A standard 5" x 7" photo will scale to approximately this size.

Exhibit 5.8

Crescendo

February, 1991 Volume 1 Number 1

New season opens with Mozart

Lorem ipsum dolor sit amet, consectetuer adipiscing elit, sed diam nonummy nibh euismod tincidunt ut laoreet dolore magna aliquam erat volutpat. Ut wisi enim ad minim veniam, quis nostrud exerci tation ullamcorper suscipit lobortis nisl ut aliquip ex ea commodo consequat. Duis autem vel eum iriure dolor in hendrerit in vulputate velit esse molestie consequat, vel illum dolore eu feugiat nulla facilisis at vero eros et accumsan et iusto odio dignissim qui blandit praesent luptatum zzril delenit augue duis dolore te feugait nulla facilisi. Lorem ipsum dolor sit amet, consectetuer adipiscing elit, sed diam nonummy nibh euismod tincidunt ut laoreet dolore magna aliquam erat volutpat. Ut wisi enim ad minim veniam, quis nostrud exerci tation ullamcorper suscipit lobortis nisl ut aliquip ex ea commodo consequat.

Duis autem vel eum iriure dolor in hendrerit in vulputate velit esse molestie consequat, vel illum dolore eu feugiat nulla facilisis at vero eros et accumsan et iusto odio dignissim qui blandit praesent luptatum zzril delenit augue duis dolore te feugait nulla facilisi. Nam liber tempor cum soluta nobis eleifend option congue nihil imperdiet doming id quod mazim placerat facer possim assum.

Lorem ipsum dolor sit amet, consectetuer adipiscing elit, sed diam nonummy nibh euismod tincidunt ut laoreet dolore magna aliquam erat volutpat. Ut wisi enim ad minim veniam, quis nostrud exerci tation ullamcorper suscipit lobortis nisl ut aliquip ex ea commodo consequat. Duis autem vel eum iriure dolor in hendrerit in vulputate velit esse molestie consequat, vel illum dolore eu feugiat nulla facilisis at vero eros et accumsan et iusto odio dignissim qui blandit praesent luptatum zzril delenit augue duis dolore te feugait nulla facilisi. Lorem ipsum dolor sit amet, consectetuer adipiscing elit, sed diam nonummy nibh euismod

tincidunt ut laoreet dolore magna aliquam erat volutpat.

Ut wisi enim ad minim veniam, quis nostrud exerci tation ullamcorper suscipit lobortis nisl ut aliquip ex ea commodo consequat. Duis autem vel eum iriure dolor in hendrerit in vulputate velit esse molestie consequat, vel illum dolore eu feugiat nulla facilisis at vero eros et accumsan et iusto odio dignissim qui blandit praesent luptatum zzril delenit augue duis dolore te feugait nulla facilisi. Lorem ipsum dolor sit amet, consectetuer adipiscing elit, sed diam nonummy nibh euismod tincidunt ut laoreet dolore magna aliquam erat volutpat.

Ut wisi enim ad minim veniam, quis nostrud exerci tation ullamcorper suscipit lobortis nisl ut aliquip ex ea commodo consequat. Duis autem vel eum iriure dolor in hendrerit in vulputate velit esse molestie consequat, vel illum dolore eu feugiat nulla facilisis at vero eros et accumsan et iusto odio dignissim qui blandit praesent luptatum zzril delenit augue duis dolore te feugait nulla

Conductor Irvin leaves for LA

Lorem ipsum dolor sit amet, consectetuer adipiscing elit, sed diam nonummy nibh euismod tincidunt ut laoreet dolore magna aliquam erat volutpat. Ut wisi enim ad minim veniam, quis nostrud exerci tation ullamcorper suscipit lobortis nisl ut aliquip ex ea commodo consequat. Duis autem vel eum iriure dolor in hendrerit in vulputate velit esse molestie consequat, vel illum dolore eu feugiat nulla facilisis at vero eros et accumsan et iusto odio dignissim qui blandit praesent luptatum zzril delenit augue duis dolore te feugait nulla facilisi. Lorem ipsum dolor sit amet, consectetuer adipiscing elit, sed diam nonummy nibh euismod tincidunt ut laoreet dolore magna aliquam erat volutpat. Ut wisi enim ad minim veniam, quis nostrud exerci tation ullamcorper suscipit lobortis nisl ut aliquip ex ea commodo consequat.

Duis autem vel eum iriure dolor in hendrerit in vulputate velit esse molestie consequat, vel illum dolore eu feugiat nulla facilisis at vero eros et

augue duis dolore te feugait nulla facilisi. Nam liber tempor cum soluta nobis eleifend option congue nihil imperdiet doming id quod mazim placerat facer possim assum.

Lorem ipsum dolor sit amet, consectetuer adipiscing elit, sed diam nonummy nibh euismod tincidunt ut laoreet dolore magna aliquam erat volutpat. Ut wisi enim ad minim veniam, quis nostrud exerci tation ullamcorper suscipit lobortis nisl ut aliquip ex ea commodo consequat. Duis autem vel eum iriure dolor in hendrerit in vulputate velit esse molestie consequat, vel illum dolore eu feugiat nulla facilisis at vero eros et accumsan et iusto odio dignissim qui blandit praesent

Five new concerts set for 1991 season

Lorem ipsum dolor sit amet, consectetuer adipiscing elit, sed diam nonummy nibh euismod tincidunt ut laoreet dolore magna aliquam erat volutpat. Ut wisi enim ad minim veniam, quis nostrud exerci tation ullamcorper suscipit lobortis nisl ut aliquip ex ea commodo consequat. Duis autem vel eum iriure dolor in hendrerit in vulputate velit esse molestie consequat, vel illum dolore eu feugiat nulla facilisis at vero eros et accumsan et iusto odio dignissim qui blandit praesent luptatum zzril delenit augue duis dolore te feugait nulla facilisi. Nam liber tempor cum soluta nobis eleifend option congue nihil imperdiet doming id quod mazim placerat facer possim assum.

Lorem ipsum dolor sit amet, consectetuer adipiscing elit, sed diam nonummy nibh euismod tincidunt ut laoreet dolore magna aliquam erat volutpat. Ut wisi enim ad minim veniam, quis nostrud exerci tation ullamcorper suscipit lobortis nisl ut aliquip ex ea commodo consequat. Duis autem vel eum iriure dolor in hendrerit in vulputate velit esse molestie consequat, vel illum dolore eu feugiat nulla facilisis at vero eros et accumsan et iusto odio dignissim qui blandit praesent luptatum zzril delenit augue duis dolore te feugait nulla facilisi. Lorem ipsum dolor sit amet, consectetuer adipiscing elit, sed diam nonummy nibh euismod tincidunt ut laoreet dolore magna aliquam erat volutpat.

Ut wisi enim ad minim veniam, quis nostrud exerci tation ullamcorper suscipit lobortis nisl ut aliquip ex ea augue duis dolore te feugait nulla facilisi. Nam liber tempor cum soluta nobis eleifend option congue nihil

Five new members

Dolor sit amet, consectetuer adipiscing elit, sed diam nonummy nibh euismod tincidunt ut laoreet dolore magna aliquam erat volutpat. Ut wisi enim ad minim veniam, quis nostrud exerci tation ullamcorper suscipit lobortis nisl ut aliquip ex ea commodo consequat.

More performances this season

Duis autem vel eum iriure dolor in hendrerit in vulputate velit esse molestie consequat, vel illum dolore eu feugiat nulla facilisis at vero eros et accumsan et iusto odio dignissim qui blandit praesent luptatum zzril delenit augue duis dolore te feugait nulla facilisi. Nam liber tempor cum soluta nobis eleifend option congue nihil imperdiet doming id quod mazim placerat facer possim assum.

Mozart makes a comeback

Lorem ipsum dolor sit amet, consectetuer adipiscing elit, sed diam nonummy nibh euismod tincidunt ut laoreet dolore magna aliquam erat volutpat. Ut wisi enim ad minim veniam, quis nostrud exerci tation ullamcorper suscipit lobortis nisl ut aliquip ex ea commodo consequat. Duis autem vel eum iriure dolor in hendrerit in vulputate velit esse molestie consequat, vel illum dolore eu feugiat nulla facilisis at vero eros et accumsan et iusto odio dignissim qui blandit praesent luptatum zzril delenit

Stephensen renews contract

Augue duis dolore te feugait nulla facilisi. Lorem ipsum dolor sit amet, consectetuer adipiscing elit, sed diam nonummy nibh euismod tincidunt ut laoreet dolore magna aliquam erat volutpat.

Free concert series

Ut wisi enim ad minim veniam, quis nostrud exerci tation ullamcorper suscipit lobortis nisl ut aliquip ex ea commodo consequat. Duis autem vel eum iriure dolor in hendrerit in Wulputate velit esse molestie consequat, vel illum dolore eu feugiat nulla facilisis at vero eros et

Exhibit 5.9

augue duis dolore te feugait nulla facilisi. Nam liber tempor cum soluta nobis eleifend option congue nihil imperdiet doming id quod mazim placerat facer possim assum.

Lorem ipsum dolor sit amet, consectetuer adipiscing elit, sed diam nonummy nibh euismod tincidunt ut laoreet dolore magna aliquam erat volutpat. Ut wisi enim ad minim veniam, quis nostrud exerci tation ullamcorper suscipit lobortis nisl ut aliquip ex ea commodo consequat. Duis autem vel eum iriure dolor in hendrerit in vulputate velit esse molestie consequat, vel illum dolore eu feugiat nulla facilisis at vero eros et accumsan et iusto odio dignissim qui blandit praesent

Five new concerts set for 1991 season

Lorem ipsum dolor sit amet, consectetuer adipiscing elit, sed diam nonummy nibh euismod tincidunt ut laoreet dolore magna aliquam erat volutpat. Ut wisi enim ad minim veniam, quis nostrud exerci tation ullamcorper suscipit lobortis nisl ut aliquip ex ea commodo consequat. Duis autem vel eum iriure dolor in hendrerit in vulputate velit esse molestie consequat, vel illum dolore eu feugiat nulla facilisis at vero eros et accumsan et iusto odio dignissim qui blandit praesent luptatum zzril delenit augue duis dolore te feugait nulla facilisi. Lorem ipsum augue duis dolore te feugait nulla facilisi. Nam liber tempor cum soluta nobis eleifend option congue nihil imperdiet doming id quod mazim placerat facer possim assum.

Lorem ipsum dolor sit amet, consectetuer adipiscing elit, sed diam nonummy nibh euismod tincidunt ut laoreet dolore magna aliquam erat volutpat. Ut wisi enim ad minim veniam, quis nostrud exerci tation ullamcorper suscipit lobortis nisl ut aliquip ex ea commodo consequat. Duis autem vel eum iriure dolor in hendrerit in vulputate velit esse molestie consequat, vel illum dolore eu feugiat nulla facilisis at vero eros et accumsan et iusto odio dignissim qui blandit praesent luptatum zzril delenit augue duis dolore te feugait nulla facilisi. Lorem ipsum dolor sit amet, consectetuer adipiscing elit, sed diam nonummy nibh euismod tincidunt ut laoreet dolore magna aliquam erat volutpat.

Ut wisi enim ad minim veniam, quis nostrud exerci tation ullamcorper suscipit lobortis nisl ut aliquip ex ea augue duis dolore te feugait nulla facilisi. Nam liber tempor cum soluta nobis eleifend option congue nihil

Lorem ipsum dolor sit amet, consectetuer adipiscing elit, sed diam nonummy nibh euismod tincidunt ut laoreet dolore magna aliquam erat volutpat. Ut wisi enim ad minim veniam, quis nostrud exerci tation ullamcorper suscipit lobortis nisl ut aliquip ex ea commodo consequat. Duis autem vel eum iriure dolor

Cello section finds new creative outlet

Lorem ipsum dolor sit amet, consectetuer adipiscing elit, sed diam nonummy nibh euismod tincidunt ut laoreet dolore magna aliquam erat volutpat. Ut wisi enim ad minim veniam, quis nostrud exerci tation ullamcorper suscipit lobortis nisl ut aliquip ex ea commodo consequat. Duis autem vel eum iriure dolor in hendrerit in vulputate velit esse molestie consequat, vel illum dolore eu feugiat nulla facilisis at vero eros et accumsan et iusto odio dignissim qui blandit praesent luptatum zzril delenit augue duis dolore te feugait nulla facilisi. Lorem ipsum augue duis dolore te feugait nulla facilisi. Nam liber tempor cum soluta nobis eleifend option congue nihil imperdiet doming id quod mazim placerat facer possim assum.

Lorem ipsum dolor sit amet, consectetuer adipiscing elit, sed diam nonummy nibh euismod tincidunt ut laoreet dolore magna aliquam erat volutpat. Ut wisi enim ad minim veniam, quis nostrud exerci tation ullamcorper suscipit lobortis nisl ut aliquip ex ea commodo consequat. Duis autem vel eum iriure dolor in hendrerit in vulputate velit esse molestie consequat, vel illum dolore eu feugiat nulla facilisis at vero eros et accumsan et iusto odio dignissim qui blandit praesent luptatum zzril delenit augue duis dolore te feugait nulla

Holtz honored at banquet

in hendrerit in vulputate velit esse molestie consequat, vel illum dolore eu feugiat nulla facilisis at vero eros et accumsan et iusto odio dignissim qui blandit praesent luptatum zzril delenit augue duis dolore te feugait nulla facilisi. Lorem ipsum augue duis dolore te feugait nulla facilisi. Nam liber tempor cum soluta nobis eleifend option congue nihil imperdiet doming id quod mazim placerat facer possim assum.

Lorem ipsum dolor sit amet, consectetuer

Exhibit 5.9

Exhibit 5.10

Crescendo

January 1991 Volume 19 Number 1

New concert season opens with Mozart

Lorem ipsum dolor sit amet, consectetuer adipiscing elit, sed diam nonummy nibh euismod tincidunt ut laoreet dolore magna aliquam erat volutpat. Ut wisi enim ad minim veniam, quis nostrud exerci tation ullamcorper suscipit lobortis nisl ut aliquip ex ea commodo consequat. Duis autem vel eum iriure dolor in hendrerit in vulputate velit esse molestie consequat, vel illum dolore eu feugiat nulla facilisis at vero eros et accumsan et iusto odio dignissim qui blandit praesent luptatum zzril delenit Lorem ipsum dolor sit amet, consectetuer adipiscing elit, sed diam nonummy nibh euismod tincidunt ut laoreet dolore magna aliquam erat volutpat. Ut wisi enim ad minim veniam, quis nostrud exerci tation ullamcorper suscipit lobortis nisl ut aliquip ex ea commodo consequat.

Duis autem vel eum iriure dolor in hendrerit in vulputate velit esse molestie consequat, vel illum dolore eu feugiat nulla facilisis at vero eros et

Lorem ipsum dolor sit amet, consectetuer adipiscing elit, sed diam nonummy nibh euismod tincidunt ut laoreet

accumsan et iusto odio dignissim qui blandit praesent luptatum zzril delenit augue duis dolore te feugait nulla facilisi. Nam liber tempor cum soluta nobis eleifend option congue nihil imperdiet doming id quod mazim placerat facer possim assum.

Lorem ipsum dolor sit amet, consectetuer adipiscing elit, sed diam nonummy nibh euismod tincidunt ut laoreet dolore magna aliquam erat volutpat.

Conductor Irvin leaves for LA

dolor sit amet, consectetuer adipiscing elit, sed diam nonummy nibh euismod tincidunt ut laoreet dolore magna aliquam erat volutpat. Ut wisi enim ad minim veniam, quis nostrud exerci tation ullamcorper suscipit lobortis nisl ut aliquip ex ea commodo consequat.

Duis autem vel eum iriure dolor in hendrerit in vulputate velit esse molestie consequat, vel illum dolore eu feugiat nulla facilisis at vero eros et accumsan et iusto odio dignissim qui blandit praesent luptatum zzril delenit Lorem ipsum dolor sit amet, consectetuer adipiscing elit, sed diam nonummy nibh euismod tincidunt ut laoreet dolore magna aliquam erat volutpat. Ut wisi enim ad minim veniam, quis nostrud exerci tation ullamcorper suscipit lobortis nisl ut aliquip ex ea commodo consequat. Duis autem vel eum iriure dolor in hendrerit in vulputate velit esse molestie consequat, vel illum dolore eu feugiat nulla facilisis at vero eros et accumsan et iusto odio dignissim qui blandit praesent luptatum zzril delenit augue duis dolore te feugait nulla facilisi. Lorem ipsum dolor sit amet, consectetuer adipiscing elit, sed diam nonummy nibh euismod tincidunt ut laoreet dolore magna aliquam erat volutpat. Ut wisi enim ad minim veniam, quis nostrud exerci tation ullamcorper suscipit lobortis nisl ut aliquip ex ea commodo consequat.

Duis autem vel eum iriure dolor in hendrerit in

Lorem ipsum dolor sit amet, consectetuer adipiscing elit, sed diam nonummy nibh euismod tincidunt ut laoreet dolore magna aliquam erat volutpat. Ut wisi enim ad minim veniam, quis nostrud exerci tation ullamcorper suscipit lobortis nisl ut aliquip ex ea commodo consequat. Duis autem vel eum iriure dolor in hendrerit in vulputate velit esse molestie consequat, vel illum dolore eu feugiat nulla facilisis at vero eros et accumsan et iusto odio dignissim qui blandit praesent luptatum zzril delenit augue duis dolore te feugait nulla facilisi. Nam liber tempor cum soluta nobis eleifend option congue nihil imperdiet doming id quod mazim placerat facer possim assum. Lorem ipsum dolor sit amet, consectetuer adipiscing elit, sed diam nonummy nibh euismod tincidunt ut laoreet dolore magna aliquam erat volutpat. Ut wisi enim ad minim veniam, quis nostrud exerci tation ullamcorper suscipit lobortis nisl ut aliquip ex ea

New accoustics better than ever

Lorem ipsum dolor sit amet, consectetuer adipiscing elit, sed diam nonummy nibh euismod tincidunt ut laoreet dolore magna aliquam erat volutpat. Ut wisi enim ad minim veniam, quis nostrud exerci tation ullamcorper suscipit lobortis nisl ut aliquip ex ea commodo consequat. Duis autem vel eum iriure dolor in hendrerit in vulputate velit esse molestie consequat, vel illum dolore eu feugiat nulla facilisis at vero eros et accumsan et iusto odio dignissim qui blandit praesent luptatum zzril delenit augue duis dolore te feugait nulla facilisi. Lorem ipsum dolor sit amet, consectetuer adipiscing elit, sed diam nonummy nibh euismod

Lorem ipsum dolor sit amet, consectetuer adipiscing elit, sed diam nonummy nibh euismod tincidunt ut laoreet

HIGHNOTES
Important late-breaking stories

Five new members

Dolor sit amet, consectetuer adipiscing elit, sed diam nonummy nibh euismod tincidunt ut laoreet dolore magna aliquam erat volutpat. Ut wisi enim ad minim veniam, quis nostrud exerci tation ullamcorper suscipit lobortis nisl ut aliquip ex ea commodo

More performances this season

Duis autem vel eum iriure dolor in hendrerit in vulputate velit esse molestie consequat, vel illum dolore eu feugiat nulla facilisis at vero eros et accumsan et iusto odio dignissim qui blandit praesent luptatum zzril delenit augue duis dolore te feugait nulla facilisi. Nam liber tempor cum soluta nobis eleifend option congue nihil imperdiet doming id quod mazim placerat facer possim assum.

Mozart makes a comeback

Lorem ipsum dolor sit amet, consectetuer adipiscing elit, sed diam nonummy nibh euismod tincidunt ut laoreet dolore magna aliquam erat volutpat. Ut wisi enim ad minim veniam, quis nostrud exerci tation ullamcorper suscipit lobortis nisl ut aliquip ex ea commodo consequat. Duis autem vel eum iriure dolor in hendrerit in vulputate velit esse molestie consequat, vel illum dolore eu feugiat nulla facilisis at vero eros et accumsan et iusto odio dignissim qui blandit praesent luptatum zzril delenit

Stephensen renews contract

Augue duis dolore te feugait nulla facilisi. Lorem ipsum dolor sit amet, consectetuer adipiscing elit, sed diam nonummy nibh euismod tincidunt ut laoreet dolore magna aliquam erat volutpat.

Free concert series

Ut wisi enim ad minim veniam, quis nostrud exerci tation ullamcorper suscipit lobortis nisl ut aliquip ex ea commodo consequat. Duis autem vel eum iriure dolor in hendrerit in Wulputate velit esse molestie consequat, vel illum dolore eu feugiat nulla facilisis at vero eros et

Exhibit 5.10

Two-column Newspaper Style

The primary difference between newspaper style and simple two-column newsletter style is the placement of the articles and the added flexibility. The simpler two-column style assumes that all stories are of equal importance and that they will be placed one after the other without jumps. Newspaper style allows for article emphasis through the use of two-column headlines and placement of articles on the page, including jumps to carry articles to other pages. This grid is still simple enough to be accomplished in a short time, yet it allows you the flexibility of emphasizing key articles.

On this grid, each page is divided into story areas assigned so as to add emphasis to the key story on the page and to suggest a reading order. This usually implies a more horizontal format rather than the strictly vertical format of the simpler version. This layout technique also requires a little more attention to detail since jumped stories must fit in on other pages. Be sure to include jump directions at the end of each article that continues elsewhere, such as "continued on page 2." And when you pick up the article on the next page, start it with an abbreviated version of the headline and continuation information, such as "Mozart series continued from page 1."

Remember that although this is a slightly different version of a two-column grid, small photos will slow your layout time if they have to be text wrapped. It is better to stick to one-column photos.

In newspaper style, headline size (point size), placement (page number or location), and width (one or two columns wide) indicates the importance you place on the story. In **Exhibit 5.12**, compare the headline at the bottom of page 1 with the headline at the top of page 2. The page 1 headline is smaller, but gains a certain importance because it is on page 1. The larger page 2 headline clearly says "start reading here." Be careful not to use a headline size that will conflict with the primary headline on the page. If the large page 2 headline were used on page 1, for example, it would conflict with the top headline and dilute the importance of both articles. If the smaller page 1

Exhibit 5.11

The opening article in this simple two-column layout finishes on page 1, followed immediately by the second article. This is the easiest two-column page to lay out since it requires no jumping. On page 2, the slightly larger, two-column headline at the bottom of the page says that this article is of equal importance to the article at the top.

Crescendo

January 1991 Volume 19 Number 1

Season opens with Mozart

Lorem ipsum dolor sit amet, consectetuer adipiscing elit, sed diam nonummy nibh euismod tincidunt ut laoreet dolore magna aliquam erat volutpat. Ut wisi enim ad minim veniam, quis nostrud exerci tation ullamcorper suscipit lobortis nisl ut aliquip ex ea commodo consequat. Duis autem vel eum iriure dolor in hendrerit in vulputate velit esse molestie consequat, vel illum dolore eu feugiat nulla facilisis at vero eros et accumsan et iusto odio dignissim qui blandit praesent luptatum zzril delenit augue duis dolore te feugait nulla facilisi. Lorem ipsum dolor sit amet, consectetuer adipiscing elit, sed diam nonummy nibh euismod tincidunt ut laoreet dolore magna aliquam erat volutpat. Ut wisi enim ad minim veniam, quis nostrud exerci tation ullamcorper suscipit lobortis nisl ut aliquip ex ea commodo consequat.

Duis autem vel eum iriure dolor in hendrerit in vulputate velit esse molestie consequat, vel illum dolore eu feugiat nulla facilisis at vero eros et accumsan et iusto odio dignissim qui blandit praesent luptatum zzril delenit augue duis dolore te feugait nulla

facilisi. Nam liber tempor cum soluta nobis eleifend option congue nihil imperdiet doming id quod mazim placerat facer possim assum.

Lorem ipsum dolor sit amet, consectetuer adipiscing elit, sed diam nonummy nibh euismod tincidunt ut laoreet dolore magna aliquam erat volutpat. Ut wisi enim ad minim veniam, quis nostrud exerci tation ullamcorper Lorem ipsum dolor sit amet, consectetuer adipiscing elit, sed diam nonummy nibh euismod tincidunt ut laoreet dolore magna aliquam erat volutpat. Ut wisi enim ad minim veniam, quis nostrud exerci tation ullamcorper suscipit lobortis nisl ut aliquip ex ea commodo consequat. Duis autem vel eum iriure dolor in hendrerit in vulputate velit esse

New acoustics better than ever

dolor sit amet, consectetuer adipiscing elit, sed diam nonummy nibh euismod tincidunt ut laoreet dolore magna aliquam erat volutpat. Ut wisi enim ad minim veniam, quis nostrud exerci tation ullamcorper suscipit lobortis nisl ut aliquip ex ea commodo consequat.

Duis autem vel eum iriure dolor in hendrerit in vulputate velit esse molestie consequat, vel illum dolore eu feugiat nulla facilisis at vero eros et accumsan et iusto odio dignissim qui blandit praesent luptatum zzril delenit augue Lorem ipsum dolor sit amet, consectetuer adipiscing elit, sed diam nonummy nibh euismod tincidunt ut laoreet dolore magna aliquam erat volutpat. Ut wisi enim ad minim veniam, quis nostrud exerci tation ullamcorper suscipit lobortis nisl ut aliquip ex ea commodo consequat. Duis autem vel eum iriure dolor in hendrerit in vulputate velit esse molestie consequat, vel illum dolore eu feugiat nulla facilisis at vero eros et accumsan et iusto odio

Lorem ipsum dolor sit amet, consectetuer adipiscing elit, sed diam nonummy nibh euismod tincidunt ut laoreet

Eugene symphony opens new era

Lorem ipsum dolor sit amet, consectetuer adipiscing elit, sed diam nonummy nibh euismod tincidunt ut laoreet dolore magna aliquam erat volutpat. Ut wisi enim ad minim veniam, quis nostrud exerci tation ullamcorper suscipit lobortis nisl ut aliquip ex ea commodo consequat. Duis autem vel eum iriure dolor in hendrerit in vulputate velit esse molestie consequat, vel illum dolore eu feugiat nulla facilisis at vero eros et accumsan et iusto odio dignissim qui blandit praesent luptatum zzril delenit augue duis dolore te feugait nulla facilisi. Nam liber tempor cum soluta nobis eleifend option congue nihil imperdiet doming id quod mazim placerat facer possim assum.

Lorem ipsum dolor sit amet, consectetuer adipiscing elit, sed diam nonummy nibh euismod tincidunt ut laoreet dolore magna aliquam erat volutpat. Ut wisi enim ad minim veniam, quis nostrud exerci tation ullamcorper suscipit lobortis nisl ut aliquip ex ea commodo consequat. Duis autem vel eum iriure dolor

Lorem ipsum dolor sit amet, consectetuer adipiscing elit, sed diam nonummy nibh euismod tincidunt ut laoreet dolore magna aliquam erat volutpat. Ut wisi enim ad minim veniam, quis nostrud exerci tation ullamcorper suscipit lobortis nisl ut aliquip ex ea commodo consequat. Duis autem vel eum iriure dolor

Lorem ipsum dolor sit amet, consectetuer adipiscing elit, sed diam nonummy nibh euismod tincidunt ut laoreet

Five new members add excitement

augue duis dolore te feugait nulla facilisi. Nam liber tempor cum soluta nobis eleifend option congue nihil imperdiet doming id quod mazim placerat facer possim assum.

Lorem ipsum dolor sit amet, consectetuer

Lorem ipsum dolor sit amet, consectetuer adipiscing elit, sed diam nonummy nibh euismod tincidunt ut laoreet

Lorem ipsum dolor sit amet, consectetuer adipiscing elit, sed diam nonummy nibh euismod tincidunt ut laoreet dolore magna aliquam erat volutpat. Ut wisi enim ad minim veniam, quis nostrud exerci tation ullamcorper suscipit lobortis nisl ut aliquip ex ea commodo consequat. Duis autem vel eum iriure dolor in hendrerit in vulputate velit esse molestie consequat, vel illum dolore eu feugiat nulla facilisis at vero eros et accumsan et iusto odio dignissim qui blandit praesent luptatum zzril delenit augue duis dolore te feugait nulla facilisi. Lorem ipsum augue duis dolore te feugait nulla facilisi. Nam liber tempor cum soluta nobis eleifend option congue nihil imperdiet doming id quod mazim placerat facer possim assum.

Lorem ipsum dolor sit amet, consectetuer adipiscing elit, sed diam nonummy nibh euismod tincidunt ut laoreet dolore magna aliquam erat volutpat. Ut wisi enim ad minim veniam, quis nostrud exerci tation ullamcorper suscipit lobortis nisl ut aliquip ex ea commodo consequat. Duis autem vel eum iriure dolor in hendrerit in vulputate velit esse molestie consequat,

headline were at the top of page 2, it would appear relatively insignificant simply because it is on page 2.

Remember, your choices of headlines in newspaper style depend on the emphasis you wish to place on the article: larger point size in one-column, larger point size in two-column, smaller point size in one-column on the front page, smaller point size in one-column on other pages, and smaller point size in two-column on pages other than page 1.

The toughest part of designing a horizontal newspaper-style page is to have all the elements in the top half run flush to the dividing line at the middle of the page. Ragged column ends will invariably leave trapped white space. And, remember, white space carries weight as does filled space, and you run the risk of having the white space focus the reader's attention where you don't want it.

Exhibit 5.12

In this example, the lead headline and picture draw the reader's eye immediately to the top of the page through the use of emphasis. You have the option of finishing the lead story on page 1 (see **Exhibit 5.13**) or continuing (jumping) to another page so that the second article can also have front-page exposure. The decision rests on the relative importance of the two articles.

Additional editorial and graphic elements have been added, such as the table of contents, a kicker (an introductory line above a headline), a deck head (an introductory line below a headline) and the news notes headline. Notice that the photos are still one-column width. This is the major drawback of two-column grids and can be remedied only by changing to a three-column grid.

Crescendo

"We've really just gotten back to the basics," says conductor Irvin

New season opens with Mozart

Lorem ipsum dolor sit amet, consectetuer adipiscing elit, sed diam nonummy nibh euismod tincidunt ut laoreet dolore magna aliquam erat volutpat. Ut wisi enim ad minim veniam, quis nostrud exerci tation ullamcorper suscipit lobortis nisl ut aliquip ex ea commodo consequat. Duis autem vel eum iriure dolor in hendrerit in vulputate velit esse molestie consequat, vel illum dolore eu feugiat nulla facilisis at vero eros et accumsan et iusto odio dignissim qui blandit praesent luptatum zzril delenit augue duis dolore te feugiat nulla facilisi. Lorem ipsum dolor sit amet, consectetuer adipiscing elit, sed diam nonummy nibh euismod tincidunt ut laoreet dolore magna aliquam erat volutpat. Ut wisi enim ad minim veniam, quis nostrud exerci tation ullamcorper suscipit lobortis nisl ut aliquip ex ea commodo consequat.

Duis autem vel eum iriure dolor in hendrerit in vulputate velit esse molestie consequat, vel illum dolore eu feugiat nulla facilisis at vero eros et accumsan et iusto odio dignissim qui blandit praesent luptatum zzril delenit augue duis dolore te feugiat nulla facilisi. Nam liber tempor cum soluta nobis eleifend option congue nihil imperdiet doming id quod mazim

Lorem ipsum dolor sit amet, consectetuer adipiscing elit, sed diam nonummy nibh euismod tincidunt ut laoreet

placerat facer possim assum.

Lorem ipsum dolor sit amet, consectetuer adipiscing elit, sed diam nonummy nibh euismod tincidunt ut laoreet dolore magna aliquam erat volutpat. Ut wisi enim ad minim veniam, quis nostrud exerci tation ullamcorper suscipit lobortis nisl ut aliquip ex ea facilisi. Lorem ipsum dolor sit amet, consectetuer adipiscing elit, sed diam nonummy nibh euismod tincidunt ut laoreet dolore magna aliquam erat volutpat.

New acoustics better than ever

Lorem ipsum dolor sit amet, consectetuer adipiscing elit, sed diam nonummy nibh euismod tincidunt ut laoreet dolore magna aliquam erat volutpat. Ut wisi enim ad minim veniam, quis nostrud exerci tation ullamcorper suscipit lobortis nisl ut aliquip ex ea commodo consequat. Duis autem vel eum iriure dolor in hendrerit in vulputate velit esse molestie consequat, vel illum dolore eu feugiat nulla facilisis at vero eros et accumsan et iusto odio dignissim qui blandit praesent luptatum zzril delenit augue duis dolore te feugiat nulla

January 1991 Volume 19 Number 1

Five new performances this season

Lorem ipsum dolor sit amet, consectetuer adipiscing elit, sed diam nonummy nibh euismod tincidunt ut laoreet dolore magna aliquam erat volutpat. Ut wisi enim ad minim veniam, quis

Lorem ipsum dolor sit amet, consectetuer adipiscing elit, sed diam nonummy nibh euismod tincidunt ut laoreet dolore magna aliquam erat volutpat. Ut wisi enim ad minim veniam, quis nostrud exerci tation ullamcorper suscipit lobortis nisl ut aliquip ex ea commodo consequat. Duis autem vel eum iriure dolor in hendrerit in vulputate velit esse molestie consequat, vel illum dolore eu feugiat nulla facilisis at vero eros et accumsan et iusto odio dignissim qui blandit praesent luptatum zzril delenit augue duis dolore te feugiat nulla facilisi. Lorem ipsum dolor sit amet, consectetuer adipiscing elit, sed diam nonummy nibh euismod tincidunt ut laoreet dolore magna aliquam erat volutpat. Ut wisi enim ad minim veniam, quis nostrud exerci tation ullamcorper suscipit lobortis nisl ut aliquip ex ea

Lorem ipsum dolor sit amet, consectetuer adipiscing elit, sed diam nonummy nibh euismod tincidunt ut laoreet

commodo consequat.

Duis autem vel eum iriure dolor in hendrerit in vulputate velit esse molestie consequat, vel illum dolore eu feugiat nulla facilisis at vero eros et

Important late-breaking stories

Five new members

Dolor sit amet, consectetuer adipiscing elit, sed diam nonummy nibh euismod tincidunt ut laoreet dolore magna aliquam erat volutpat. Ut wisi enim ad minim veniam, quis nostrud exerci tation ullamcorper suscipit lobortis nisl ut aliquip ex ea commodo consequat.

More performances this season

Duis autem vel eum iriure dolor in hendrerit in vulputate velit esse molestie consequat, vel illum dolore eu feugiat nulla facilisis at vero eros et accumsan et iusto odio dignissim qui blandit praesent luptatum zzril delenit augue duis dolore te feugiat nulla facilisi. Nam liber tempor cum soluta nobis eleifend option congue nihil imperdiet doming id quod mazim placerat facer possim assum.

Mozart makes a comeback

Lorem ipsum dolor sit amet, consectetuer adipiscing elit, sed diam nonummy nibh euismod tincidunt ut laoreet dolore magna aliquam erat volutpat. Ut wisi enim ad minim veniam, quis nostrud exerci tation ullamcorper suscipit lobortis nisl ut aliquip ex ea commodo consequat. Duis autem vel eum iriure dolor in hendrerit in vulputate velit esse molestie consequat, vel illum dolore eu feugiat nulla facilisis at vero eros et accumsan et iusto odio dignissim qui blandit luptatum zzril delenit

Stephensen renews contract

Augue duis dolore te feugiat nulla facilisi. Lorem ipsum dolor sit amet, consectetuer adipiscing elit, sed diam nonummy nibh euismod tincidunt ut laoreet dolore magna aliquam erat volutpat.

Free concert series

Ut wisi enim ad minim veniam, quis nostrud exerci tation ullamcorper suscipit lobortis nisl ut aliquip ex ea commodo consequat. Duis autem vel eum iriure dolor in Wulputate velit esse molestie consequat, vel illum dolore eu feugiat nulla facilisis at vero eros et

Crescendo

January 1991 Volume 19 Number 1

Season opens with Mozart

Lorem ipsum dolor sit amet, consectetuer adipiscing elit, sed diam nonummy nibh euismod tincidunt ut laoreet dolore magna aliquam erat volutpat. Ut wisi enim ad minim veniam, quis nostrud exerci tation ullamcorper suscipit lobortis nisl ut aliquip ex ea commodo consequat. Duis autem vel eum iriure dolor in hendrerit in vulputate velit esse molestie consequat, vel illum dolore eu feugiat nulla facilisis at vero eros et accumsan et iusto odio dignissim

The opening baton

Lorem ipsum dolor sit amet, consectetuer adipiscing elit, sed diam nonummy nibh
Lorem ipsum dolor sit amet, consectetuer adipiscing elit, sed diam nonummy nibh

Lorem ipsum dolor sit amet, consectetuer adipiscing elit, sed diam nonummy nibh euismod tincidunt ut laoreet dolore magna aliquam erat volutpat. Ut wisi enim ad minim veniam, quis nostrud exerci tation ullamcorper suscipit lobortis nisl ut aliquip ex ea commodo consequat. Duis autem vel eum iriure dolor in hendrerit in vulputate velit esse molestie consequat, vel illum dolore eu feugiat nulla facilisis at vero eros et accumsan et iusto odio dignissim qui blandit praesent luptatum zzril delenit augue duis dolore te feugait nulla facilisi. Lorem ipsum dolor sit amet, consectetuer adipiscing elit, sed diam nonummy nibh euismod tincidunt ut laoreet dolore magna aliquam erat volutpat. Ut wisi enim ad minim veniam, quis nostrud exerci tation ullamcorper suscipit lobortis nisl ut aliquip ex ea commodo consequat.

Sound better than ever

Lorem ipsum dolor sit amet, consectetuer adipiscing elit, sed diam nonummy nibh euismod tincidunt ut laoreet dolore magna aliquam erat volutpat. Ut wisi enim ad minim veniam, quis nostrud exerci tation ullamcorper suscipit lobortis nisl ut aliquip ex ea commodo consequat. Duis autem vel eum iriure dolor in hendrerit in vulputate velit esse molestie consequat, vel illum dolore eu feugiat nulla facilisis at vero eros et accumsan et iusto odio dignissim qui blandit praesent luptatum zzril delenit augue duis dolore te feugait nulla facilisi. Lorem ipsum dolor sit amet, consectetuer adipiscing elit, sedLorem ipsum dolor sit amet, consectetuer adipiscing elit, sed

Bach festival draws crowd

Lorem ipsum dolor sit amet, consectetuer adipiscing elit, sed diam nonummy nibh euismod tincidunt ut laoreet dolore magna aliquam erat volutpat. Ut wisi enim ad minim veniam, quis nostrud exerci tation ullamcorper suscipit lobortis nisl ut aliquip ex ea commodo consequat. Duis autem vel eum iriure dolor in hendrerit in vulputate velit esse molestie consequat, vel illum dolore eu feugiat nulla facilisis at vero eros et accumsan et iusto odio dignissim qui blandit praesent luptatum zzril delenit augue duis dolore te feugait nulla facilisi. Lorem ipsum dolor sit amet, consectetuer adipiscing
Lorem ipsum dolor sit amet, consectetuer adipiscing elit, sed diam nonummy nibh euismod tincidunt ut laoreet dolore magna aliquam erat volutpat. Ut wisi enim ad minim veniam, quis nostrud exerci tation ullamcorper suscipit lobortis nisl ut aliquip ex ea commodo consequat. Duis autem vel eum iriure dolor in hendrerit in

New conductor selected

ad minim veniam, quis nostrud exerci tation ullamcorper suscipit lobortis nisl ut aliquip ex ea commodo consequat. Duis autem vel eum iriure dolor in hendrerit in vulputate velit esse molestie consequat, vel illum dolore eu feugiat nulla facilisis at vero eros et accumsan et iusto odio dignissim qui blandit praesent luptatum zzril delenit augue duis dolore te feugait nulla facilisi. Lorem ipsum dolor sit amet, consectetuer adipiscing elit, sed diam nonummy nibh euismod tincidunt ut laoreet dolore magna aliquam erat volutpat. Ut
Lorem ipsum dolor sit amet, consectetuer adipiscing elit, sed diam nonummy nibh euismod tincidunt ut laoreet dolore magna aliquam erat volutpat. Ut wisi enim

Lorem ipsum dolor sit amet, consectetuer adipiscing elit, sed diam nonummy nibh euismod tincidunt ut laoreet dolore magna aliquam erat volutpat. Ut wisi enim

HIGH NOTES
Late-breaking stories

Five new members
Dolor sit amet, consectetuer adipiscing elit, sed diam nonummy nibh euismod tincidunt ut laoreet dolore magna aliquam erat volutpat. Ut wisi enim ad minim

More to hear this season
Duis autem vel eum iriure dolor in hendrerit in vulputate velit esse molestie consequat, vel illum dolore eu feugiat nulla facilisis at vero eros et accumsan et iusto odio dignissim qui blandit praesent luptatum zzril delenit augue duis dolore te feugait nulla facilisi. Nam

Mozart makes a comeback
Lorem ipsum dolor sit amet, consectetuer adipiscing elit, sed diam nonummy nibh euismod tincidunt ut laoreet dolore magna aliquam erat volutpat. Ut wisi enim ad minim veniam, quis nostrud exerci tation ullamcorper suscipit lobortis nisl ut aliquip ex ea commodo consequat. Duis autem

Stephensen renews contract
Augue duis dolore te feugait nulla facilisi. Lorem ipsum dolor sit amet, consectetuer adipiscing elit, sed diam nonummy nibh

Free concert series
Ut wisi enim ad minim veniam, quis nostrud exerci tation ullamcorper suscipit lobortis nisl ut aliquip ex ea commodo consequat. Duis autem vel eum iriure dolor in hendrerit in Wulputate velit esse molestie consequat, vel illum dolore eu feugiat nulla facilisis at

Exhibit 5.13

Three-column Grids

The three-column grid is probably the most popular of all grids, both for newsletters and for other publications, such as magazines. Chief among the reasons for its popularity is the flexibility you gain in placing articles and pictures. As mentioned earlier, a three-column grid allows you to adjust the emphasis of headlines and other editorial and graphic devices through the choice of one-, two-, or three-column widths. In addition, you can use smaller and more vertical pictures without requiring text wraparounds. The three-column page manages all of this without being unduly complex or difficult to build.

Exhibit 5.13 is the simplest version of a three-column grid. Like the simple two-column grid, articles in this version follow one after the other with one-column headlines for each. The starting point for the reader is assumed to be the top left of the page since that is the natural starting point when no other elements lead the eye. In this case, the large photo at the bottom left of the page vies for first look. If this is your intent, then you will have accomplished your goal. In order for your reader to realize that the large photo is part of the first story, the article must take up both columns. If the second story's headline began in the second column, the reader might become confused.

Notice that the caption is constrained to one column, to the upper left of the photo and at the bottom of the first column. This placement further bonds the relationship of the story to the graphic since the eye naturally follows the first column to the photograph.

In the more sophisticated version in **Exhibit 5.14**, several features are added, including a jump of the second story on page 1 (notice the jumpline on the top of page 2) and a pull quote.

Pull quotes are useful both as editorial and as design elements. Editorially, a pull quote draws attention to your article by highlighting an interesting quote. As a design element, a pull quote can help fill space. If, for instance, you have several inches left over on your page, simply add a pull quote to the middle of the article in the length you need to take up the extra space.

Crescendo

January 1991 Volume 19 Number 1

Season opens with Mozart

Lorem ipsum dolor sit amet, consectetuer adipiscing elit, sed diam nonummy nibh euismod tincidunt ut laoreet dolore magna aliquam erat volutpat. Ut wisi enim ad minim veniam, quis nostrud exerci tation ullamcorper suscipit lobortis nisl ut aliquip ex ea commodo consequat. Duis autem vel eum iriure dolor in hendrerit in vulputate velit esse molestie consequat, vel illum dolore eu feugiat nulla facilisis at vero eros et accumsan et iusto odio dignissim qui blandit praesent luptatum zzril delenit augue duis dolore te feugait nulla facilisi. Lorem ipsum dolor sit amet, consectetuer adipiscing

The opening baton

Lorem ipsum dolor sit amet, consectetuer adipiscing elit, sed diam nonummy nibh Lorem ipsum dolor sit amet, consectetuer adipiscing elit, sed diam nonummy nibh

Lorem ipsum dolor sit amet, consectetuer adipiscing elit, sed diam nonummy nibh euismod tincidunt ut laoreet dolore magna aliquam erat volutpat. Ut wisi enim ad minim veniam, quis nostrud exerci tation ullamcorper suscipit lobortis nisl ut aliquip ex ea commodo consequat. Duis autem vel eum iriure dolor in hendrerit in vulputate velit esse molestie consequat, vel illum dolore eu feugiat nulla facilisis at vero eros et accumsan et iusto odio dignissim qui blandit praesent luptatum zzril delenit augue duis dolore te feugait nulla facilisi. Lorem ipsum dolor sit amet, consectetuer adipiscing elit, sedLorem ipsum dolor sit amet, consectetuer adipiscing elit, sed diam nonummy nibh euismod tincidunt ut laoreet dolore magna aliquam erat volutpat. Ut wisi enim ad minim veniam, quis nostrud exerci tation ullamcorper suscipit lobortis nisl ut aliquip ex ea commodo consequat. Duis autem vel eum iriure dolor sed diam nonummy nibh euismod tincidunt ut laoreet dolore magna

Sound better than ever

Lorem ipsum dolor sit amet, consectetuer adipiscing elit, sed diam nonummy nibh euismod tincidunt ut laoreet dolore magna aliquam erat volutpat. Ut wisi enim ad minim veniam, quis nostrud exerci tation ullamcorper suscipit lobortis nisl ut aliquip ex ea commodo consequat. Duis autem vel eum iriure dolor in hendrerit in vulputate velit esse molestie consequat, vel illum dolore eu feugiat nulla facilisis at vero eros et accumsan et iusto odio dignissim qui blandit praesent luptatum zzril delenit augue duis dolore te feugait nulla facilisi. Lorem ipsum dolor sit amet, consectetuer adipiscing elit, sed diam nonummy nibh euismod tincidunt ut laoreet dolore magna aliquam erat volutpat. Ut wisi enim ad minim veniam, quis nostrud exerci tation ullamcorper suscipit lobortis nisl ut aliquip ex ea

In This Issue:

Mozart season

Continued from page 1

Lorem ipsum dolor sit amet, consectetuer adipiscing elit, sed diam nonummy nibh euismod tincidunt ut laoreet dolore magna aliquam erat volutpat. Ut wisi enim ad minim veniam, quis nostrud exerci tation ullamcorper suscipit

From the opening baton to the last, lingering note, this season will be a winner.

lobortis nisl ut aliquip ex ea commodo consequat, vel illum dolore eu feugiat nulla facilisis at vero eros et accumsan et iusto odio dignissim qui blandit praesent luptatum zzril delenit augue duis dolore te feugait nulla facilisi. Lorem ipsum dolor sit amet, consectetuer adipiscing

State-of-the-art acoustics

Lorem ipsum dolor sit amet, consectetuer adipiscing elit, sed diam nonummy nibh euismod tincidunt ut laoreet dolore magna aliquam erat

Lorem ipsum dolor sit amet, consectetuer adipiscing elit, sed diam nonummy nibh euismod tincidunt ut laoreet dolore magna aliquam erat volutpat. Ut wisi enim ad minim veniam, quis nostrud exerci tation ullamcorper suscipit lobortis nisl ut aliquip ex ea commodo consequat. Duis autem vel eum iriure dolor in hendrerit in vulputate velit esse molestie consequat, vel illum dolore eu feugiat nulla facilisis at vero eros et accumsan et iusto odio dignissim qui blandit praesent luptatum zzril delenit augue duis dolore te feugait nulla facilisi. Lorem ipsum dolor sit amet, consectetuer adipiscing elit, sed diam nonummy nibh euismod tincidunt ut laoreet dolore magna aliquam erat volutpat. Ut

HIGH NOTES
Late-breaking stories

Five new members

Dolor sit amet, consectetuer adipiscing elit, sed diam nonummy nibh euismod tincidunt ut laoreet dolore magna aliquam erat volutpat. Ut wisi enim ad minim

More to hear this season

Duis autem vel eum iriure dolor in hendrerit in vulputate velit esse molestie consequat, vel illum dolore eu feugiat nulla facilisis at vero eros et accumsan et iusto odio dignissim qui blandit praesent luptatum zzril delenit augue duis dolore te feugait nulla facilisi. Nam

Mozart makes a comeback

Lorem ipsum dolor sit amet, consectetuer adipiscing elit, sed diam nonummy nibh euismod tincidunt ut laoreet dolore magna aliquam erat volutpat. Ut wisi enim ad minim veniam, quis nostrud exerci tation ullamcorper suscipit lobortis nisl ut aliquip ex ea commodo consequat. Duis autem

Stephensen renews contract

Augue duis dolore te feugait nulla facilisi. Lorem ipsum dolor sit amet, consectetuer adipiscing elit, sed diam nonummy nibh

Free concert series

Ut wisi enim ad minim veniam, quis nostrud exerci tation ullamcorper suscipit lobortis nisl ut aliquip ex ea commodo consequat. Duis autem vel eum iriure dolor in hendrerit in Wulputate velit esse molestie consequat, vel illum dolore eu feugiat nulla facilisis at

Exhibit 5.14

Lorem ipsum dolor sit amet, consectetuer adipiscing elit, sed diam nonummy nibh euismod tincidunt ut laoreet dolore magna aliquam erat volutpat. Ut wisi enim ad minim veniam, quis nostrud exerci tation ullamcorper

'From the opening baton to the last, lingering note, this season will be a winner.'

suscipit lobortis nisl ut aliquip ex ea commodo consequat. Duis autem vel eum iriure dolor in hendrerit in vulputate velit esse molestie consequat, vel illum dolore eu feugiat nulla facilisis at vero eros et accumsan et iusto odio dignissim qui blandit praesent luptatum zzril delenit

---

Lorem ipsum dolor sit amet, consectetuer adipiscing elit, sed diam nonummy nibh euismod tincidunt ut laoreet dolore magna aliquam erat volutpat. Ut wisi enim ad minim veniam, quis nostrud exerci tation ullamcorper

'From the opening baton to the last, lingering note, this season will be a winner.'

suscipit lobortis nisl ut aliquip ex ea commodo consequat. Duis autem vel eum iriure dolor in hendrerit in vulputate velit esse molestie consequat, vel illum dolore eu feugiat nulla facilisis at

---

Lorem ipsum dolor sit amet, consectetuer adipiscing elit, sed diam nonummy nibh euismod tincidunt ut laoreet dolore magna aliquam erat volutpat. Ut wisi enim ad minim veniam, quis nostrud exerci tation ullamcorper

'From the opening baton to the last, lingering note, this season will be a winner.'

suscipit lobortis nisl ut aliquip ex ea commodo consequat. Duis autem vel eum iriure dolor in

Exhibit 5.15

As a design element, a pull quote can be used to take up space on a page. The normal restrictions for trapped white space don't apply here as the increased white space can be used as a point of emphasis. Notice that the extra white space falls below the pull quote.

Three-column Newspaper Style

A step up in complexity, the three-column newspaper style grid takes advantage of a great variety of editorial and graphic effects. This is probably the most versatile newsletter grid to work with.

Exhibit 5.16, the easiest version in this style, begins the page with a two-column wide photo with its caption immediately below, also two columns wide. The thin rule and the added space below the caption helps to separate the caption visually from the two-column headline below it. Notice, too, that this version makes use of bylines—the names of the authors of the articles—usually preceding the article. In some instances, the byline can be placed following the article. Whichever style you use, make sure you stick with it for consistency.

Page 2 illustrates balance achieved through photo placement. Even though the top photo is twice the size of the bottom photo, balance is gained by placing the smaller, vertical photo in the center of the page. When using more than one large photo on a single page, be sure to separate them with as much space as possible. If the photos relate to the same article, and must be placed close together, some other balancing device must be used, such as a large headline at the opposite end of the page. Remember, the points of heaviest emphasis are the top and bottom of a page.

In **Exhibit 5.17**, notice that the table of contents is aligned with the adjacent article creating a uniform page division. Since the table of contents is usually fairly flexible, you can adjust its length to match most articles. A rule above both elements also accentuates the page division. Make sure not to leave any white space between the two halves of the page since this will unnecessarily draw the reader's eye away from the top of the page, your intended starting point.

Alignment of elements is extremely important for an orderly looking newsletter. For instance, photos should align with the tops of articles or adjacent headlines if possible.

Notice that portrait-style photos (also called mug shots) are well suited to a three-column format. Since most mug shots are fairly boring in content, they usually don't need to be larger than half a column on a three-column grid. Since a three-column grid is easily divisible into 6 columns, this allows easy placement of mug shots. Remember to crop and scale photos such as a series of mug shots so that the tops and bottoms align.

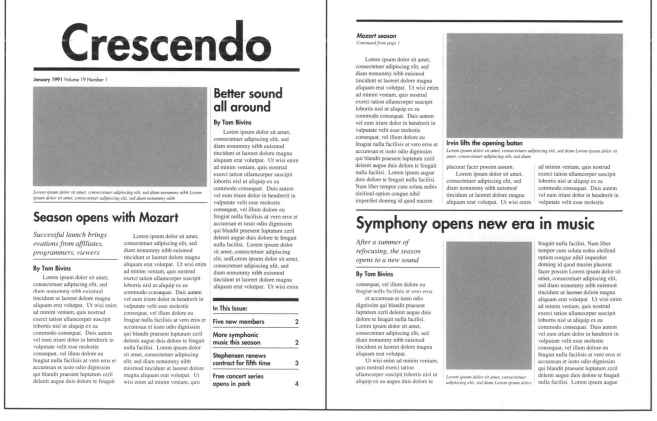

Exhibit 5.16

Exhibit 5.18 is a more sophisticated version of the three-column newspaper style grid. Two columns are devoted to the lead story while the third column is used for a news notes-style column. This design replicates a similar device used by such newspapers as the *Wall-Street Journal*. This type of column (really an expanded table of contents) is extremely useful if you know that a key audience for your newsletter will be busy people who are skimming for the most important news.

The white space following the news notes headline on page 2 draws attention to the top of the page more effectively than a longer or larger headline might. Also notice the grouping of the four photos on the bottom half of the page. These serve to balance out the large area of white at the top of the page. Remember, when grouping pictures, make sure to indicate in the caption the order in which they should be viewed. Normally, a photo grouping such as this will be viewed clockwise from the upper left.

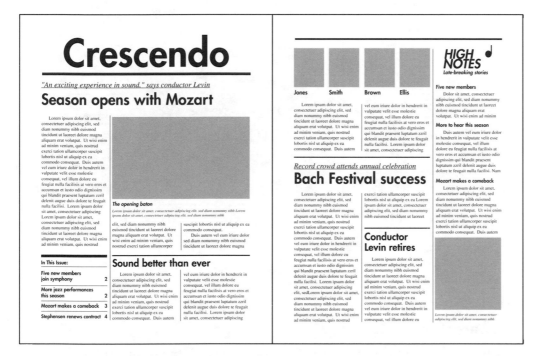

Exhibit 5.17

Exhibit 5.18

Crescendo

New season opens with Mozart

Commentary by Leonard Irvin

Nommodo consequat. Duis autem vel eum iriure dolor in hendrerit in vulputate velit esse molestie consequat, vel illum dolore eu feugiat nulla facilisis at vero eros et accumsan et iusto odio dignissim qui blandit praesent luptatum zzril delenit augue duis dolore te feugait nulla facilisi. Lorem ipsum dolor sit amet, consectetuer adipiscing elit, sed diam nonummy nibh euismod tincidunt ut laoreet dolore magna aliquam erat volutpat.

Ut wisi enim ad minim veniam, quis nostrud exerci tation ullamcorper suscipit lobortis nisl ut aliquip ex ea augue duis dolore te feugait nulla facilisi. Nam liber tempor cum soluta nobis eleifend option congue nihil imperdiet doming id quod mazim placerat facer possim Lorem ipsum dolor sit amet, consectetuer adipiscing elit, sed diam nonummy nibh euismod tincidunt ut laoreet dolore magna aliquam erat

22 Years Ago

Lorem ipsum dolor sit amet, consectetuer adipiscing elit, sed diam nonummy nibh euismod tincidunt ut laoreet dolore magna aliquam erat volutpat. Ut wisi enim ad minim veniam, quis nostrud exerci tation ullamcorper suscipit lobortis nisl ut aliquip ex ea commodo consequat. Duis autem vel eum iriure dolor in hendrerit in vulputate velit esse molestie consequat, vel illum dolore eu feugiat nulla facilisis at vero eros et accumsan et iusto odio dignissim qui blandit praesent luptatum zzril delenit augue duis dolore te feugait nulla facilisi. Lorem ipsum dolor sit amet, consectetuer adipiscing elit, sed diam nonummy nibh euismod tincidunt ut laoreet dolore magna aliquam erat volutpat. Ut wisi enim

In This Issue:

From the Editor's Desk

Lorem ipsum dolor sit amet, consectetuer adipiscing elit, sed diam nonummy nibh euismod tincidunt ut laoreet dolore magna aliquam erat volutpat. Ut wisi enim ad minim veniam, quis nostrud exerci tation ullamcorper suscipit lobortis nisl ut aliquip ex ea commodo consequat. Duis autem vel eum iriure dolor in hendrerit in vulputate velit esse molestie consequat, vel illum dolore eu feugiat nulla facilisis at vero eros et accumsan et iusto odio dignissim qui blandit praesent luptatum zzril delenit augue duis dolore te feugait nulla facilisi. Lorem ipsum augue duis dolore te feugait nulla facilisi. Nam liber tempor cum soluta nobis eleifend option congue nihil imperdiet doming id quod mazim placerat facer possim assum.

Lorem ipsum dolor sit amet, consectetuer adipiscing elit, sed diam nonummy nibh euismod tincidunt ut laoreet dolore magna aliquam erat volutpat. Ut wisi enim ad minim veniam, quis nostrud exerci tation ullamcorper suscipit lobortis nisl ut aliquip ex ea commodo consequat. Duis autem vel eum iriure dolor in hendrerit in vulputate velit esse molestie consequat, vel illum dolore eu feugiat nulla facilisis at vero eros et accumsan et iusto odio dignissim

Commentary, *continued from page 1*

Lorem ipsum dolor sit amet, consectetuer adipiscing elit, sed diam nonummy nibh euismod tincidunt ut laoreet dolore magna aliquam erat volutpat. Ut wisi enim ad minim veniam, quis nostrud exerci tation ullamcorper suscipit lobortis nisl ut aliquip ex ea commodo consequat. Duis autem vel eum iriure dolor in hendrerit in vulputate velit esse molestie consequat, vel illum dolore eu feugiat nulla facilisis at vero eros et accumsan et iusto odio dignissim qui blandit praesent luptatum zzril

Exploration is the key

delenit augue duis dolore te feugait nulla facilisi. Lorem ipsum augue duis dolore te feugait nulla facilisi. Nam liber tempor cum soluta nobis eleifend option congue nihil imperdiet doming id quod mazim placerat facer possim assum.

Lorem ipsum dolor sit amet, consectetuer adipiscing elit, sed diam nonummy nibh euismod tincidunt ut laoreet dolore magna aliquam erat volutpat. Ut wisi enim ad minim veniam, quis nostrud exerci tation ullamcorper suscipit lobortis nisl ut aliquip ex ea commodo consequat. Duis autem vel eum iriure dolor in hendrerit in vulputate velit esse molestie consequat, vel illum dolore eu feugiat nulla facilisis at vero eros et accumsan et iusto odio dignissim qui blandit praesent luptatum zzril delenit augue duisLorem ipsum dolor sit amet, consectetuer adipiscing elit, sed diam nonummy nibh euismod tincidunt ut laoreet dolore magna aliquam erat volutpat. Ut wisi enim ad minim veniam, quis nostrud exerci tation ullamcorper suscipit lobortis nisl ut aliquip ex ea commodo

Lorem ipsum dolor sit amet, consectetuer adipiscing elit, sed diam nonummy nibh euismod tincidunt ut laoreet dolore magna aliquam erat volutpat. Ut wisi enim ad minim veniam, quis nostrud exerci tation

HIGH NOTES
Late-breaking stories

Five new members

Dolor sit amet, consectetuer adipiscing elit, sed diam nonummy nibh euismod tincidunt ut laoreet dolore magna aliquam erat volutpat. Ut wisi enim ad minim

Performances this season

Duis autem vel eum iriure dolor in hendrerit in vulputate velit esse molestie consequat, vel illum dolore eu feugiat nulla facilisis at vero eros et accumsan et iusto odio dignissim qui blandit praesent luptatum zzril delenit augue duis dolore te feugait nulla facilisi. Nam

Mozart makes a comeback

Lorem ipsum dolor sit amet, consectetuer adipiscing elit, sed diam nonummy nibh euismod tincidunt ut laoreet dolore magna aliquam erat volutpat. Ut wisi enim ad minim veniam, quis nostrud exerci tation ullamcorper suscipit lobortis nisl ut aliquip ex ea commodo consequat. Duis autem

Stephensen renews contract

Augue duis dolore te feugait nulla facilisi. Lorem ipsum dolor sit amet, consectetuer adipiscing elit, sed diam nonummy nibh

Free concert series

Ut wisi enim ad minim veniam, quis nostrud exerci tation ullamcorper suscipit lobortis nisl ut aliquip ex ea commodo consequat. Duis autem vel eum iriure dolor in hendrerit in Wulputate velit esse molestie consequat, vel illum dolore eu feugiat nulla facilisis at

Exhibit 5.19

Unequal Columns with a Three-column Grid

The three-column grid can be useful for designing one of the most used front-page formats—a wide column for the lead story plus a narrower single column for sidebar-type information. The three-column grid allows you to designate two of the columns for a single story either to the right or left of the page. The remaining single column can then be used for a variety of purposes: a newsbriefs column, editor's column, expanded table of contents, masthead information, or sidebars accompanying the primary article.

Exhibit 5.19 features a single topic newsletter designed to fit into two of the three available columns. Normally, you will want to raise the point size in order to facilitate tracking in this wider format. For example, if your standard body text is 10/12, you might want to run this column 12/14 or even 14/15.

This format may be used just for the front page, with the rest of the newsletter using a standard three-column format, or it may be continued throughout the newsletter.

Notice the initial capital letter at the beginning of the article. This is a fairly common typographic device used to draw the eye to the beginning of the story. When you use initial caps, just be sure that the point size is different enough to prevent it from conflicting with the headline above it. In this case, the byline, in an even smaller typeface than the headline, comes between the headline and the initial cap.

Exhibit 5.20 shows a similarly constructed front page except that the two-column spread is divided horizontally into separate featurettes, each separated by a thin rule. This is an excellent way to set up a feature on a group of individuals. It is usually best to allow for equal amounts of space for each section when setting up a page like this. A standard, vertical 5" x 7" mug shot works perfectly in this grid since it is reducible to half of one of the columns. This front page utilizes, from left to right, one-half column, one-and-one-half columns, and one column.

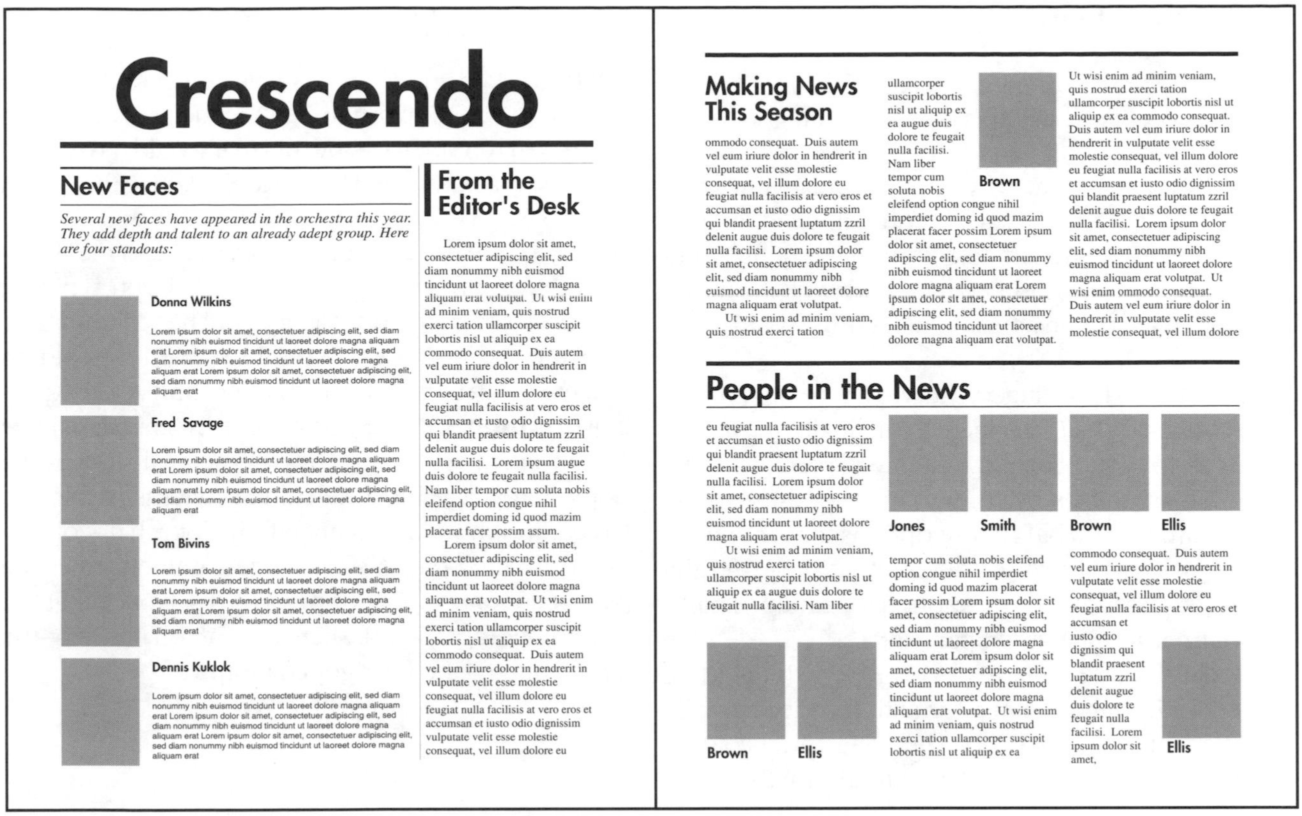

Crescendo

New Faces

Several new faces have appeared in the orchestra this year. They add depth and talent to an already adept group. Here are four standouts:

Donna Wilkins

Lorem ipsum dolor sit amet, consectetuer adipiscing elit, sed diam nonummy nibh euismod tincidunt ut laoreet dolore magna aliquam erat Lorem ipsum dolor sit amet, consectetuer adipiscing elit, sed diam nonummy nibh euismod tincidunt ut laoreet dolore magna aliquam erat

Fred Savage

Lorem ipsum dolor sit amet, consectetuer adipiscing elit, sed diam nonummy nibh euismod tincidunt ut laoreet dolore magna aliquam erat Lorem ipsum dolor sit amet, consectetuer adipiscing elit, sed diam nonummy nibh euismod tincidunt ut laoreet dolore magna aliquam erat

Tom Bivins

Lorem ipsum dolor sit amet, consectetuer adipiscing elit, sed diam nonummy nibh euismod tincidunt ut laoreet dolore magna aliquam erat Lorem ipsum dolor sit amet, consectetuer adipiscing elit, sed diam nonummy nibh euismod tincidunt ut laoreet dolore magna aliquam erat

Dennis Kuklok

Lorem ipsum dolor sit amet, consectetuer adipiscing elit, sed diam nonummy nibh euismod tincidunt ut laoreet dolore magna aliquam erat Lorem ipsum dolor sit amet, consectetuer adipiscing elit, sed diam nonummy nibh euismod tincidunt ut laoreet dolore magna aliquam erat

From the Editor's Desk

Lorem ipsum dolor sit amet, consectetuer adipiscing elit, sed diam nonummy nibh euismod tincidunt ut laoreet dolore magna aliquam erat volutpat. Ut wisi enim ad minim veniam, quis nostrud exerci tation ullamcorper suscipit lobortis nisl ut aliquip ex ea commodo consequat. Duis autem vel eum iriure dolor in hendrerit in vulputate velit esse molestie consequat, vel illum dolore eu feugait nulla facilisi. Lorem ipsum augue duis dolore te feugait nulla facilisi. Nam liber tempor cum soluta nobis eleifend option congue nihil imperdiet doming id quod mazim placerat facer possim assum.

Lorem ipsum dolor sit amet, consectetuer adipiscing elit, sed diam nonummy nibh euismod tincidunt ut laoreet dolore magna aliquam erat volutpat. Ut wisi enim ad minim veniam, quis nostrud exerci tation ullamcorper suscipit lobortis nisl ut aliquip ex ea commodo consequat. Duis autem vel eum iriure dolor in hendrerit in vulputate velit esse molestie consequat, vel illum dolore eu feugait nulla facilisi at vero eros et accumsan et iusto odio dignissim vulputate velit esse molestie consequat, vel illum dolore eu

Making News This Season

ommodo consequat. Duis autem vel eum iriure dolor in hendrerit in vulputate velit esse molestie consequat, vel illum dolore eu feugait nulla facilisi at vero eros et accumsan et iusto odio dignissim qui blandit praesent luptatum zzril delenit augue duis dolore te feugait nulla facilisi. Lorem ipsum dolor sit amet, consectetuer adipiscing elit, sed diam nonummy nibh euismod tincidunt ut laoreet dolore magna aliquam erat volutpat.

Ut wisi enim ad minim veniam, quis nostrud exerci tation

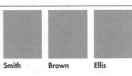

ullamcorper suscipit lobortis nisl ut aliquip ex ea augue duis dolore te feugait nulla facilisi. Nam liber tempor cum soluta nobis eleifend option congue nihil imperdiet doming id quod mazim placerat facer possim Lorem ipsum dolor sit amet, consectetuer adipiscing elit, sed diam nonummy nibh euismod tincidunt ut laoreet dolore magna aliquam erat Lorem ipsum dolor sit amet, consectetuer adipiscing elit, sed diam nonummy nibh euismod tincidunt ut laoreet dolore magna aliquam erat volutpat.

Brown

Ut wisi enim ad minim veniam, quis nostrud exerci tation ullamcorper suscipit lobortis nisl ut aliquip ex ea commodo consequat. Duis autem vel eum iriure dolor in hendrerit in vulputate velit esse molestie consequat, vel illum dolore eu feugait nulla facilisis at vero eros et accumsan et iusto odio dignissim qui blandit praesent luptatum zzril delenit augue duis dolore te feugait nulla facilisi. Lorem ipsum dolor sit amet, consectetuer adipiscing elit, sed diam nonummy nibh euismod tincidunt ut laoreet dolore magna aliquam erat volutpat. Ut wisi enim ad minim veniam, quis nostrud exerci tation ullamcorper suscipit lobortis nisl ut aliquip ex ea commodo consequat. Duis autem vel eum iriure dolor in hendrerit in vulputate velit esse molestie consequat, vel illum dolore

People in the News

eu feugait nulla facilisis at vero eros et accumsan et iusto odio dignissim qui blandit praesent luptatum zzril delenit augue duis dolore te feugait nulla facilisi. Lorem ipsum dolor sit amet, consectetuer adipiscing elit, sed diam nonummy nibh euismod tincidunt ut laoreet dolore magna aliquam erat volutpat.

Ut wisi enim ad minim veniam, quis nostrud exerci tation ullamcorper suscipit lobortis nisl ut aliquip ex ea feugait nulla facilisi. Nam liber

Jones **Smith** **Brown** **Ellis**

tempor cum soluta nobis eleifend option congue nihil imperdiet doming id quod mazim placerat facer possim Lorem ipsum dolor sit amet, consectetuer adipiscing elit, sed diam nonummy nibh euismod tincidunt ut laoreet dolore magna aliquam erat Lorem ipsum dolor sit amet, consectetuer adipiscing elit, sed diam nonummy nibh euismod tincidunt ut laoreet dolore magna aliquam erat volutpat. Ut wisi enim ad minim veniam, quis nostrud exerci tation ullamcorper suscipit lobortis nisl ut aliquip ex ea commodo

Brown **Ellis**

commodo consequat. Duis autem vel eum iriure dolor in hendrerit in vulputate velit esse molestie consequat, vel illum dolore eu feugait nulla facilisis at vero eros et accumsan et iusto odio dignissim qui blandit praesent luptatum zzril delenit augue duis dolore te feugait nulla facilisi. Lorem ipsum dolor sit amet,

Ellis

Exhibit 5.20

Page 2 features half-column photos in full-column display. This will require wrapping text around the photo or placing the caption next to the photo instead of beneath it. Remember, though, that if the photo is a mug shot (a head and shoulders shot of a person) the caption should only be the person's name, and this isn't enough to fill the space next to the photo.

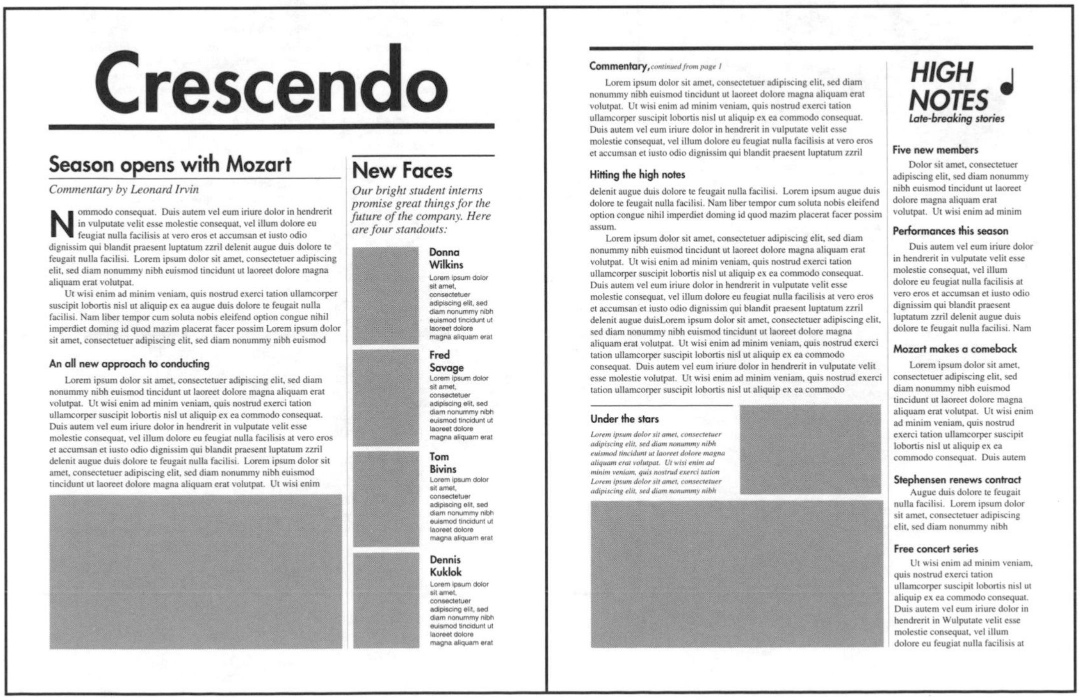

Crescendo

Season opens with Mozart

Commentary by Leonard Irvin

Nommodo consequat. Duis autem vel eum iriure dolor in hendrerit in vulputate velit esse molestie consequat, vel illum dolore eu feugait nulla facilisis at vero eros et accumsan et iusto odio dignissim qui blandit praesent luptatum zzril delenit augue duis dolore te feugait nulla facilisi. Lorem ipsum dolor sit amet, consectetuer adipiscing elit, sed diam nonummy nibh euismod tincidunt ut laoreet dolore magna aliquam erat volutpat.

Ut wisi enim ad minim veniam, quis nostrud exerci tation ullamcorper suscipit lobortis nisl ut aliquip ex ea augue duis dolore te feugait nulla facilisi. Nam liber tempor cum soluta nobis eleifend option congue nihil imperdiet doming id quod mazim placerat facer possim Lorem ipsum dolor sit amet, consectetuer adipiscing elit, sed diam nonummy nibh euismod

An all new approach to conducting

Lorem ipsum dolor sit amet, consectetuer adipiscing elit, sed diam nonummy nibh euismod tincidunt ut laoreet dolore magna aliquam erat volutpat. Ut wisi enim ad minim veniam, quis nostrud exerci tation ullamcorper suscipit lobortis nisl ut aliquip ex ea commodo consequat. Duis autem vel eum iriure dolor in hendrerit in vulputate velit esse molestie consequat, vel illum dolore eu feugait nulla facilisis at vero eros et accumsan et iusto odio dignissim qui blandit praesent luptatum zzril delenit augue duis dolore te feugait nulla facilisi. Lorem ipsum dolor sit amet, consectetuer adipiscing elit, sed diam nonummy nibh euismod tincidunt ut laoreet dolore magna aliquam erat volutpat. Ut wisi enim

New Faces

Our bright student interns promise great things for the future of the company. Here are four standouts:

Donna Wilkins

Lorem ipsum dolor sit amet, consectetuer adipiscing elit, sed diam nonummy nibh euismod tincidunt ut laoreet dolore magna aliquam erat

Fred Savage

Lorem ipsum dolor sit amet, consectetuer adipiscing elit, sed diam nonummy nibh euismod tincidunt ut laoreet dolore magna aliquam erat

Tom Bivins

Lorem ipsum dolor sit amet, consectetuer adipiscing elit, sed diam nonummy nibh euismod tincidunt ut laoreet dolore magna aliquam erat

Dennis Kuklok

Lorem ipsum dolor sit amet, consectetuer adipiscing elit, sed diam nonummy nibh euismod tincidunt ut laoreet dolore magna aliquam erat

Commentary, *continued from page 1*

Lorem ipsum dolor sit amet, consectetuer adipiscing elit, sed diam nonummy nibh euismod tincidunt ut laoreet dolore magna aliquam erat volutpat. Ut wisi enim ad minim veniam, quis nostrud exerci tation ullamcorper suscipit lobortis nisl ut aliquip ex ea commodo consequat. Duis autem vel eum iriure dolor in hendrerit in vulputate velit esse molestie consequat, vel illum dolore eu feugait nulla facilisis at vero eros et accumsan et iusto odio dignissim qui blandit praesent luptatum zzril

Hitting the high notes

delenit augue duis dolore te feugait nulla facilisi. Lorem ipsum augue duis dolore te feugait nulla facilisi. Nam liber tempor cum soluta nobis eleifend option congue nihil imperdiet doming id quod mazim placerat facer possim assum.

Lorem ipsum dolor sit amet, consectetuer adipiscing elit, sed diam nonummy nibh euismod tincidunt ut laoreet dolore magna aliquam erat volutpat. Ut wisi enim ad minim veniam, quis nostrud exerci tation ullamcorper suscipit lobortis nisl ut aliquip ex ea commodo consequat. Duis autem vel eum iriure dolor in hendrerit in vulputate velit esse molestie consequat, vel illum dolore eu feugait nulla facilisis at vero eros et accumsan et iusto odio dignissim qui blandit praesent luptatum zzril delenit augue duisLorem ipsum dolor sit amet, consectetuer adipiscing elit, sed diam nonummy nibh euismod tincidunt ut laoreet dolore magna aliquam erat volutpat. Ut wisi enim ad minim veniam, quis nostrud exerci tation ullamcorper suscipit lobortis nisl ut aliquip ex ea commodo consequat. Duis autem vel eum iriure dolor in hendrerit in vulputate velit esse molestie consequat, vel illum dolore eu feugait nulla facilisis at vero eros et accumsan et iusto odio dignissim qui blandit praesent luptatum zzril delenit augue duis dolore te feugait nulla facilisi.

Under the stars

Lorem ipsum dolor sit amet, consectetuer adipiscing elit, sed diam nonummy nibh euismod tincidunt ut laoreet dolore magna aliquam erat volutpat. Ut wisi enim ad minim veniam, quis nostrud Lorem ipsum dolor sit amet, consectetuer adipiscing elit, sed diam nonummy nibh

HIGH NOTES

Late-breaking stories

Five new members

Dolor sit amet, consectetuer adipiscing elit, sed diam nonummy nibh euismod tincidunt ut laoreet dolore magna aliquam erat volutpat. Ut wisi enim ad minim

Performances this season

Duis autem vel eum iriure dolor in hendrerit in vulputate velit esse molestie consequat, vel illum dolore eu feugait nulla facilisis at vero eros et accumsan et iusto odio dignissim qui blandit praesent luptatum zzril delenit augue duis dolore te feugait nulla facilisi. Nam

Mozart makes a comeback

Lorem ipsum dolor sit amet, consectetuer adipiscing elit, sed diam nonummy nibh euismod tincidunt ut laoreet dolore magna aliquam erat volutpat. Ut wisi enim ad minim veniam, quis nostrud exerci tation ullamcorper suscipit lobortis nisl ut aliquip ex ea commodo consequat. Duis autem

Stephensen renews contract

Augue duis dolore te feugait nulla facilisi. Lorem ipsum dolor sit amet, consectetuer adipiscing elit, sed diam nonummy nibh

Free concert series

Ut wisi enim ad minim veniam, quis nostrud exerci tation ullamcorper suscipit lobortis nisl ut aliquip ex ea commodo consequat. Duis autem vel eum iriure dolor in hendrerit in Wulputate velit esse molestie consequat, vel illum dolore eu feugait nulla facilisis at

Exhibit 5.21

This layout features another way to use the single column on page 1. Page 2 shows grouped photos with the caption taking up enough space to define an even page division.

Four-column Grids

The restrictions inherent in a four-column grid make it slightly less flexible than a three-column grid. Some of those restrictions include the narrowness of the columns for text. Unless you use a relatively small point size, 10/11 for instance, you will encounter an increase in hyphenation. Justification might help, but in narrow columns, justified text tends to leave white spaces, called rivers, between various words and lines.

Don't be discouraged, however, from trying a four-column format. The increase in flexibility may be worth it to you. For example, you can vary the emphasis of articles by using one, two, three, or all four columns. You have more options for varying the column widths of text for different articles. And the single columns are narrow enough to handle pictures without requiring text wraparounds.

Exhibit 5.22 features a page-length table of contents with a little extra information added to make it a kind of newsbriefs column. The three-column wide photo focuses the reader's attention at the top of the page, where it belongs. The smaller, vertical photo at the bottom helps balance the heavy page top.

Page 2 includes two articles stacked so as to shorten the column length of the articles. They could have been run side-by-side, but that would have given the page an extremely vertical look. Notice the colum widths are one, one, and two. Using a two-column spread for the notes column gives it a "read me" look.

Four-column grids are excellent if you typically use a great many photographs. The column size allows photos of one-, two-, three-, or four-column widths—both horizontal (landscape) and vertical (portrait). **Exhibit 5.23** demonstrates this flexibility. Page 1 is an example of a nearly symmetrical front page. Copy is restricted to one-column widths, while the large top photo is balanced by four half-column photos in the bottom story. Page 2 demonstrates the placement of a variety of photo sizes. Notice that the related photographs all share a common border—the left margin of the far right column.

Exhibit 5.22

Crescendo

"An exciting approach to an old friend," says conductor Irvin.

Season opens with Mozart

Lorem ipsum dolor sit amet, consectetuer adipiscing elit, sed diam nonummy nibh euismod tincidunt ut laoreet dolore magna aliquam erat volutpat. Ut wisi enim ad minim veniam, quis nostrud exerci tation ullamcorper suscipit lobortis nisl ut aliquip ex ea commodo consequat. Duis autem vel eum iriure dolor in hendrerit in vulputate velit esse molestie consequat, vel illum dolore eu feugiat nulla facilisis at vero eros

Lorem ipsum dolor sit amet, consectetuer adipiscing elit, sed diam nonummy nibh euismod tincidunt ut laoreet dolore magna aliquam erat volutpat. Ut wisi enim

et accumsan et iusto odio dignissim qui blandit praesent luptatum zzril delenit augue duis dolore

cum soluta nobis eleifend option congue nihil imperdiet doming id quod mazim placerat facer possim assum.

Lorem ipsum dolor sit amet, consectetuer adipiscing elit, sed diam nonummy nibh euismod tincidunt ut laoreet dolore magna aliquam erat volutpat. Ut wisi enim ad minim veniam, quis nostrud exerci tation ullamcorper suscipit lobortis nisl ut aliquip ex ea commodo consequat. Duis autem vel eum iriure

te feugait nulla facilisi. Lorem ipsum augue duis dolore te feugait nulla facilisi. Nam liber tempor

New additions add excitement

Lorem ipsum dolor sit amet, consectetuer adipiscing elit, sed diam nonummy nibh euismod tincidunt ut laoreet dolore magna aliquam erat volutpat. Ut wisi enim ad minim veniam, quis nostrud exerci tation ullamcorper suscipit lobortis nisl ut aliquip ex ea commodo consequat. Duis autem vel eum iriure dolor in hendrerit in vulputate velit esse molestie consequat, vel

Kuklok **Davis** **Wales** **Roderick**

illum dolore eu feugiat nulla facilisis at vero eros et accumsan et iusto odio dignissim qui blandit praesent luptatum zzril delenit augue duis dolore te feugait nulla facilisi. Lorem ipsum augue duis dolore te feugait nulla

facilisi. Nam liber tempor cum soluta nobis eleifend option congue nihil imperdiet doming id quod mazim placerat facer possim assum.

Lorem ipsum dolor sit amet, consectetuer adipiscing elit, sed diam

In This Issue:

2 /Performances this season add interest
Lorem ipsum dolor sit amet, consectetuer adipiscing elit, sed

3 / Stephensen signs contract for season
Lorem ipsum dolor sit amet, consectetuer adipiscing elit, sed

3 / Free concert series in the park
Lorem ipsum dolor sit amet, consectetuer adipiscing elit, sed

Symphony opens new era of excitement

Diverse is intended to keep the many audiences on the edge of their seats

Lorem ipsum dolor sit amet, consectetuer adipiscing elit, sed diam nonummy nibh euismod tincidunt ut laoreet dolore magna aliquam erat volutpat. Ut wisi enim ad minim veniam, quis nostrud exerci tation ullamcorper suscipit lobortis nisl ut aliquip ex ea commodo consequat. Duis autem vel eum iriure dolor in hendrerit in vulputate velit esse molestie consequat, vel illum dolore eu feugiat nulla facilisis at vero eros et accumsan et iusto odio dignissim qui blandit

praesent luptatum zzril delenit augue duis dolore te feugait nulla facilisi. Lorem ipsum augue duis dolore te feugait nulla facilisi. Nam liber tempor cum soluta nobis eleifend option congue nihil imperdiet doming id quod mazim placerat facer possim assum.

Lorem ipsum dolor sit amet, consectetuer

adipiscing elit, sed diam nonummy nibh euismod tincidunt ut laoreet dolore magna aliquam erat volutpat. Ut wisi enim ad minim veniam, quis

nostrud exerci tation ullamcorper suscipit lobortis nisl ut aliquip ex ea commodo consequat. Duis autem vel eum iriure dolor in hendrerit in vulputate velit esse

Molestie consequat, vel illum dolore eu feugiat nulla facilisis at vero eros et accumsan et iusto odio dignissim qui blandit praesent luptatum zzril

Lorem ipsum dolor sit amet, consectetuer adipiscing elit, sed diam nonummy nibh euismod tincidunt ut laoreet dolore magna aliquam erat volutpat. Ut wisi enim

The proof is in the listening
Acoustics mean sound

nonummy nibh euismod tincidunt ut laoreet dolore magna aliquam erat volutpat. Ut wisi enim ad minim veniam, quis nostrud exerci tation ullamcorper suscipit lobortis nisl ut aliquip ex ea commodo consequat. Duis autem vel eum iriure dolor in hendrerit in esse molestie consequat, vel illum dolore eu feugiat nulla facilisis at vero eros et accumsan et iusto odio

dignissim qui blandit praesent luptatum zzril delenit augue duis dolore te feugait nulla facilisi. Lorem ipsum dolor sit amet, consectetuer adipiscing elit, sed diam nonummy nibh euismod tincidunt ut laoreet dolore magna aliquam erat volutpat.

Ut wisi enim ad minim veniam, quis nostrud exerci tation ullamcorper suscipit lobortis nisl ut aliquip ex

Free concert series opens in the park

ea augue duis dolore te feugait nulla facilisi. Nam liber tempor cum soluta nobis eleifend option congue nihil imperdiet doming id quod mazim placerat facer possim Lorem ipsum dolor sit amet, consectetuer adipiscing elit, sed diam nonummy nibh euismod tincidunt ut laoreet dolore magna aliquam erat feugait nulla facilisi. Nam liber tempor

Lorem ipsum dolor sit amet, consectetuer adipiscing elit, sed diam nonummy nibh euismod tincidunt ut laoreet dolore magna aliquam erat volutpat. Ut wisi enim Lorem ipsum dolor sit amet, consectetuer adipiscing elit, sed diam nonummy nibh

Exhibit 5.23

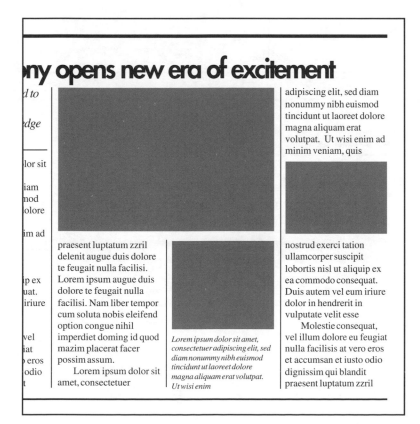

ny opens new era of excitement

d to

dge

lor sit

iam
mod
olore

im ad

praesent luptatum zzril delenit augue duis dolore te feugait nulla facilisi. Lorem ipsum augue duis dolore te feugait nulla facilisi. Nam liber tempor cum soluta nobis eleifend option congue nihil imperdiet doming id quod mazim placerat facer possim assum.

Lorem ipsum dolor sit amet, consectetuer

Lorem ipsum dolor sit amet, consectetuer adipiscing elit, sed diam nonummy nibh euismod tincidunt ut laoreet dolore magna aliquam erat volutpat. Ut wisi enim

adipiscing elit, sed diam nonummy nibh euismod tincidunt ut laoreet dolore magna aliquam erat volutpat. Ut wisi enim ad minim veniam, quis

nostrud exerci tation ullamcorper suscipit lobortis nisl ut aliquip ex ea commodo consequat. Duis autem vel eum iriure dolor in hendrerit in vulputate velit esse

Molestie consequat, vel illum dolore eu feugiat nulla facilisis at vero eros et accumsan et iusto odio dignissim qui blandit praesent luptatum zzril

p ex
uat.
iriure

vel
iat
o eros
odio
t

Exhibit 5.24
A closer look at page 2 of **Exhibit 5.23** shows the relationship of the photo spread. Notice how the photos share a common margin between columns three and four. This design device aids the reader in psychologically accepting the association of the three photos to each other and the story they are part of. Notice, also, how the joint caption serves to inscribe a natural border between it, the adjacent columns and the bottom half of the page.

Five-column Grids

The five-column grid is probably most appropriate for larger formats, such as tabloid-size newsletters; however, it can also be used for the standard newsletter size to solve unusual layout problems. Beginners should avoid this format since it takes a fairly well-developed design sense to make the most of its attributes.

Typically, you will want text columns to be two columns wide. An 8½" x 11" page with five text columns would require extremely small type and be legible only to those with extremely good vision, a magnifying glass, or perhaps to eagles.

Exhibit 5.25 is similar to a four- or three-column grid that uses one column for sidebars, newsbriefs, extended tables of contents, or similar additional and stand-alone information. Notice that on both pages the photos flow into the narrow column, helping tie the elements together. This narrow column, if used on the outside of the page, can be used to insert small photos, pull quotes, or captions

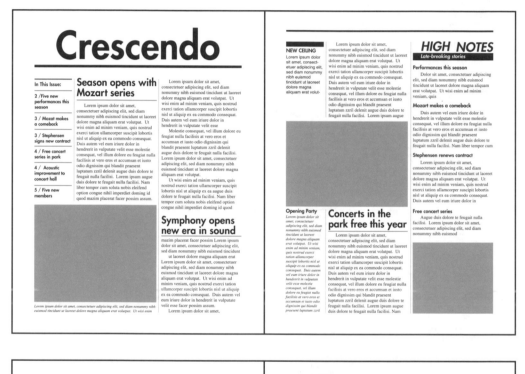

Exhibit 5.25

Exhibit 5.26

This is a rather extreme example of specialty layout. The small column in the center of the page is used for sidebar-type information—either a brief, accompanying story, or an extremely long caption. This type of design should be used sparingly.

Designing the Front Page

The front page of your newsletter is the key to your entire publication. It will be the deciding factor in whether it is read or not. On the front page will be your banner, your nameplate telling who the newsletter is for, the feature or lead story, graphic aids, and perhaps a table of contents.

Since a newsletter uses a self-contained cover, you will not have the luxury of using a full-page bleed (a photograph that covers the entire page and runs over the edges) the way a magazine does. You won't usually have full-color options. You won't be able to use other magazine devices such as surprinting (printing teasers over the cover photo) to entice readers inside. In short, since your newsletter has to utilize every square inch of space economically, the cover has to serve both as an attention-getter and the place you begin your editorial matter. This dual role doesn't allow for much in the way of attention-grabbing devices, so you have to make the most of what you do have.

What's in a Name?

A good banner speaks to your readers in both its style and its literal meaning. The first step toward designing an effective banner for your newsletter is to come up with a name. This is not an easy proposition. Words have both denotative and connotative meaning. The denotative meaning is a word's literal definition—its dictionary meaning. A word's connotative meaning is what the reader brings to it by way of prior experiences with the word. The connotative meaning of a word can play funny tricks on perception. For example, the word *stock* will probably mean something quite different to a market analyst than it does to a rancher. The difference certainly has a denotative basis, but probably stems more from the *association* each of these readers has with it—or its connotation.

When you choose a name for your newsletter, you should pick something that plays both on its denotative and its connotative meanings. In other words, if your newsletter name can have more than one meaning, and both are consistent with its purpose and content, you have scored a major coup. Here are some examples.

Fast Break—A newsletter for the women's basketball team at the University of Oregon.

Benefacts—A newsletter of employee benefit news from Weyerhaeuser Corporation.

House Calls—A community newsletter of Sacred Heart General Hospital.

In the Pink—A community health newsletter of Good Samaritan Hospital.

Pulse Beat—A community health newsletter of McKenzie-Willamette Hospital.

Heartbeat Quarterly—Another community health newsletter from Sacred Heart General Hospital (having *heart* in your organization's name opens up a number of possibilities for a hospital newsletter).

Random Lengths—A timber industry publication. Random lengths refers to a specific cut of lumber.

Springfield Composites—A newsletter of the Springfield, Oregon, Weyerhaeuser plant. Composites refers to the type of wood product produced by this plant—primarily, plywood.

On the other hand, many newsletters take a simpler approach. For example, there are a number of standard words signifying "communications" that are often used in names.

Briefs	Issues	Profiles
Bulletin	Link	Reporter
Byline	Monthly	Reports
Capsule	News	Scene
Channels	Newsline	Times
Daily	Notes	Weekly
Digest	On line	

These words can be combined with other specific modifiers to focus your name or make it unique to your newsletter. For example:

Portland Business Briefs
Pacific Bulletin
Northridge Reporter
Faculty Profiles
University On line

Don't feel bad if you can't come up with the most inspirational name ever seen in the civilized world. Remember, the name of your newsletter is supposed to say something about its content and its intended audience. If it doesn't, it is self-defeating.

Designing the Banner

Once you've settled on a name, you have to think of the most effective way to display it. Designing a

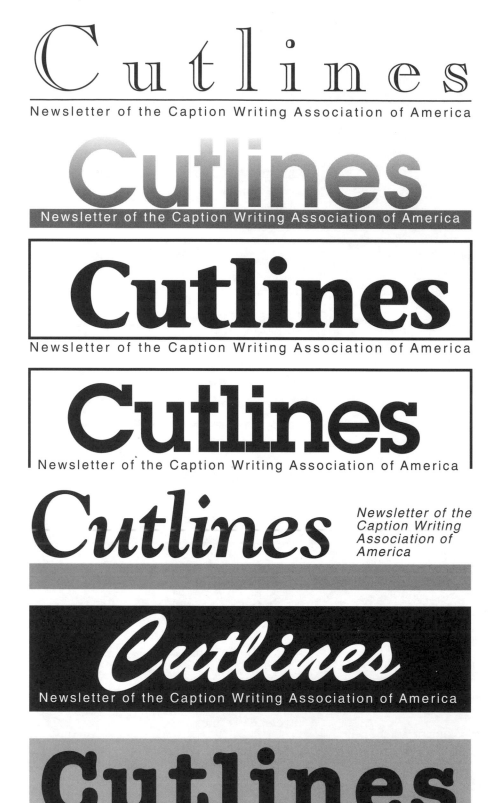

Exhibit 5.27

A banner changes in subtle ways every time you change the type. Each of these banners says something different about the newsletter it heads up. Italic and script typefaces imply informality while outline serif imparts an antique formality. If you were choosing a banner for a newsletter aimed at writers, which of these would come the closest to setting an appropiate nonverbal theme?

banner isn't easy. For years, most great looking banners were produced by graphic artists or calligraphers. These banners required a number of preliminary sketches, plenty of review, and usually a tidy investment in time and money. Most successful newsletter publishers will tell you that a well-designed banner is worth all that trouble. The payoff in name recognition alone can be worth it. Once your readers begin to associate your banner with your message, you've accomplished an important part of your job. Remember, a good banner acts as an enticement to those not already familiar with your newsletter, a reminder to those who are, and a sign that you care enough about your readers to add the quality a good banner imparts.

A banner is really only a word, or a couple of words. Therefore, the easiest banner to design is composed of plain type. Many of the most striking banners are fairly plain and make use of simple typography.

Today, with the aid of computers, you can take a stab at designing your own banner. Even without a computer, you can work up rough sketches of your ideas. You can even finalize them with press type (a rub-down lettering that comes in sheets in practically every type style and size). Although this is tedious and takes a bit of practice, many a newsletter has been born with a press-type banner.

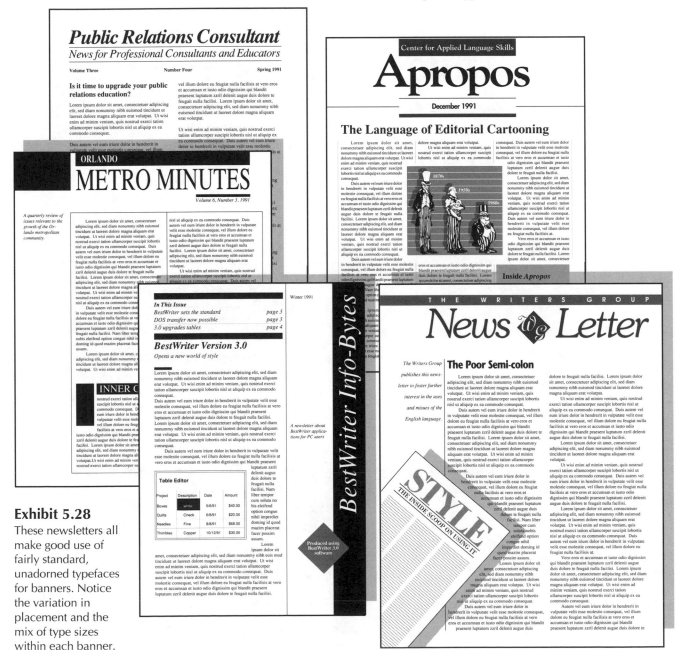

Exhibit 5.28

These newsletters all make good use of fairly standard, unadorned typefaces for banners. Notice the variation in placement and the mix of type sizes within each banner.

The Evolution of a Banner

Assume you are developing a banner for a newsletter for your local symphonic band. The band is a less formal organization than the symphony orchestra of which it is a part; therefore, you need a banner that imparts this informality and the fact that the newsletter is for a music group. You've already picked a name— *In Tune*. It meets the requirements for a consistent denotative and connotative message. *In Tune* refers both to a musical term and to the fact of being in touch through information.

The first step is to decide on a type face. You will need something that implies the informality of your theme. A normal, roman type face is too formal.

In Tune

Of course, you can italicize it to add a touch of informality.

In Tune

But your best bet is to pick a script or calligraphic face. Here are a few choices.

In Tune Brush Script

In Tune Kaufmann

In Tune Linotext

Once you have decided on a typeface. You must think in larger terms about how you want it displayed. Many banners are enclosed in a box, typically horizontal from margin to margin. This shape lends itself easily to a musical staff, which is horizontal and can conform to practically any height you need. There are five lines, including the outside of the box, evenly spaced.

You usually find musical notes on a staff, and that attractive device known as a clef that looks a lot like an ampersand gone crazy.

By some creative arranging of these various elements (all drawn in a computer illustration program called *FreeHand*, by Aldus Corporation) we now have an interesting banner. Notice the drop shadow behind the elements. This graphic effect makes the elements look as if they are floating slightly above the staff. This is an interesting, but often overused, design device.

The addition of the nameplate information immediately below the banner finishes off the design.

This banner, by the way, was designed by a student in a newsletter class.

Exhibit 5.29

All of these banners were originally designed for real clients by students in a newsletter class. The finished banners were accomplished on a Macintosh computer using Aldus *FreeHand.* The type faces are all included in the Adobe Type Library, while several of the banners make use of computer clip art.

If you do have a computer that can handle large type sizes, try a few banners on your own. But before you begin, whether it's with a computer or the old-fashioned way, you must have an idea of where you want to go. There are several things to consider.

- You need to keep it simple. Don't use two words if one will do. Don't use fancy type if plain type will do. Don't use a long word if a short word will do.

- Fit the type to the other non-verbal messages in your newsletter. If your newsletter is conservative, pick a conservative type face (more on this under typography). If it is informal, pick an informal type face.

- If you use color—and the banner is a great place to use it—make sure the color complements the rest of your look. Conservative colors for conservative newsletters, brighter colors for more informal newsletters.

- Make sure the banner design you decide on has visual impact. This usually means size, but can mean color, typeface, or other characteristics. Remember, the banner is the first thing your readers will see.

- If your newsletter is one of a number of publications your organization produces, it may be important for it to reflect a consistency of design. You may want to incorporate your organization's logo, or type style, or colors into your banner.

- Consider printing. If you are quick copying your newsletter, avoid large black areas, too fine a line, or too busy a design. You want a banner that will look as good on every copy as it does on your pasteup.

- Consider adding graphic elements to your banner other than type. Logos, rules, and other illustrative matter is okay as long as it doesn't conflict with your name or crowd the overall design.

If you are at all leery of tackling banner design on your own, hire a graphic artist. The money you pay now will return to you in reader response later. Remember, however, that a newsletter distribution of 100 copies per issue may not be worth paying $200 for a banner design. Or, as you can see from several of the banners on the preceding page, an artist may not be needed. Some of the simplest banners can be designed right at your own desk.

Exhibit 5.30
Not all banners have to display creative artwork and fancy typefaces. The examples below, all developed as options for a new newsletter, make good use of simple type faces. The two on the left are (top) flush left Times Roman, and (bottom) Avant Garde centered. On the right, additional tint blocks help dress up the Palatino type.

Other Front-page Elements

Although the banner is the most striking aspect of a newsletter front page, there are other elements that will aid you in drawing and satisfying reader attention.

Table of Contents

A table of contents is not absolutely necessary. After all, most newsletters are only four pages long. However, a table of contents can be used for more than just information. It is frequently utilized as a design element—to help balance the page, create white space, impart a newspaper style through page division, or as a focal point for newsbriefs. All of these uses are based on positioning.

For example, if the table of contents is placed in the left column, it tends to draw immediate attention. This is a good placement for a newsbriefs column or an expanded table of contents including teasers for the stories inside.

Placed horizontally across the bottom of the page, the table of contents can replicate newspaper style, especially if the items are boxed in some way. Several newspapers, most notably the *Christian Science Monitor,* use this style.

Placed at the bottom of the page in one or two of three columns, the table of contents can act as a page divider, especially if aligned with an adjacent article.

Placed to the outside—either in a separate, narrower column or in the bottom right corner—the table of contents acts as an exit point for the reader and a taste of what's to come.

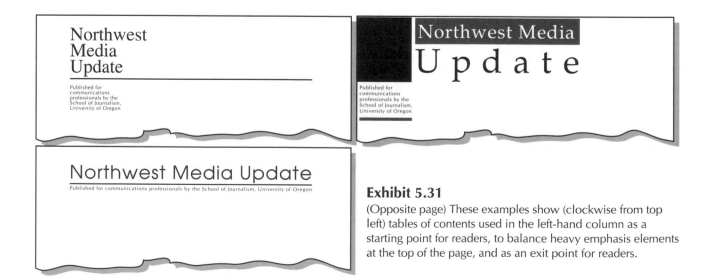

Exhibit 5.31
(Opposite page) These examples show (clockwise from top left) tables of contents used in the left-hand column as a starting point for readers, to balance heavy emphasis elements at the top of the page, and as an exit point for readers.

the Newsletter

Newsletter for employees and friends of the Associated Products Corporation

INSIDE

Duis autem vel eum iriure dolor in hendrerit in vulputate velit esse molestie
3

New headquarters opens with a bang

Lorem ipsum dolor sit amet, consectetuer adipiscing elit, sed diam nonummy nibh euismod tincidunt ut laoreet dolore magna aliquam erat volutpat. Ut wisi enim ad minim veniam, quis nostrud exerci tation ullamcorper suscipit lobortis nisl ut aliquip ex ea commodo consequat.

Duis autem vel eum iriure dolor in hendrerit in vulputate velit esse molestie consequat, vel illum dolore eu feugiat nulla facilisis at vero eros et accumsan et iusto odio dignissim qui blandit praesent luptatum zzril delenit augue duis dolore te feugait nulla facilisi. Lorem ipsum dolor sit amet, consectetuer adipiscing elit, sed diam nonummy nibh euismod tincidunt ut laoreet dolore magna aliquam erat volutpat.

Ut wisi enim ad minim veniam, quis nostrud exerci tation ullamcorper suscipit lobortis nisl ut aliquip ex ea commodo consequat.

Duis autem vel eum iriure dolor in hendrerit in vulputate velit esse molestie consequat, vel illum dolore eu feugiat nulla facilisis at vero eros et accumsan et iusto odio dignissim qui blandit praesent luptatum zzril delenit augue duis dolore te feugait nulla facilisi.

Nam liber tempor cum soluta nobis eleifend option congue nihil imperdiet doming id quod mazim placerat facer possim assum.

Lorem ipsum dolor sit amet, consectetuer adipiscing elit, sed diam nonummy nibh euismod tincidunt ut laoreet dolore magna aliquam erat volutpat. Ut wisi enim ad minim veniam, quis nostrud exerci tation ullamcorper suscipit lobortis nisl ut aliquip ex ea commodo consequat.

Duis autem vel eum iriure dolor in hendrerit in vulputate velit esse molestie

consequat, vel illum dolore eu feugiat nulla facilisis at vero eros et accumsan et iusto odio dignissim qui blandit praesent luptatum zzril delenit augue duis dolore te feugait nulla facilisi. Lorem ipsum dolor sit amet, consectetuer adipiscing elit, sed diam nonummy nibh euismod tincidunt ut laoreet dolore magna aliquam erat volutpat.

Ut wisi enim ad minim veniam, quis nostrud exerci tation ullamcorper suscipit lobortis nisl ut aliquip ex ea commodo consequat.

Duis autem vel eum iriure dolor in hendrerit in vulputate velit esse molestie consequat, vel illum dolore eu feugiat nulla facilisis at vero eros et accumsan et iusto odio dignissim qui blandit praesent luptatum zzril delenit augue duis dolore te feugait nulla facilisi.

Lorem ipsum dolor sit amet, consectetuer adipiscing elit, sed diam nonummy nibh euismod tincidunt ut laoreet dolore magna aliquam erat volutpat.

Ut wisi enim ad minim veniam, quis nostrud exerci tation ullamcorper suscipit lobortis nisl ut aliquip ex ea commodo consequat. Duis autem vel eum iriure dolor in hendrerit in vulputate velit esse molestie

---

the Newsletter

Newsletter for employees and friends of the Associated Products Corporation

INSIDE

New headquarters opens with a bang

Lorem ipsum dolor sit amet, consectetuer adipiscing elit, sed diam nonummy nibh euismod tincidunt ut laoreet dolore magna aliquam erat volutpat. Ut wisi enim ad minim veniam, quis nostrud exerci tation ullamcorper suscipit lobortis nisl ut aliquip ex ea commodo consequat.

Duis autem vel eum iriure dolor in hendrerit in vulputate velit esse molestie consequat, vel illum dolore eu feugiat nulla facilisis at vero eros et accumsan et iusto odio dignissim qui blandit praesent luptatum zzril delenit augue duis dolore te feugait nulla facilisi.

Ut wisi enim ad minim veniam, quis nostrud exerci tation ullamcorper suscipit lobortis nisl ut aliquip ex ea commodo consequat.

Duis autem vel eum iriure dolor in hendrerit in vulputate velit esse molestie consequat, vel illum dolore eu feugiat nulla facilisis at vero eros et accumsan et iusto odio dignissim qui blandit praesent luptatum zzril delenit augue duis dolore te feugait nulla facilisi.

Nam liber tempor cum soluta nobis eleifend option congue nihil imperdiet doming id quod mazim placerat facer possim assum.

Lorem ipsum dolor sit amet, consectetuer adipiscing elit, sed diam nonummy nibh euismod tincidunt ut laoreet dolore magna aliquam erat volutpat. Duis autem vel eum iriure dolor in hendrerit in vulputate velit esse molestie

consequat, vel illum dolore eu feugiat nulla facilisis at vero eros et accumsan et iusto odio dignissim qui blandit praesent luptatum zzril delenit augue duis dolore te feugait nulla facilisi. Lorem ipsum dolor sit amet, consectetuer adipiscing elit, sed diam nonummy nibh euismod tincidunt ut laoreet dolore magna aliquam erat volutpat.

Ut wisi enim ad minim veniam, quis nostrud exerci tation ullamcorper suscipit lobortis nisl ut aliquip ex ea commodo consequat. Duis autem vel eum iriure dolor in hendrerit in vulputate velit esse molestie consequat, vel illum dolore eu feugiat nulla facilisis at vero eros et accumsan et iusto odio dignissim qui blandit praesent luptatum zzril delenit augue duis dolore te feugait nulla facilisi.

Lorem ipsum dolor sit amet, consectetuer adipiscing elit, sed diam nonummy nibh euismod tincidunt ut laoreet dolore magna aliquam erat volutpat.

Ut wisi enim ad minim veniam, quis nostrud exerci tation ullamcorper suscipit lobortis nisl ut aliquip ex ea commodo consequat. Duis autem vel eum iriure dolor in hendrerit in vulputate velit esse molestie

---

the Newsletter

Newsletter for employees and friends of the Associated Products Corporation

New headquarters opens with a bang

Lorem ipsum dolor sit amet, consectetuer adipiscing elit, sed diam nonummy nibh euismod tincidunt ut laoreet dolore magna aliquam erat volutpat. Ut wisi enim ad minim veniam, quis nostrud exerci tation ullamcorper suscipit lobortis nisl ut aliquip ex ea commodo consequat.

Duis autem vel eum iriure dolor in hendrerit in vulputate velit esse molestie consequat, vel illum dolore eu feugiat nulla facilisis at vero eros et accumsan et iusto odio dignissim qui blandit praesent luptatum zzril delenit augue duis dolore te feugait nulla facilisi. Lorem ipsum dolor sit amet, consectetuer adipiscing elit, sed diam nonummy nibh euismod tincidunt ut laoreet dolore magna aliquam erat volutpat.

Ut wisi enim ad minim veniam, quis nostrud exerci tation ullamcorper suscipit lobortis nisl ut aliquip ex ea commodo consequat.

Duis autem vel eum iriure dolor in hendrerit in vulputate velit esse molestie consequat, vel illum dolore eu feugiat nulla facilisis at vero eros et accumsan et iusto odio dignissim qui blandit praesent luptatum zzril delenit augue duis dolore te feugait nulla facilisi.

augue duis dolore te feugait nulla facilisi.

Nam liber tempor cum soluta nobis eleifend option congue nihil imperdiet doming id quod mazim placerat facer possim assum.

Lorem ipsum dolor sit amet, consectetuer adipiscing elit, sed diam nonummy nibh euismod tincidunt ut laoreet dolore magna aliquam erat volutpat. Ut wisi enim ad minim veniam, quis nostrud exerci tation ullamcorper suscipit lobortis nisl ut aliquip ex ea commodo consequat.

Duis autem vel eum iriure dolor in hendrerit in vulputate velit esse molestie consequat, vel illum dolore eu feugiat nulla facilisis at vero eros et accumsan et iusto odio dignissim qui blandit praesent luptatum zzril delenit augue duis dolore te feugait nulla facilisi. Lorem ipsum dolor sit amet, consectetuer adipiscing elit, sed diam nonummy nibh euismod tincidunt ut laoreet dolore magna aliquam erat volutpat.

Ut wisi enim ad minim veniam, quis nostrud exerci tation ullamcorper suscipit nisl ut aliquip ex ea commodo consequat. Duis autem vel

eum iriure dolor in hendrerit in vulputate velit esse molestie consequat, vel illum dolore eu feugiat nulla facilisis at vero eros et accumsan et iusto odio dignissim qui blandit praesent luptatum zzril delenit augue duis dolore te feugait nulla facilisi.

Lorem ipsum dolor sit amet, consectetuer adipiscing elit, sed diam nonummy nibh euismod tincidunt ut laoreet dolore magna aliquam erat volutpat.

Ut wisi enim ad minim veniam, quis nostrud exerci tation ullamcorper suscipit lobortis nisl ut aliquip ex ea commodo consequat. Duis autem vel eum iriure dolor in hendrerit in vulputate velit esse molestie consequat, vel illum dolore eu feugiat nulla facilisis at vero eros et accumsan et iusto odio dignissim qui blandit praesent luptatum zzril delenit augue duis dolore te feugait nulla facilisi.

Lorem ipsum dolor sit amet, consectetuer adipiscing elit, sed diam nonummy nibh euismod tincidunt ut laoreet dolore magna aliquam erat volutpat.

Ut wisi enim ad minim veniam, quis nostrud exerci tation ullamcorper

---

the Newsletter

Newsletter for employees and friends of the Associated Products Corporation

New headquarters opens with a bang

Lorem ipsum dolor sit amet, consectetuer adipiscing elit, sed diam nonummy nibh euismod tincidunt ut laoreet dolore magna aliquam erat volutpat. Ut wisi enim ad minim veniam, quis nostrud exerci tation ullamcorper suscipit lobortis nisl ut aliquip ex ea commodo consequat.

Duis autem vel eum iriure dolor in hendrerit in vulputate velit esse molestie consequat, vel illum dolore eu feugiat nulla facilisis at vero eros et accumsan et iusto odio dignissim qui blandit praesent luptatum zzril delenit augue duis dolore te feugait nulla facilisi. Lorem ipsum dolor sit amet, consectetuer adipiscing elit, sed diam nonummy nibh euismod tincidunt ut laoreet dolore magna aliquam erat volutpat.

Ut wisi enim ad minim veniam, quis nostrud exerci tation ullamcorper suscipit lobortis nisl ut aliquip ex ea commodo consequat.

Duis autem vel eum iriure dolor in hendrerit in vulputate velit esse molestie consequat, vel illum dolore

congue nihil imperdiet doming id quod mazim placerat facer possim assum. Lorem ipsum dolor sit amet, consectetuer adipiscing elit, sed diam nonummy nibh euismod tincidunt ut laoreet dolore magna aliquam erat volutpat. Ut wisi enim ad minim veniam, quis nostrud exerci tation ullamcorper suscipit lobortis nisl ut aliquip ex ea commodo consequat.

Duis autem vel eum iriure dolor in hendrerit in vulputate velit esse molestie consequat, vel illum dolore

Lorem ipsum dolor sit amet, consect etuer adipis cing elit, sed diam

eu feugiat nulla facilisis at vero eros et accumsan et iusto odio dignissim qui blandit praesent luptatum zzril delenit augue duis dolore te feugait nulla facilisi. Lorem ipsum dolor sit amet, consectetuer adipiscing elit, sed diam nonummy nibh euismod tincidunt ut laoreet dolore magna aliquam erat volutpat. Ut wisi enim ad minim veniam, quis nostrud exerci tation ullamcorper suscipit lobortis nisl ut aliquip ex ea commodo consequat. Duis autem vel eum iriure dolor in hendrerit in vulputate velit esse molestie consequat, vel illum dolore eu feugiat nulla facilisis at vero eros et accumsan et iusto odio dignissim qui blandit praesent luptatum zzril delenit augue duis dolore te feugait nulla

illum dolore eu feugiat nulla facilisis at vero eros et accumsan et iusto odio dignissim qui blandit praesent luptatum zzril delenit augue duis dolore te feugait nulla facilisi.

Lorem ipsum dolor sit amet, consectetuer adipiscing elit, sed diam nonummy nibh euismod tincidunt ut laoreet dolore magna aliquam erat volutpat.

Ut wisi enim ad minim veniam, quis nostrud exerci tation ullamcorper suscipit lobortis nisl ut aliquip ex ea commodo consequat. Duis autem vel eum iriure dolor in hendrerit in vulputate velit esse molestie consequat, vel illum dolore eu feugiat nulla facilisis at vero eros et accumsan et iusto odio dignissim qui blandit praesent luptatum zzril delenit augue duis dolore te

feugait nulla facilisi.

Lorem ipsum dolor sit amet, consectetuer adipiscing elit, sed diam nonummy nibh euismod tincidunt ut laoreet dolore magna aliquam erat volutpat.

Ut wisi enim ad minim veniam, quis nostrud exerci tation ullamcorper suscipit lobortis nisl ut aliquip ex ea commodo consequat. Duis autem vel eum iriure dolor in hendrerit in vulputate velit esse molestie Lorem ipsum dolor sit amet, consectetuer adipiscing elit, sed diam nonummy nibh euismod tincidunt ut laoreet dolore magna aliquam erat volutpat.

Ut wisi enim ad minim veniam, quis nostrud exerci tation ullamcorper suscipit lobortis nisl ut aliquip ex ea commodo consequat. Duis autem vel eum iriure dolor in hendrerit in vulputate velit

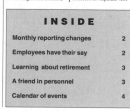

Remember, if you decide to use a table of contents, use it in each issue. Like any other standing column, it serves to aid consistency and can frustrate readers if it appears only sporadically.

Primary or feature headline

The front page is normally the place in which you use your largest headline. This large headline normally accompanies your newsletter's feature story. The headline should draw immediate attention to the feature article, yet not conflict with the banner. This is especially important if you are using a similar typeface in your banner and headlines, or if your banner type is particularly small.

You can reduce conflict in three ways. You can make sure your headline typeface doesn't repeat your banner typeface. You can make sure your type size is sufficiently smaller than your banner type. Or, if your emphasis is hurt by reducing the type size, you can create more white space between it and the banner. In any event, keep enough space between your headline and the banner so that the top of your page doesn't become crowded or top heavy.

Graphic elements

Photographs and other graphic elements, such as artwork, should support your front page, not overwhelm it. Some newsletters rely on large graphic elements to "sell" the front page. This is fine, as long as the artwork or photography complements the message of your newsletter or the theme of a particular issue.

Most of the time, photos and artwork will be of a size that they will be used primarily for balance—or will have to be counterbalanced by other elements on the page, such as the table of contents, white space, or headlines. Remember, graphic elements tend to draw the reader's attention first. If they are not the primary emphasis of your front page, don't place them too high or make them too large.

As you saw previously under the section on grids, all of the front-page elements must create harmony for the reader. This harmony comes from the proper understanding and use of the principles of design: balance, proportion, sequence, emphasis, and unity.

Exhibit 5.32
Headline type too close in size or type face to your banner will conflict with and detract from both element (top). Solutions include lowering type size and changing typeface (middle) and just changing type face while allowing slightly more white space between banner and headline (bottom).

Exhibit 5. 33
This tabloid-size newsletter shows the use of large photographs as artistic focus points. Use this technique sparingly since its tends to overpower your message. Obviously, the photos have to have meaning in context with the feature story.

Using Swipe Files

One of the best ways to stimulate your creative juices is to consult a swipe file. A swipe file is a collection of your favorite pieces done by other people or companies. They will help you a great deal with design, layout ideas and writing style as well as with communicating your ideas to typesetters and printers. You may find a particular newsletter, for instance, that is exactly the right size and design for the publication you want to produce. You may decide to use similar paper, ink color, or even design. Most graphic artists, designers, and printers use ideas generated from a variety of sources. However, don't plagiarize your source. Don't steal the artwork right off the source newsletter. Be careful to differentiate between emulation and plagiarism. If you do decide that you must "borrow" directly from another piece, obtain permission from its originator in advance of the publication of your piece.

You will find that many newsletters look alike—some, remarkably so. That's for two reasons. There are only a limited number of design formats available to newsletters, and designs are not usually copyrightable. What really prevents newsletter designers from using an identical design is potential reader confusion. You don't want your readers to mistake your newsletter for something else. Ultimately, it is in your best interest to be as original as you can. Develop your own design and get your readers used to it. Their familiarity with your design will pay off in the long run.

Typography

Working with type is a pleasure for some, a chore for others. The process of selecting and working with type can be a bewildering experience for the beginner. However, the payoff is a more readable, attractive, and memorable newsletter.

Typography is one of those areas in which novices feel as though they've fallen into very deep water without a life preserver. There are literally thousands of typefaces from which to choose, and many thousands more variations on these faces. The first time you confront a printer or typesetter with your raw copy can be a humbling experience. Your conversation might go something like this:

Printer: What typeface are you using for your body copy?

You: Garamond.

Printer: Light, book, regular, italic, demi-bold, demi-bold italic, bold, bold italic? Which?

You: Huh?

Printer: How about point size?

You: I want something big enough to read easily, but not too big?

Printer: 10 point? 12 Point? 14 point?

You: Uh... 12 point will be fine... I guess.

Printer: Leading?

You: What?

Printer: Leading. How much leading do you want?

You: Uh... I don't know. Whatever looks good.

And you haven't even gotten to headlines yet.

You get the picture. You have to know quite a bit about type just to have your newsletter printed. And you have to know even more about type just to pick the face for your newsletter. For example, is your newsletter going to be read by older people? You'll probably need a larger typeface. Do you have a lot of information and not much space? You'll probably need a smaller typeface. Is your newsletter formal or informal? Should you use serif or sans serif type? The same typeface for headlines as for body copy? How many typefaces can you use in one publication? Should you give up this hair-brained idea of publishing a newsletter while there's still a chance to preserve your sanity?

Don't despair. Understanding type requires *some* knowledge, but not a *lot* of knowledge. There are those who will tell you that you practically have to know how to design your own type in order to pick it for a publication. In reality, all you need to know is just enough to get your newsletter off on the right foot, and keep it there. After that, anything else you learn about type is just gravy.

Types of Type

There really is a bewildering array of choices facing you; however, if you learn a few basics now, that array can be narrowed down to just a few choices for you and your newsletter.

The first thing to know is how to classify type. Let's start with the most general, and useful, classification for publication purposes. First of all, type is measured in points (in type, this is a vertical measure-

Exhibit 6.1
Although you don't need to know all of the information contained in this example, it helps to be aware of the various characteristics of type so that you can begin to understand how various typefaces differ in their design and how those differences affect your newsletter.

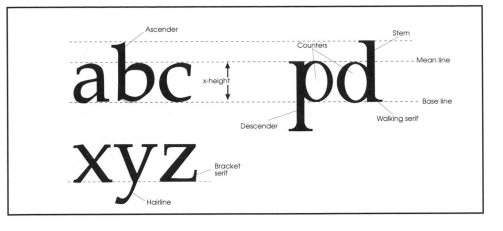

ment). There are 72 points in an inch. Imagine trying to designate 11-point type in inches and you know why printers and typesetters have traditionally used a different scale. Small type, up to 14 points, is called *body type*. Type that is 14 points and above is called *display type* (normally headlines). Most typefaces come in both body and display sizes; however, there are subtle differences between the sizes. For instance, the loop (or hole) in a lower-case *e* is proportionally smaller in larger sizes because it's easier to see. In a smaller size, say 10 points, the loop is larger so that it doesn't fill in with ink when printed.

Next, type can be broken down into five other, fairly broad categories: serif, sans serif, italic, script, and novelty.

1. *Serif*. Most serif faces are distinguished by a variation in thick and thin strokes, and by serifs—the lines that cross the end strokes of the letters. Serif type can be further broken down into *romans* and *slab* or *square serif* faces. Romans have the traditional thick and thin strokes while slab serif faces have relatively uniform strokes and serifs. Serif faces are usually considered easier to read, especially in body type sizes.

Times
Serifs are the small lines that cross the end strokes of the letters in serif type.

Lubalin
Square or slab serifs have fairly uniform thicknesses of both the letter strokes and their serifs.

2. *Sans serif*. These are faces without serifs (*sans*, from the French, meaning *without*). They are usually, but not always, distinguished by uniformity of strokes. They usually impart a more modern look to a publication, especially if used as display type. Setting body type in sans serif is unwise since the uniformity of the strokes tends to darken your page and makes for difficult reading. There are some exceptions. Optima, for example, has some variation in stroke and reads fairly well in smaller sizes. Stone Sans, a new face designed by Sumner Stone of Adobe Systems, makes excellent use of both thin and thick strokes.

Helvetica
In this example of sans serif type (Helvetica), notice the uniformity of stroke width. This is characteristic of most, but not all, sans serif type.

Optima
Optima is one of several sans serif typefaces with some interesting variation in stroke width. This variation (along with a hint of serifs) tends to make the face more readable.

3. *Italics*. Some typographers don't consider italics a separate category of type since most typefaces today come with an italic version. However, *true* italic versions of many typefaces are completely different from their upright versions. Since the advent of desktop publishing, editors have had the option of italicizing a typeface with a simple keystroke.

This method typically only slants the existing face; it does not always create a true italic version of that face. Only by selecting a face that has been designed specifically as an italic do we get true italics. Because they are slanted, italics tend to impart an informality and speed to your message. But, because of the slant, they are more difficult to read and should be used for accent only. Also, italic refers only to a version of a serif face. A slanted version of a sans serif face is called *oblique*. Like italics, true obliques are designed as separate *fonts* (a complete alphabet, number series and set of punctuation points and miscellaneous marks) and are not simply the original face at a slant.

Type Type

Note that there is quite a bit of difference between a true italic face (Goudy italic) left, and a slanted version of the upright face, right. Type designers would just as soon you didn't mess with their original designs by distorting their typefaces.

Type Type

There is a significant amount of variance among italic faces. You can see from these two examples (Palatino on the left and Times on the right) that type designers can create rather elegant nuances in their italic faces.

Type Type

Sans serif typefaces don't have italic versions *per se*. Instead, they have obliques. Like italics, obliques are specifically designed to be set at a slant. They are not simply slanted versions of the upright face.

4. *Script.* These typefaces attempt to replicate handwriting or calligraphy. Use them sparingly, if at all. They are useful for certificates, greeting cards, invitations and the like, but not very useful for newsletters. They can make good banner type if used creatively, or sometimes even good speciality headline type.

Brush Script
Lino Script
Kaufman
Chancery

These four examples of script face range from calligraphic brush style, to calligraphic pen style, to near-handwriting style, to the more chiseled look of Zapf Chancery.

5. *Novelty type.* This refers to the huge variety of "cute" typefaces that seem to be favorites of most novices. Outline type, type with drop shadows, ornate type, type made up of animals, people, vines, or practically every imaginable non-traditional object, is called novelty type. This type has little or no real value in newsletter publication except in rare circumstances in which you wish to impart a particular message in a novel way. As with any other category of type, novelty types say something specific about your message.

Open Face
Black Face
University
Roman
STENCIL

Novelty faces run the range from moderately usable under certain circumstances (such as the ones shown here) to totally silly and unacceptable for newsletter publication.

How to Select Type

For our purposes, let's assume you will be using typeset copy rather than typewritten copy. There are several questions to ask yourself when selecting a typeface for your newsletter.

1. **Can I use just one typeface?** The safest route to take is to stick with one typeface. Using a single face lends your newsletter unity and consistency. You will need to pick one that comes in as many variations as possible. These variations include: style, weight and size (both horizontal and vertical).

   Most typefaces come in *regular* and/or *light* versions. These are sometimes called *book* or *text*. They also come in *upright* (roman) and *italic* or *oblique*. In addition, they may have *demi-bold* and *bold* versions in both upright and italic or oblique (or these versions may be called *heavy* or *black*; or heavy and black versions may be in addition to bold). And the semi-bold and bold versions may come as extended and/or condensed (referring to the width of the letters).

The greater the variety, the more flexibility you have in a single typeface. For example, you could use the regular version for body type, the bold version for headlines, and the regular italic version for captions, pull quotes and subheads (in different point sizes).

2. **Can I use more than one typeface?** Novices with access to a computer and a type library of twenty faces tend to use all twenty just because they have them. Try to limit yourself to no more than two different typefaces in a publication. And be aware that they shouldn't conflict with each other. This is the most difficult part of using more than one face. Here are a few guidelines to remember.

Exhibit 6.2

The two examples below are both set in variations of a new family of typefaces designed by Sumner Stone, simply called Stone. The one on the left has a headline of Stone Sans semi-bold and body copy of Stone Serif. The example on the right has a headline of Stone Sans bold, with body copy of Stone Informal. Both copy blocks are set 12/14.

DGA Wins UL Certificate

The sign on the door reads "Grade 'A' UL Central Station." To the people at Dallas General Alarm (DGA) and to the hundreds of businesses and homes they protect, this means the availability of some of the best alarm and intrusion detection systems in the country. In fact, almost every improvement made at DGA over the past few years has had as its goal the attainment of UL certification.

In 1924, Underwriters Laboratories, Inc. began offering a means of identifying burglar alarm systems that met acceptable minimum standards. The installing company can apply for investigation of their services and, if found qualified, may be issued UL certification.

DGA Wins UL Certificate

The sign on the door reads "Grade 'A' UL Central Station." To the people at Dallas General Alarm (DGA) and to the hundreds of businesses and homes they protect, this means the availability of some of the best alarm and intrusion detection systems in the country. In fact, almost every improvement made at DGA over the past few years has had as its goal the attainment of UL certification.

In 1924, Underwriters Laboratories, Inc. began offering a means of identifying burglar alarm systems that met acceptable minimum standards. The installing company can apply for investigation of their services and, if found qualified, may be issued UL certification.

- If your body type is serif, try a sans serif for headlines. Two *different* serif faces will probably conflict with one another.

- If you are using a light body type (as opposed to its regular version), use a regular or semi-bold headline type. You don't want your headline weight to overpower your text weight.

- Above all, don't pick your type just by looking at a type chart. Have a page set, complete with body copy and headlines, to see for yourself whether your two faces are going to harmonize or not.

3. **Where do I go to select type**? If you are working on a computer, you probably have anywhere from two to a hundred choices, depending on the sophistication of your desktop publishing system. Stick with what you've got. It's easier and saves a lot of frustration in the long run. If all you've got is Times Roman, use it. If you've got Times Roman and Helvetica, use Times for the body copy and Helvetica for the headlines. Under no circumstances use Helvetica for the body copy. It is not very readable set in blocks of small type. If you are lucky enough to have access to a larger type library on computer, explore your options by experimenting with several combinations, printing out a page with each one.

And don't forget to try several different point sizes for body copy. There can be a great deal of variation in readability between 12-point Times and 12-point Palatino, as well as between 12-point Palatino and 10-point Palatino.

Be aware that your type will also look different when printed on a dot-matrix printer, a laser printer, and an imagesetter. Decide which one you're going to use to print your final camera-ready copy and check its print quality against your type choice. Typefaces with thin serifs may not print as well on a dot-matrix printer as on a laser printer, or as well on a laser writer as on an imagesetter. Bold or heavy faces (especially if condensed) will tend to clog and fill on dot-matrix and laser printers, but will print cleanly on an imagesetter.

If you don't have access to computer type, check with your printer or typesetter for samples of type set in copy blocks and as display type. Most printers can provide you with more than just a type chart.

Other Considerations

Just because you've finally decided on a typeface or faces doesn't mean your job's done. There are several other considerations you'll have to deal with: line length, leading, and alignment. Let's look at them one at a time.

Line Length

This has to do with how wide you want your columns to be and what size type to use to gain the most readability from your body copy. Two-hundred years ago, newspapers were often printed in 10-point type, spread from margin to margin across the page. Even hand-written documents were often produced with extremely long lines. Take a look at the Declaration of Independence in full size. The average line length is nearly a foot wide! And the size of the writing is no bigger than that in an average letter to a friend. Maybe folks in 1776 didn't have any trouble reading lines of that length, but readers today sure do.

Today's readers tire easily. We are more used to short copy and graphic support. Perhaps television viewing has spoiled us. Whatever the reason, your newsletter has to accommodate today's reading habits. And, to do this, you must reach a happy medium. Lines that are too long are tiring because we have too few visual pauses, while lines that are too short make us read in stops and starts.

The simplest method of determining line length is to double the point size of your type. The resulting number will be the recommended width of your line in *picas* (a printer's measure of width). Thus, using 12-*point* type for your body copy indicates using a 24-*pica* line length. Keep in mind, however, that because of design differences, all 12-point type *isn't* the same size. For example, a 12-point line of Palatino will have fewer characters than a 12-point line of Times. So a line of 12-point Palatino 24 picas wide may look more spacious than a line of 12-point Times set the same width.

Given this peculiarity, a more accurate method of calculating line length is to measure the width of a lowercase typeface *a* to *z*, then add half of that measure to the width to get your line measure. So, if a lowercase alphabet of Times Roman at 12 point measures 12 picas (it does), just add 6 and 12 for a line length of 18. This number is really an average line length. The minimum line length would be the width of the alphabet, 12 picas, and the maximum would be double that, or 24 picas. Since determining line length this way is based on the actual width of the letters in your typeface, suggested line length will vary more than if you use the first method. Either way, you will probably be close.

Exhibit 6.3

Notice how difficult it is to track the longer lines set in 10-point type below. The narrower column, still in 10-point type, is much easier to read, while the right-hand column, set in 12-point type, is easier still.

Leading

Leading (pronounced *ledding*) refers to the space between lines of type. Too little leading and your copy seems cramped and hard to read. Too much leading and your copy looks open and disjointed (and also as if you ran out of something to say). The easiest way to determine leading is simply to add two points to your type size. So, 12-point type would be leaded 14 points. That means that the space between your lines will be the height of your type plus two points. If you were writing this down for a printer, you would put 12/14 (if you were telling your printer, you would say "twelve on fourteen").

Although it is standard to lead two points, one point leading is not uncommon. If you are trying to save space, try reducing your leading by one point. The effect on readability will usually be negligible

The sign on the door reads "Grade 'A' UL Central Station." To the people at Dallas General Alarm (DGA) and to the hundreds of businesses and homes they protect, this means the availability of some of the best alarm and intrusion detection systems in the country. In fact, almost every improvement made at DGA over the past few years has had as its goal the attainment of UL certification.

In 1924, Underwriters Laboratories, Inc. began offering a means of identifying burglar alarm systems that met acceptable minimum standards. The installing company can apply for investigation of their services and, if found qualified, may be issued UL certification.

To the customer, this certification can mean a large reduction (sometimes up to 70 percent) in insurance premiums, depending on the exact grade and extent of the UL-approved service used.

However, Dallas General Alarm doesn't sell only UL service. "We sell and lease our systems on the merit of the system and the particular need of the customer," says Dave Michaels, Director of Quality Control for DGA. "Of course, those who do have the UL Grade 'A' system installed can usually pay the extra cost entailed with the savings they make on insurance alone."

What makes this Grade "A" system so effective that insurance companies charging sometimes thousands of dollars a year in coverage are willing to cut 40, 60 or even 70 percent off their premiums?

"The UL people are really tight on their standards," says Michaels. "They conduct a number of 'surprise' inspections of DGA on a regular basis. If we fall down in any of their requirements, we get our certification cancelled."

DGA has its own tight security system consisting of television monitors on all doors and verbal contact with people entering their offices. The central control room is always manned and locked. A thick, glass window allows the operators on duty to check personally all people entering the premises. Other UL requirements are extra fire proofing for the building itself and a buried cable containing the thousands of telephone lines used to monitor the various alarm systems which run out of the building. The cable is unmarked, preventing the adventurous burglar from cutting

The over-a-thousand customers who either lease or buy alarm or detection systems from DGA range from some of the biggest businesses in Dallas to private residences. In addition, all of the schools in the Dallas area are monitored from the DGA central station against break-in and vandalism.

The monitoring devices, located at the DGA central control, vary from a simple paper tape printout to actual voice communication with the premises being protected. For instance, the card-key system used by Atlantic Richfield Company allows access to certain areas through the use of a magnetic card inserted into a slot in the door. Access is forbidden to those lacking the proper clearance and the number and time of the attempted access are printed out at the DGA central station.

while the space saving will be substantial. Sometimes, copy is set *solid*. That is, the leading equals the point size of the type. Sometimes, copy uses *minus leading*, or less leading than the point size of the type. Solid leading is okay for typefaces with short ascenders and descenders and can save quite a bit of space; however, minus leading should be reserved for special effects with display type, usually sans serif.

When setting leading for headlines, be aware that at larger sizes, standard leading may result in too much space between lines. Most of the time, you will want to reduce the leading to solid. If ascenders and descenders bump, increase it a point.

CEO Jones says she'll back pay increase

CEO Jones says she'll back pay increase

CEO Jones says she'll back pay increase

Exhibit 6.5
These 24-point headlines show the difference tighter leading can make at larger type sizes. The top headline is leaded 26 points, the middle 24 (solid), and the bottom17 (minus).

Exhibit 6.4
The text below is 10-point Times leaded (from left to right) 14, 11, and 10 (set solid).

The sign on the door reads "Grade 'A' UL Central Station." To the people at Dallas General Alarm (DGA) and to the hundreds of businesses and homes they protect, this means the availability of some of the best alarm and intrusion detection systems in the country. In fact, almost every improvement made at DGA over the past few years has had as its goal the attainment of UL certification.

In 1924, Underwriters Laboratories, Inc. began offering a means of identifying burglar alarm systems that met acceptable minimum standards. The installing company can apply for investigation of their services and, if found qualified, may be issued UL certification.

To the customer, this certification can mean a large reduction (sometimes up to 70 percent) in insurance premiums, depending on the exact grade and extent of the UL-approved service used.

However, Dallas General Alarm doesn't sell only UL service. "We sell and lease our systems on

The sign on the door reads "Grade 'A' UL Central Station." To the people at Dallas General Alarm (DGA) and to the hundreds of businesses and homes they protect, this means the availability of some of the best alarm and intrusion detection systems in the country. In fact, almost every improvement made at DGA over the past few years has had as its goal the attainment of UL certification.

In 1924, Underwriters Laboratories, Inc. began offering a means of identifying burglar alarm systems that met acceptable minimum standards. The installing company can apply for investigation of their services and, if found qualified, may be issued UL certification.

To the customer, this certification can mean a large reduction (sometimes up to 70 percent) in insurance premiums, depending on the exact grade and extent of the UL-approved service used.

However, Dallas General Alarm doesn't sell only UL service. "We sell and lease our systems on the merit of the system and the particular need of the customer," says Dave Michaels, Director of Quality Control for DGA. "Of course, those who do have the

The sign on the door reads "Grade 'A' UL Central Station." To the people at Dallas General Alarm (DGA) and to the hundreds of businesses and homes they protect, this means the availability of some of the best alarm and intrusion detection systems in the country. In fact, almost every improvement made at DGA over the past few years has had as its goal the attainment of UL certification.

In 1924, Underwriters Laboratories, Inc. began offering a means of identifying burglar alarm systems that met acceptable minimum standards. The installing company can apply for investigation of their services and, if found qualified, may be issued UL certification.

To the customer, this certification can mean a large reduction (sometimes up to 70 percent) in insurance premiums, depending on the exact grade and extent of the UL-approved service used.

However, Dallas General Alarm doesn't sell only UL service. "We sell and lease our systems on the merit of the system and the particular need of the customer," says Dave Michaels, Director of Quality Control for DGA. "Of course, those who do have the

Alignment

Alignment refers to the way your copy is arranged in relation to column margins. The two most typical alignments are *flush left* (sometimes called *ragged right*) and *justified.* Flush right copy is getting to be quite common for newsletters. It imparts a less formal look, involves less hyphenation, and takes up more space.

Justified copy looks more formal, is more hyphenated, and takes up less space. However, when using justified copy, keep in mind that the width of your columns severely affects *word spread.* The narrower your columns, the more your words will separate from one another in order to maintain justification. Computers allow for minute adjustments to word and letter spacing to help correct this spread, but the best way to avoid it is to keep your columns at the average or maximum width for your type size.

There are other alignment possibilities, such as *flush right* and *centered.* Flush right copy should be avoided simply because it is difficult to read. It is, however, sometimes useful for very brief text blocks such as pull quotes that appear in outside left margins. Centered body text should always be avoided. Centered headlines are not in fashion these days, although centered pull quotes are still found quite a bit.

The best idea is to pick either flush left or justified for your body copy and don't deviate. Stick with flush left for headlines. And use either flush left or justified for pull quotes and captions.

Exhibit 6.6

Notice that the justified text (left) takes up less space than the flush left text (center). The flush right text (right) is nearly impossible to track.

The sign on the door reads "Grade 'A' UL Central Station." To the people at Dallas General Alarm (DGA) and to the hundreds of businesses and homes they protect, this means the availability of some of the best alarm and intrusion detection systems in the country. In fact, almost every improvement made at DGA over the past few years has had as its goal the attainment of UL certification.

In 1924, Underwriters Laboratories, Inc. began offering a means of identifying burglar alarm systems that met acceptable minimum standards. The installing company can apply for investigation of their services and, if found qualified, may be issued UL certification.

To the customer, this certification can mean a large reduction (sometimes up to 70 percent) in insurance premiums, depending on the exact grade and extent of the UL-approved service used.

However, Dallas General Alarm doesn't sell only UL service. "We sell and lease our systems on the merit of the system and the particular need of the customer," says Dave Michaels, Director of Quality Control for DGA. "Of course, those who do have the UL

The sign on the door reads "Grade 'A' UL Central Station." To the people at Dallas General Alarm (DGA) and to the hundreds of businesses and homes they protect, this means the availability of some of the best alarm and intrusion detection systems in the country. In fact, almost every improvement made at DGA over the past few years has had as its goal the attainment of UL certification.

In 1924, Underwriters Laboratories, Inc. began offering a means of identifying burglar alarm systems that met acceptable minimum standards. The installing company can apply for investigation of their services and, if found qualified, may be issued UL certification.

To the customer, this certification can mean a large reduction (sometimes up to 70 percent) in insurance premiums, depending on the exact grade and extent of the UL-approved service used.

However, Dallas General Alarm doesn't sell only UL service. "We sell and lease our systems on the merit of the system and the particular need of the customer," says Dave Michaels, Director of Quality Control for DGA.

The sign on the door reads "Grade 'A' UL Central Station." To the people at Dallas General Alarm (DGA) and to the hundreds of businesses and homes they protect, this means the availability of some of the best alarm and intrusion detection systems in the country. In fact, almost every improvement made at DGA over the past few years has had as its goal the attainment of UL certification.

In 1924, Underwriters Laboratories, Inc. began offering a means of identifying burglar alarm systems that met acceptable minimum standards. The installing company can apply for investigation of their services and, if found qualified, may be issued UL certification.

To the customer, this certification can mean a large reduction (sometimes up to 70 percent) in insurance premiums, depending on the exact grade and extent of the UL-approved service used.

However, Dallas General Alarm doesn't sell only UL service. "We sell and lease our systems on the merit of the system and the particular need of the customer,"

Style Conventions in Headline Type

Avoid all-uppercase headlines (or all-uppercase anything, for that matter). Lines set all upper case are very difficult to read and leading becomes a real problem. Style preferences change according to what's popular or in vogue. For example, it used to be the norm to run headlines in what is known as *up style*. That is, all significant words are capitalized. These days, however, the trend is toward *down style*. Only the first word and any proper nouns are capitalized. Although the choice is yours, down style *is* easier to read.

Another style peculiarity in headline type has to do with the use of quotation marks. It is standard to use single quotes in display type, not the usual double quotes. No one seems to know exactly why, but it has been common practice in headline writing in newspapers for years. However, if you do decide to use double quotes, no one other than an old newspaper hand will probably notice.

Copyfitting

Basically, copyfitting means fitting your typeset copy into a prescribed space. This requires careful planning. Until the advent of desktop publishing, copyfitting was a tedious process involving a number of complicated steps. Even today, if you are without a page-layout program, copyfitting will have to be done by someone—and that someone is usually you. Whether you set your type on a computer and then paste it in place on your layout, or send it out to be typeset, you will need to know something about copyfitting if you want everything to go together properly.

There are two ways to work copyfitting: either predetermine your space requirements, then fit your copy to your space needs; or determine your space allotment based on how much copy you have. To be honest, either way has worked for me. In fact, I usually let my story length dictate my space allotment. However, the other way around is less risky, since you know beforehand that all your stories will be included in your newsletter. The worst you'd have to do is edit them to fit the space requirements. If you choose to set your space allotment based on story length, you stand a good chance of having to leave an entire story out. The decision is yours.

In any event, the first thing you must do is get yourself a typesetter's ruler. They are usually made of metal and have measures in inches, picas, and points.

It is much easier to use a ruler than to try to convert from inches to picas.

Let's assume for this first example that you will be copyfitting to a predetermined space, then we'll work it the other way around. In order to fit copy to a predetermined amount of space, you must have a finished dummy layout of your newsletter, complete with grids and placement marks for each item you will include in this issue. Photos and illustrations will have been blocked in, as well as space for headlines, captions, pull quotes, and copy blocks. Your dummy layout is your roadmap through copyfitting. You will use it to determine how much space you have to fill with your copy. Based on your dummy, you will need to:

1. Determine the column width and depth of the typeset copy. Remember, type is measured in points (72 points = 1 inch). Points indicate the vertical size of a letter. The point size of a given alphabet is determined by the size of its capitals— usually anywhere from 6 to 72 points. Type size for publications, for instance, usually ranges from 8 to 12 points. The point size you choose is determined to a great extent by readability. Anything below 8 points is pretty difficult to read.

2. Select the typeface, type size, and amount of leading to be used.

3. Obtain a character-per-pica (CPP) count for the typeface. *Character-per-pica count* (CPP) tells us how many characters of a given typeface of a given point size that will fit into a pica. A pica is a typesetter's measurement used to indicate the space into which the copy will be fit (6 picas = 1 inch). Measured horizontally or vertically, one pica equals 12 points. Thus, one line of 12-point type would take up one pica vertically. If a block of type is set solid, 100 lines of 12-point type would take up 100 picas or about 16⅔ inches. Character-per-pica count is the horizontal measurement and is usually determined by consulting a type book or a typesetter. Most type books include a CPP. The CPP for 10-point Helvetica, for instance, is 2.4 which means that you can get 2.4 characters of 10-point Helvetica into one pica measured horizontally. If your copy is 10 picas wide and is set in 10-point Helvetica, then the number of characters per line will be 24.

4. Determine how many lines of copy you'll have to type to fit your requirements by using these four steps.

Step 1. Take your typesetter's ruler and measure the column width and depth of the first article in your newsletter. Let's say you have to fill a total space 18 picas wide by 105 picas deep.

Step 2. Select a typeface, size and leading. Let's assume that you will have your copy set in Garamond 12-point with 12-point leading (set solid—12/12). Thus, since there are 12 points in a pica, the depth in picas will equal the number of typeset lines—six lines to an inch.

Step 3. Let's say that you've checked the character per pica count (CPP) for Garamond and it is 1.8.

Step 4. If your typewriter gives you 10 characters per inch, set it to a 60-space line or 60 characters per line. Now, to determine now many lines at 60 characters each you will have to type to fill the article space, use this formula (always rounding decimals to the nearest whole number).

1. CPP **x** column width = CPL (characters per line)

   $1.8 \times 18 = 32.4$ or 32 CPL

2. CPL **x** depth of proposed copy = Total characters (Remember, this is assuming that you are setting 12-point Garamond so depth in picas will equal number of actual typeset lines.)

   $32 \times 105 = 3360$ characters

3. Typed lines needed will equal total characters divided by typewriter characters per line, thus:

   $\dfrac{3360}{60} = 56$ typewritten lines

If you had decided to use a typeface that is 12-point leaded 1 (12/1), you would have to compensate for the difference in point size including leading and the depth in picas. The CPP remains the same, so step one remains the same.

2. $\dfrac{\text{Depth of article in picas} \times 12}{\text{point size} + \text{leading}}$ = Lines of type

   $\dfrac{105 \times 12}{(12 + 1)} = 96.92$ or 97 lines of type

3. Lines of type **x** CPL = Total characters

   $97 \times 32 = 3104$ total characters

4. Typed lines needed will equal total characters divided by typewriter characters per line.

   $\dfrac{3104}{60} = 51.7$ or 58 typewritten lines

If you decide to approach copyfitting from the opposite perspective—allocate space according to already written copy—you can do it one of two ways.

If you know the copy width

Suppose you want to set 2500 characters of original copy in 12-point Garamond leaded 12 points (set solid). You know that your copy width when set in type will be 20 picas (basically, a two-column grid). How many lines of copy will you have?

1. CPP **x** line width (in picas) = CPL (characters per line)

   $1.8 \times 20 = 36$ CPL

2. $\dfrac{\text{Total characters in original copy}}{\text{CPL}}$ = Number of lines

   $\dfrac{2500}{36} = 69.44$ or 69 lines

In this case, line number equals depth in picas. Since the type is 12-point set solid, each line equals a pica.

Now, you have 69 lines of copy set in 12-point Garamond and you decide to lead it 1 point. What will the depth be in picas?

1. (Point size + leading) **x** number of lines = Depth in points

   $(12 + 1) \times 69 = 897$ points

2. $\dfrac{\text{Depth in points}}{12}$ = Depth in picas

   $\dfrac{572}{12} = 74.75$ or 75 picas

Marking the Copy

Typesetters can't read minds, although sometimes they come very close. In order for your instructions to get across to the typesetter, you must mark your copy indicating type style, size, and any other information pertinent to how you want your finished typeset copy to look. Some necessary indications are:

- Name of type style (font or typeface—Garamond, Helvetica, Bodoni Bookface, etc.)
- Weight of the typeface (bold, medium, light, etc.)
- Point size and leading
- Column width and depth
- Special instructions such as flush right or flush left, etc.

On the first page of copy, indicate any instructions pertaining to all copy. For instance, if you want all copy to be flush left, this is the place to indicate it. For each block of copy requiring a separate notation, indicate that instruction in the left margin, directly next to the relevant copy.

Designate your type style, point size, leading, margin format and column by using a shorthand notation understood by most typesetters and printers.

First, draw a horizontal line with a vertical line crossing it left of center:

- In the upper right quarter, indicate type style and weight (medium, bold, italic, etc.)

$$\frac{\quad |\; Helvetica}{\quad |\quad}$$

- In the upper left quarter, specify point size.

$$\frac{10\; |\; Helvetica}{\quad |\quad}$$

- In the lower left quarter, indicate leading.

$$\frac{10\; |\; Helvetica}{12\; |\quad}$$

- In the lower right quarter, indicate margin format and column width.

$$\frac{10\; |\; Helvetica}{12\; |\; [18\; picas]}$$

- Special column designations should be indicated if needed (center, stacked, etc.). Flush right/left is indicated by [or], ragged right/left by ⌇ or ⌇ .

Exhibit 6.7

When you mark your copy for typesetting, make sure your marks are placed close to the copy they refer to. If in doubt, draw a line from the mark to the copy and circle the copy.

New Widget Works Wonders $\frac{18\,\backslash\,Times\ Bold}{19\,\backslash\,Centered}$

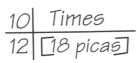

$$\frac{10|\; Times}{12|\; [18\ picas]}$$

　　"We think 'Plaget' will revolutionize

designers think about widgets from now on.

Raoul Simpson, materials engineer for REPC

Simpson and his team who are credited with

a "revolutionary" new plastic widget which

to REPC president Paul Johnson, will have

impact on a number of industries.

Style Sheets

In order to maintain consistency in your newsletter from issue to issue, you will need to develop a *style sheet*. A style sheet is a listing of all of the type specifications you use in your newsletter. It should be as complete as possible, and every member of your staff should have a copy. Style sheets are especially important if you are sick or on vacation and someone else has to produce an issue or two of your newsletter. It will tell them at a glance what it probably took you hours to determine when you first started. **Exhibit 6.8** shows a typical style sheet.

Some Type Samples

On the following page are a number of the most standard typefaces used in newsletters. Each is designated as usable for body copy and/or display type. Most can be used for captions. All are available both from computer type libraries and from your printer/typesetter. A number of variations of Helvetica are shown to demonstrate the kind of variety a typeface can have.

Exhibit 6.8
A style sheet should contain everything a total stranger would need to know to publish your newsletter.

Style Sheet: On Line
Newsletter of the Public Relations Student Society of America, University of Oregon Chapter

Page size—11 by 17 inches, one-page, front and back, vertical tabloid layout. Margins 3/4 on all sides. Folded in thirds for mailing. Self-mailer on bottom third of back page.

Grid—Five columns for normal text layout. Four or five columns for boxed or feature items. One pica between columns with a hairline rule.

Body text—10-point Times, auto leaded, flush left, first indents 1/4 inch.

Captions—9-point Times italic, flush left, run width of photo, 1/2 pica beneath photo.

Lead article headline—24-point Optima bold, set solid, reversed on 40% screen. Run full width of page (five columns).

Two and three-column heads—18-point Optima bold, leaded 19, flush left running width of article. Reversed on 40% screen.

Pull quotes—14-point Optima italic, centered, one to three-column width as needed. Two-point line one pica above and one-point line below as needed to fill space.

Masthead copy—9-point Optiman, flush left, one-column width..

Paper—60 lb. white, semi-matt finish.

Ink color—Black ink run on Pre-printed blanks with banner in PMS 4515. Standing heads and banner created on Freehand.

Times Roman (for body copy & display)
The quick brown fox jumped over the
lazy dogs. 1234567890&

Bookman (for body copy & display)
The quick brown fox jumped over
the lazy dogs.1234567890&

Garamond (body copy & display)
The quick brown fox jumped over the
lazy dogs.1234567890&

Goudy (body copy & display)
The quick brown fox jumped over the
lazy dogs.1234567890&

Korinna (display)
The quick brown fox jumped over
the lazy dogs.1234567890&

Lubalin Graph (display)
The quick brown fox jumped over
the lazy dogs.1234567890&

Baskerville (body copy & display)
The quick brown fox jumped over the
lazy dogs.1234567890&

Palatino (body copy & limited display)
The quick brown fox jumped over the
lazy dogs.1234567890&

Souvenir (display & limited body copy)
The quick brown fox jumped over the
lazy dogs.1234567890&

Stone Serif (body copy & display)
The quick brown fox jumped over
the lazy dogs.1234567890&

Stone Informal (display & limited
body copy)
The quick brown fox jumped over
the lazy dogs.1234567890&

Avant Garde (display)
The quick brown fox jumped over
the lazy dogs. 1234567890&

Futura (display)
The quick brown fox jumped over the
lazy dogs. 1234567890&

Optima (display & limited body copy)
The quick brown fox jumped over the
lazy dogs. 1234567890&

Stone Sans (display & limited body copy)
The quick brown fox jumped over
the lazy dogs. 1234567890&

Helvetica Light (display)
The quick brown fox jumped over the
lazy dogs. 1234567890&

Helvetica Light Oblique
The quick brown fox jumped over the
lazy dogs. 1234567890&

Helvetica Regular
The quick brown fox jumped over the
lazy dogs. 1234567890&

Helvetica Black
The quick brown fox jumped
1234567890&

Helvetica Black Oblique
The quick brown fox jumped
1234567890&

Helvetica Regular Condensed
The quick brown fox jumped over the lazy dogs.
1234567890&

Helvetica Black Condensed
The quick brown fox jumped over the
lazy dogs. 1234567890&

Working with Computer Type

Probably the single most revolutionary breakthrough in computer technology, for newsletter editors at least, has been the ability to set type. With a little practice, *almost* anyone can set their own type for publication.

Millions of dollars a year are spent setting copy in type. In fact, quite a large percentage of any print production budget goes into typesetting. Computer typesetting has cut down on cost and time. Before, you had to type your copy, spec it for copyfitting, mark it, take it to the typesetter, wait until it was typeset, proof the type, have the typesetter make any necessary corrections, and then paste it up. Now, typesetting, corrections and additions, and pasteup can all be done by one person at the same time. And costs can often be cut by a third or more.

Smart typesetters and printers have been quick to keep themselves in the production chain by offering valuable services such as Linotronic output or some other computer-assisted production function. Many printers and typesetters now accept computer disks or direct feeds from your computer.

Desktop publishing has probably been of the most benefit to the smaller or single-person office. What once took a number of intermediaries to accomplish can now be done by one person. There are some basics you have to know, however, before you can handle computer type successfully.

Digital Fonts

Digital fonts are computer-designed and -generated typefaces, and although type generated on the computer should be identical to type set the conventional way, it's not. First of all, computer-set type is standardized. That is, the eccentricities and flourishes of hand-designed typefaces are often sacrificed when the type is digitized. What this means to the true type afficionado is that many of the built-in irregularities that give typefaces their distinctive charm are missing.

For example, some of the older typefaces had different length descenders for different letter or word combinations or leading. For example, a *y* on a line above a word with an ascender such as a *d* might need to have a version with a shortened ascender, while set above an *o* it might need a longer descender. This slight irregularity from letter to letter within the same face is what adds the charm to traditional type.

Bit-mapped and Outline Fonts

Your computer's printer also affects your finished product. Let's assume that for most newsletters, daisy-wheel and dot-matrix printers are ruled out. If you are outputting directly to a printer for final copy, you'll want to use a laser printer. And, you will most likely use one of two technologies—a printer based on Apple's LaserWriter or one based on Hewlett-Packard's LaserJet. Both will give you quick, clean copy, but each handles type differently.

The LaserJet-type printer stores type in its memory as bit maps (dot patterns) that restrict the printer to specific sizes. If the printer has information on 12-point Helvetica then it will only print 12-point Helvetica. It won't print 24-point Helvetica. If you want other sizes or other fonts, you have to provide them either through cartridges or software that is downloadable (can be loaded from your computer into your printer). The only problem with downloadable fonts—and it affects both types of printers—is that the more information you download to your printer, the less memory it has. A standard laser printer with 1 megabyte or less of RAM (Random Access Memory, which is what your printer or computer uses while you're working) will quickly run out of memory.

Exhibit 6.9

Outline fonts (left) are stored as mathematic values allowing the printer to perform adjustments of almost any sort on the type. The fonts print out "object oriented," that is, they appear as unbroken curved and straight lines instead of the ragged bit-mapped fonts (right). Although on some laser printers, bit-mapped fonts show up as near letter perfect, under a magnifying glass you will see the ragged edges. When used as display type, the raggedness is even more apparent.

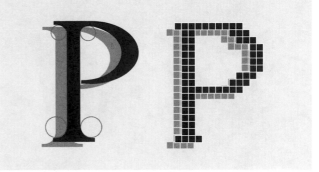

LaserWriter-type printers use an outline method of storing type shapes. That allows you to scale your type to any size, rotate it, distort it, print it backwards, or anything else you want. This is important to desktop publishers who need to have the flexibility to work with type in all its forms. But, recent advances in hardware and software have allowed the LaserJet-type printers to approximate the capabilities of the LaserWriter-type printers.

WYSIWYG

Another problem peculiar to desktop publishing is WYSIWYG (pronounced wizzy-wig), or "what you see is what you get." Many computers and computer monitors promise WYSIWYG, but when it comes to type, few deliver. The problem is that most monitors build images out of tiny squares called pixels. Computer type fonts appear on the screen as composites of these pixels regardless of whether you are using a LaserJet-type printer or a LaserWriter-type printer. The result is that you can't often tell from your screen what your type is going to look like or, especially, how it's going to fit until you print it out. This is mostly, though not exclusively, true of display type. The larger the point size, the more distorted it will tend to be on your screen.

One method of cutting down on distortion at larger point sizes is to load screen font versions of your typefaces in the largest available sizes.

Exhibit 6.10

Left is a screen font much as it might appear on a Macintosh screen. As you can see, the bit-mapping at this size can cause you trouble if you are trying to align characters or kern. The printer-produced version on the right (from an outline-font printer) is proof that what you see on your screen isn't always what you get.

Screen and printer fonts

Type fonts for the Macintosh computer, for instance, come in both printer and screen versions. You have to have both to operate efficiently. Basically, the printer-font version is loaded into (or is already resident in) your printer and becomes available when you use it. Depending on your system, fonts can be loaded in a number of ways. Placing them into the system file allows some programs to load them as needed (which frees up printer memory after each font is used). Manually downloading them as you need them ties up quite a bit of printer memory which then can only be cleared by reinitializing the printer. Placing them in separate files for downloading later, storing them on a separate hard disk, or using printer cartridges are other options.

The screen-font version has to be loaded into your computer system or program so that you can get a representation of that font on your screen. To save memory space, most people load a minimum of point sizes—usually 10, 12, and 14 points in each font. As long as some point size is loaded, you can scale up or down to any point size you need. However, unless you've loaded a screen font in the exact (or near exact) point size you ultimately scale to, your screen type is going to look extremely ragged.

The problem, of course, is WYSIWYG. It is impossible to kern, for example, with large point sizes on the screen. All you can do is do it, print it, look at it printed out, and do it again. But, help is on the horizon. Already there are several programs (including Adobe *Type Manager*) available that help reduce the disparity between the type you see on the screen and the type that comes out of your printer.

Choosing Computer Type

Once you have decided on how your newsletter is to look, you can decide on the typefaces, styles and sizes you want to use. The precautions and guidelines that apply to traditional type also apply to selecting computer type. Some faces and styles go with certain types of messages and others don't.

The computer typographer can choose from among hundreds of faces available through dozens of software manufacturers in a range of prices. One word of warning. It is usually best to stick to the traditional faces manufactured (or digitized) under auspices of the original designers or their agents. For instance, of the hundreds of faces available from International Typeface Corporation (ITC), dozens of these have been packaged by Adobe Systems. As you become more familiar with type and aware of the vast array of faces available for the computer, you will undoubtedly be tempted to purchase some of the many cloned faces. These are basically altered copies of already existing faces. Since most typefaces are copyrighted, all you have to do is alter one letter slightly in order to market a clone.

The difference between an original typeface and its clone isn't readily apparent to everyone; however, such things as line thickness, legibility at smaller point sizes, and clarity of individual characters can be important to your final product. We're not saying to avoid everything but brand-name type, but at least consider the best for your newsletters. After all, a lot of design skill went into the original typeface. Use that to your advantage.

Copyfitting on the Computer

Copyfitting used to require patience, a ruler, patience, a calculator (or knowledge of math), patience, knowledge of type-fitting formulas and measurements, patience, and more patience. With a computer, all you need is a little know-how. Under the traditional (read "old-fashioned") method, you decided on column width and type size and the typesetter gave it back to you set that way. Unless you had a lot of money to waste, your copy might as well have been carved in stone. If you suddenly decided you needed 18 pica-wide columns instead of 24 pica-wide columns, you paid to typeset the whole thing over again.

Now, all you do is pick a point size and column width and, voila!—it's done. And, if you don't like it, you can do it again. It only takes seconds. Naturally, some planning is necessary up front. It might be fun to sit in front of your computer for hours playing with column width and point size, but you're probably on a deadline. Once you have a basic design in mind and have set up the grid (see **Chapter 5** for details on grids), copyfitting becomes a breeze.

For most, but not all, page-layout programs, copy is imported directly from a word processing program and then positioned on your page. That's why it's important to choose a compatible word processing program and to follow a few basic guidelines when writing your document.

- Use a program from the same system type. That is, don't write your story on a PC system and try to transfer it to a Macintosh system. It's usually too much trouble. If you're using *PageMaker*

for the Macintosh, write your copy on a Macintosh-based word processing program such as *Macwrite* or Microsoft *Word* for the Macintosh.

- Keep formatting within your word-processed document to a minimum. It is usually easier to write in word processing and format in your page-layout program. Some minimal formatting can be done, but most of it will be lost when you import it into your page-layout program.

- Don't justify your copy in your word processing program. It will seldom match your final column width and will probably only confuse you when you go to place it on the page. Usually, there is no need to hyphenate either. Remember, your final formatting will be done in your page-layout program.

- Don't worry about faces, styles, sizes, and so on. You can assign them in your page-layout program. If you do use a specific style (bold subheads for instance) you might lose it anyway when you import the copy or set a new global style from your page-layout program's style sheet (see below).

- Set headlines and subheads for articles and other copy right in with your word-processed document. Even if their style is lost during the transfer process, they will serve as designators as you begin to format. You can always re-bold as you go along. Another option is to set display type, such as headlines for feature stories, separately in your page-layout program. It is then more easily manipulated since it is a separate element.

Once you've imported the copy, you can place it, fit it, and change face, style, leading, spacing and size till your heart's content.

A Word about Style Sheets

If your page-layout program has them, use them. In a nutshell, style sheets are electronic menus in which you designate how you want your copy to appear in its various incarnations. It remembers each description and on command will change designated text to the selected style. For example, *PageMaker* includes a style sheet on which you can pre-set typeface, size, style, leading, tab sets, indents, alignment, and a number of other designations for any of several categories such as *body text, headlines, captions* and *subheads.* You can also add categories, such as *pull quotes,* to suit your particular newsletter's needs.

To use a style sheet, you simply select the portion of text you want to set a certain style and then choose that style from the **style menu** In an instant, the original text conforms to your pre-set style.

Display Type

Display type is handled pretty much the same way as body copy. You can manipulate each of these elements to suit your needs. There are some special considerations you should be aware of, however.

- Don't always assume that the typeface you use for body copy will be just fine at 24 or 36 points. Some faces are better suited to headlines than others. The key to the proper display type is clarity. If it's clear, then check out the aesthetics.

- Be aware that the larger the point size, the more obvious the leading will be if set at *auto.* For example, a stacked, 36-point headline with auto leading is going to look very "loose" to the trained eye. The trick is to reduce the leading until the stack tightens up somewhat. Be careful not to let descenders bump the tops of ascenders in the lines below.

- Don't justify headlines. In longer headlines, this will create unsightly spaces between words. To center them, use the alignment command for centering rather than manually placing a

flush-left headline in the center of a column. Aligning each headline will insure consistency.

- Designate in advance exactly where you want your headline to appear. In *PageMaker,* for example, if you want to extend it beyond your column width, simply place the text tool at the starting point and, by depressing the mouse button, drag a dotted square to the farthest right-hand point you want your headline to extend to. When you type, your headline will ignore column indicators and continue to the designated point. Or, you can drag the handle out to the needed width (see **Exhibit 6.11**).

It's best to set up style sheets for each of your categories of display type. It will save you time and frustration, especially if you are working on a multi-page document or setting up a template to be used from issue to issue. Suppose you're working on a 16-page tabloid full of headlines, subheads, pull quotes, and captions. From page to page, you can't seem to remember if that second-level subhead was 14-point italic or 12-point italic bold. You have to keep "flipping" back to previous pages to check it out. If you set up a style sheet with each of these designations, you don't have to keep checking. For instance, you might have a headline style set for 36-point Helvetica bold, a first-level subhead of 18-point Times italic, a second-level subhead of 18-point Times italic underlined, and pull quotes of 14-point Helvetica bold italic. In addition, each of these

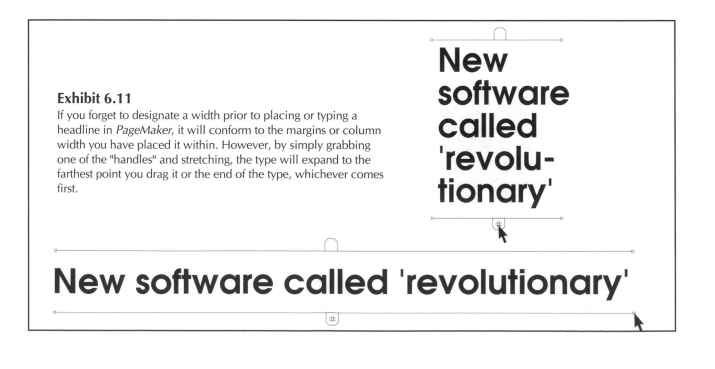

Exhibit 6.11
If you forget to designate a width prior to placing or typing a headline in *PageMaker,* it will conform to the margins or column width you have placed it within. However, by simply grabbing one of the "handles" and stretching, the type will expand to the farthest point you drag it or the end of the type, whichever comes first.

elements will contain information on leading and alignment. Setting these up in advance will save you a lot of heartburn.

Kerning

Kerning, of particular concern when dealing with display type, refers to the amount of space between letters (or sometimes words). Layout problems usually account for a certain amount of automatic kerning between pairs of letters in any given typeface. For example, in some faces *o* and *e* will fit differently when paired than *t* and *e*. But, discrepancies in letter spacing at larger sizes are more apparent.

This was a problem with earlier versions of most page-layout programs. Headlines often looked awkwardly spaced. For instance, an uppercase *T* might aesthetically fit closer to a lowercase *o* in a headline than the automatic-kerned setting allowed. The newer

Exhibit 6.12
At a larger size, the word *Toy* (top) has an unsightly spread between the *T* and the *o*. By manually kerning in *PageMaker*, we can tighten both the *o* and the *y* slightly (center). If we are not careful, however, or if we rely on the screen for accuracy, we might over kern (bottom).

versions have compensated for this by adding manual kerning, which lets you tighten that space to your specifications. See **Exhibit 6.12** for an example of how kerning works.

Using Initial Caps

In most page-layout programs, initial caps can present some problems. In *Ventura Publisher* dropped caps are created and aligned automatically with a few key strokes. In other programs, such as *PageMaker*, using them is more difficult. You can either designate the actual first letter of your body copy by bolding it and raising the point size (which requires manually adjusting the leading between the line in which the cap appears and the line below it), or creating the cap as a separate piece of copy and placing it in the body copy (which requires moving the body copy to compensate for the space). See **Exhibit 6.13**.

Exhibit 6.13
Although programs such as *Ventura Publisher* allow you to set guidelines for raised initial caps, *PageMaker* requires that you manually set the leading between lines. The procedure, which is simple, eliminates the problem seen in the top example. Raising the point size of a single letter set into a body of text increases the leading between the line it is on and the following line based on the point size of the raised letter, not the body copy. To avoid the gap, simply set the leading for the block manually. *PageMaker* calculates its auto leading at 120 percent of point size, regardless of the face. So 12-point Times will be auto-leaded at 14.4 points. Since *PageMaker* doesn't allow for increments of leading less than .5, you must set your manual leading at 14.5. This allows the lines to remain leaded properly despite the raised initial cap. Make sure that your leading is set to "proportional" not "top of caps" in the type menu under "spacing." An alternative method on the Macintosh is to type in the letter you want in *PageMaker*, bold and size it, copy it to the scrapbook file, then place it by accessing the system folder and scrapbook file. The resulting placement icon will have a number on it representing the number of items in the scrapbook. Place only the last item (the first number showing on the icon), then "unload" the icon by clicking on the arrow in the toolbox. The letter can now be treated as a graphic by using the textwrap function of *PageMaker*.

I was a fresh, new journalist, and needed a *nom de guerre*; so I confiscated the ancient mariner's discarded one, and have done my best to make it remain what it was in his hands—a sign and symbol and warrant that whatever is found in its company may be gambled on as being the

I was a fresh, new journalist, and needed a *nom de guerre*; so I confiscated the ancient mariner's discarded one, and have done my best to make it remain what it was in his hands – a sign and symbol and warrant that whatever is found in its company may be gambled on as being the petrified truth.

After all is said and done, the cereal box is the only object between you and your purchase decision. However, it is a formidable obstacle, especially if its brightly colored motif beckons to that unsuspecting victim of packaging—your five-year-old child.

Graphic Elements

A great deal of the attraction of any newsletter is directly attributable to the way it uses graphcis. Illustration, photography, and simple graphic devices such as lines and tint blocks, all aid readers in their understanding and enjoyment of your message.

Graphic elements are generally used to indicate points of emphasis in a newsletter. For example, your banner is the first graphic device usually seen by a reader. It indicates both the name of your newsletter and the starting point. It is used to catch your readers' attention and to introduce them to the opening page. Most graphic devices are used similarly.

In addition to being used as points of emphasis, graphics tend to stop readers or give them a resting place—a point at which to linger for a moment—in the midst of your copy. As with other non-verbal aspects of your newsletter, a good graphic also says something about your theme, or helps establish a mood. The one thing you don't want your graphic to be is mere filler—something you stuck in because you had some white space left over. A good graphic has to contribute to your newsletter the way every other element in the publication does.

The first decision every editor has to make is how much space to devote to graphic elements and how much to editorial matter. Basically, graphics should be used as support for editorial content. Your target audience will rarely be subscribing to your newsletter for its look alone. Sacrificing important editorial matter for an eye-catching graphic will probably be a mistake. However, enhancing your content, or making it more appealing through the creative use of graphics might just make your message more memorable than it otherwise would have been. In fact, although there are numerous successful newsletters that are virtually graphics-free, most of them could benefit from a more interesting look—the kind of look only good graphics can provide.

There are basically three types of graphic elements: design elements—such as type, rules, boxes, and tint blocks—illustration, and photography. Let's look at these one at a time.

Design Elements as Graphics

A number of elements already mentioned can be used as graphic devices to draw attention, give the reader pause, or simply add continuity to your message. Among the most common design element used as a graphic is type.

Type as Design

Type is most often used as body copy or headlines, and we tend to treat it only in certain ways. However, type can also be used effectively as a design tool—to draw attention, to break up long blocks of copy by creating space, and as a decorative element or illustration with its own inherent artistic value.

Initial caps

One of the easiest methods of indicating a starting point for the reader is to make use of a very ancient device known as the *initial cap.* Originally, scribes used highly decorative initial letters as illustration fine enough to be viewed as separate artwork. Today, the initial cap is used either as a raised or dropped letter of a size and weight different enough from the body copy to draw attention to it. Often, this initial cap is even from a different typeface, increasing the emphasis.

The raised initial cap is accomplished simply by raising the point size of the first letter of the first word in an article. The dropped initial cap is literally dropped into the text, creating its own boundary. Surrounding letters are either set off in equal dis-

After a hard day's work at the office, there is only one place you want to go—home. Home is a safe haven from the rigors of the daily grind and a place where you can be at ease, at least

Over his office door is a sign that reads "knock only if no answer is required." This is your first hint that this is a man who doesn't want to be disturbed—no matter what the reason.

Running the gauntlet aptly describes the daily process of gaining approvals for every piece of writing you produce as the editor of the company newsletter. It is a process fraught with frustration.

Behold the office computer. You arrived one day to find it sitting on your desk, staring blankly at you from an amber-lighted screen, its unknown potential firmly locked up in an unintelligible manual.

Exhibit 7.1
Here are five variations of the initial letter. They are the raised initial letter, contoured initial letter, straitjacketed initial letter, and a boxed initial letter.

tances from the dropped cap or in varying distances according to the shape of the initial letter (see **Exhibit 7.1**).

Pull quotes

A second way to use type as a graphic element is to create space in lengthy copy blocks. This allows you to fill space in a shorter article in order for it to come out even at the bottom of a page, for instance. Using type as a space-creation device also focuses your readers' attention and allows them to rest briefly before reading on in a lengthy article.

The most common space-creation method utilizing type is the *pull quote*. A pull quote is also an editorial device that utilizes a quote from within an article as a focal point or teaser to concentrate reader interest or entice further reading. As a graphic device, pull quotes are usually a larger point size, different weight or slant, and often aligned differently from the body copy. Pull quotes can be set off further by the use of rules above and below the quote, boxes surrounding the quote, or tint blocks under the quote.

When using rules with pull quotes, the top and bottom lines can be of different thicknesses for an enhanced effect. The bottom rule can be pulled down to create as much white space as you need to fill out your article (see **Exhibit 7.2**). Pull quotes can also extend from one-column widths to full-page widths. Generally, the wider the pull quote, the larger the type; however, do not increase the type size so much that it conflicts with headlines on the same page.

Remember, a pull quote should add something to your page and to the article in which it appears. See the section on writing pull quotes in **Chapter 8** for details on how best to use them.

Reverses

Reverses involve printing white letters over dark backgrounds, usually black. Because computer layout has made reverses as easy to accomplish as regular type, editors tend to overuse them. Basically, reverses should be reserved for display type. For example, some newsletters gain emphasis by revers-

Reverses should be in bold type sizes 14-points and larger for legibility.

"A pull quote can be used at the top of a page as a kind of headline introducing the key idea on that page."

Lorem ipsum dolor sit amet, consectetuer adipiscing elit, sed diam nonummy nibh euismod tincidunt ut laoreet dolore magna aliquam erat volutpat. Ut wisi enim ad minim veniam, quis nostrud exerci tation ullamcorper suscipit lobortis nisl ut aliquip ex ea commodo consequat.

Duis autem vel eum iriure dolor in hendrerit in vulputate velit esse molestie consequat, vel illum dolore eu feugiat nulla facilisis at vero eros et accumsan et iusto odio dignissim qui blandit praesent luptatum zzril delenit augue duis dolore te feugait nulla facilisi.

"A pull quote can can be used in a one-column format with extended white space following."

"Pull quotes can be used to balance other pull quotes or other graphic elements on the page."

"A pull quote can extend across two columns breaking up a copy-heavy page and creating more white space."

Lorem ipsum dolor sit amet, consectetuer adipiscing elit, sed diam nonummy nibh euismod tincidunt ut laoreet dolore magna aliquam erat volutpat. Ut wisi enim ad minim veniam, quis nostrud exerci tation ullamcorper suscipit lobortis nisl ut aliquip ex ea commodo consequat.

Exhibit 7.2

Pull quotes (clockwise from top left) used as an introduction to the page; to add white space; one-column used to balance a picture in the far right column; across two columns.

ing headlines against tint blocks. Reverses, like other graphic elements, tend to draw the eye immediately. Use them for emphasis only. Under no circumstances use regular body type as a reverse. It severely impedes reading and serves no purpose. A good rule of thumb is to use only bold letters in reverse, and no smaller than fourteen points.

Type as Art

The final way to use type as a graphic device is as a piece of art. Calligraphers and other designers have used type as a decorative device for thousands of years. Don't underestimate the power of type as an illustration; however, don't overuse it either. Occasionally, an extra-large letter or word, expertly executed, can really draw attention to your page. Or a logo device (which is really what your banner is) composed of type can impart a quick image where 10,000 words might fail.

The trick to using type as an illustration is to hire an artist or designer to execute it for you. Hours of

Exhibit 7.3
The example above is a simple use of type as art; however, the mere raising of a letter to an abnormally large size doesn't necessarily make it a piece of art. How you use it graphically determines its value as illustration.

playing on a computer can result in some interesting type designs; however, only a true designer can use type correctly as decoration.

Rules, Boxes, and Tint Blocks

Lines, or *rules*, are the most common and simplest of design elements. They can be used to break up your page into sections, separate columns of copy from one another, indicate beginnings and ends, or simply underscore a point that needs emphasis. There are a few simple ground rules to follow when using lines.

- Always use hairlines between columns. Anything thicker detracts from the copy. Justified copy doesn't usually gain anything from rules since justification inscribes a natural line between columns. Rules between columns also add a more formal look to your newsletter. When using vertical lines, always stop them one pica short of other elements, such as photographs or horizontal lines. Never allow vertical and horizontal lines to meet.

- Use lines of four-point thickness or greater at the beginning of articles only. Thick lines usually indicate a starting point. A combination of thick and thin lines can be used creatively as standing head indicators.

President's Message

- Use lines of one- to two-point thickness to separate pages horizontally, as in newspaper-style grids. These lines can also be used at the beginning and end of tables of contents, and above or below captions to separate them from body copy.

- When using horizontal lines to separate elements on a page, try to keep to a single line if possible. Several short lines will tend to fragment your page.

- Use single horizontal lines of one or two points at the bottom of a page to *anchor* the page. If no page number or other device comes between your text columns and the bottom of the page, the copy often looks as if it is heading off the bottom of the page. There is a difference, however, between an

Lorem ipsum dolor sit amet, consectetuer adipiscing elit, sed diam nonummy nibh euismod tincidunt ut laoreet dolore magna aliquam erat volutpat. Ut wisi enim ad minim veniam, quis nostrud exerci tation ullamcorper suscipit lobortis nisl ut aliquip ex ea commodo consequat. Duis autem vel eum iriure dolor in hendrerit in vulputate velit esse molestie consequat, vel illum dolore eu feugiat nulla facilisis at vero eros et accumsan et iusto odio dignissim qui blandit praesent luptatum zzril delenit augue duis dolore te feugait nulla facilisi. Lorem ipsum dolor sit amet, consectetuer adipiscing elit, sed diam nonummy nibh euismod

tincidunt ut laoreet dolore magna aliquam erat volutpat. Ut wisi enim ad minim veniam, quis nostrud exerci tation ullamcorper suscipit lobortis nisl ut aliquip ex ea commodo consequat.

Duis autem vel eum iriure dolor in hendrerit in vulputate velit esse molestie consequat, vel illum dolore eu feugiat nulla facilisis at vero eros et accumsan et iusto odio dignissim qui blandit praesent luptatum zzril delenit augue duis dolore te feugait nulla facilisi. Nam liber tempor cum soluta nobis eleifend option congue nihil imperdiet doming id quod mazim placerat facer possim assum.

Lorem ipsum dolor sit amet, consectetuer adipiscing elit, sed diam nonummy nibh euismod tincidunt ut laoreet

dolore magna aliquam erat volutpat. Ut wisi enim ad minim veniam, quis nostrud exerci tation ullamcorper suscipit lobortis nisl ut aliquip ex ea commodo consequat. Duis autem vel eum iriure dolor in hendrerit in vulputate velit esse molestie consequat, vel illum dolore eu feugiat nulla facilisis at vero eros et accumsan et iusto odio dignissim qui blandit praesent luptatum zzril delenit nulla facilisi. Lorem ipsum dolor sit amet, consectetuer adipiscing elit, sed diam nonummy nibh euismod tincidunt ut laoreet dolore magna aliquam erat volutpat.

Ut wisi enim ad minim veniam, quis nostrud exerci tation ullamcorper suscipit

lobortis nisl ut aliquip ex ea commodo consequat. Duis autem vel eum iriure dolor in hendrerit in vulputate velit esse molestie consequat, vel illum dolore eu feugiat nulla facilisis at vero eros et accumsan et iusto odio dignissim qui blandit praesent luptatum zzril delenit augue duis dolore te feugait nulla facilisi. Lorem ipsum dolor sit amet, consectetuer adipiscing elit, sed diam nonummy nibh euismod tincidunt ut laoreet dolore magna aliquam erat volutpat.

Ut wisi enim ad minim veniam, quis nostrud exerci tation ullamcorper suscipit lobortis nisl ut aliquip ex ea commodo consequat. Duis autem vel eum iriure dolor in hendrerit in vulputate velit esse molestie consequat, vel illum dolore eu feugiat nulla facilisis at vero eros et accumsan et iusto odio dignissim qui blandit praesent luptatum zzril delenit augue duis dolore te feugait nulla facilisi.

Lorem ipsum dolor sit amet, consectetuer adipiscing elit, sed diam nonummy nibh euismod tincidunt ut laoreet dolore magna aliquam erat volutpat. Ut wisi enim ad minim veniam, quis nostrud exerci

tation ullamcorper suscipit lobortis nisl ut aliquip ex ea commodo consequat. Duis autem vel eum iriure dolor in hendrerit in vulputate velit esse molestie consequat, vel illum dolore eu feugiat nulla facilisis at.

Vero eros et accumsan et iusto odio dignissim qui blandit praesent luptatum zzril delenit augue duis dolore te feugait nulla facilisi. Lorem ipsum dolor sit amet, consectetuer adipiscing elit, sed diam nonummy nibh euismod tincidunt ut laoreet dolore magna aliquam erat volutpat. Ut wisi enim ad minim veniam, quis

4

Exhibit 7.4

Placing a bottom rule to anchor your page is useful if your columns don't bump the bottom margin, yet come close to being equal. On the other hand, radically uneven columns with some other anchoring device, such as a page number, can impart a more open, less formal look to your page.

artistic use of white space and an unanchored page bottom. If your pages consistently are open at the bottom, with lots of white space acting as counterweight to other design elements, a line may create trapped white space instead of anchoring your page. The closer uneven columns come to the bottom margin, the more you might need a line to anchor them. Extremely uneven columns, if handled well, simply impart a sense of openness. An anchoring line adds more formality to your publication.

Boxes are also one of the most common design elements in newsletter publication. They can be used to surround and set off everything from a table of contents to whole articles. There is no hard and fast rule for when to use a box. Basically, you use them to draw attention to editorial content, to separate editorial items on a page, or to balance other elements on a page.

When you add a tinted screen behind an article in a box, it is called a *tint block*. Tint blocks can be run either with or without a line around them. As a basic rule of thumb, don't use a screen any darker than 30 percent, and avoid large screens if your newsletter is

Exhibit 7.5

When using tint blocks, take care that your type will read well over the percentage screen you've chosen. Top to bottom are 20, 30, 50, and 60 percent screens.

Lorem ipsum dolor sit amet, consectetuer adipiscing elit, sed diam nonummy nibh euismod tincidunt ut laoreet dolore magna aliquam erat volutpat. Ut wisi enim ad minim veniam, quis nostrud exerci tation ullamcorper suscipit lobortis nisl ut aliquip ex ea commodo consequat. Duis autem vel eum iriure dolor in hendrerit in vulputate velit esse molestie consequat, vel illum dolore eu feugiat nulla facilisis at vero eros et accumsan et iusto odio dignissim qui blandit praesent luptatum zzril delenit augue duis dolore te feugait nulla facilisi. Lorem ipsum dolor sit amet, consectetuer adipiscing elit, sed diam nonummy nibh euismod tincidunt ut laoreet dolore magna aliquam erat volutpat. Ut wisi enim ad minim veniam, quis nostrud exerci tation ullamcorper suscipit lobortis nisl ut aliquip ex ea commodo consequat.

Duis autem vel eum iriure dolor in hendrerit in vulputate velit esse molestie consequat, vel illum dolore eu feugiat nulla facilisis at vero eros et accumsan et iusto odio dignissim qui blandit praesent luptatum zzril delenit augue duis dolore te feugait nulla facilisi. Nam liber tempor cum soluta nobis eleifend option congue nihil imperdiet doming id quod mazim placerat facer possim assum.

going to be quick copied. Screens tend to muddy when photocopied. Also, test the readability of any copy you print over your screen before going to print. Light or small typefaces and those with thin serifs tend to get lost in screens.

Illustration

Roughly speaking, *illustration* is anything created by an artist or illustrator. The biggest decision you have to make regarding illustration (once you've decided to use it) is whether or not to hire an illustrator. With the wealth of good clip art available these days, you

don't have to hire someone to create art for you. However, much of what passes for clip art (specifically art that is packaged for sale in large quantities), both in traditional form on photo-reproducible paper and on computer disks, is a poor substitute for original artwork. Let's look at clip art first.

Clip art can be obtained from a number of sources.

- **Published collections**. Almost any bookstore has a selection of books of thematic clip art. These are usually collections of nineteenth century engravings of subjects ranging from animals to industrial scenes, and everything in between. For most of us, these collections are interesting, but of little use. As with most clip art, it takes something of a design flare to be able to use it successfully. However, when used creatively (and often with a sense of humor) these collections can be a good source of art (see **Exhibit 7.6**).

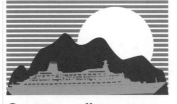

Exhibit 7.6

Many pieces of clip art are composites of several elements. In the clip art seen here, the entire piece is used in the newlsetter on the left, while only the ship and moon, enlarged and cropped, are used in the newsletter on the right. Creative sizing and cropping of clip art, especially if the cropped image seems to begin or run off the page, can add sophistication to your page. Clip art run too small can make your page look amateurish.

- **Clip books**. Clip books are published as complete sets (usually sorted thematically) or on a monthly subscription basis. One of the most successful (and one of the best) publishers of clip art is Dynamic Graphics. They publish clip art in complete collections based on themes such as sports, jobs, humor, school, holidays, etc. They also run a subscription service through which you receive a publication full of clip art each month as well as a newsletter with suggestions on how to use it. Dynamic Graphics, as well as others in the business, nowadays provide clip art on computer disk in addition to the traditional hard copy formats. The major drawback is cost. Whether purchased in thematic sets or by the month, this type of art can run you hundreds of dollars.

If you do opt for clip art, there are a few things you need to know.

- Generally speaking, the more you pay for it, the better it will be. This is true for traditional as well as computer clip art. If you have a choice between cheap clip art or no art at all, choose no art at all.

- When purchasing clip art, select thematically if possible. A giant compendium of multiple themes may be fun to thumb through, but you'll probably only use a fraction of it. Pick a collection that matches the theme of your newsletter, then purchase complementary smaller collections as you need them. For example, if you publish a newsletter for a school district, buy school-related clip art. It will probably contain everything from teachers to textbooks to school athletics.

- Never use clip art in its original size or configuration. Creative cropping and sizing of clip art can lend an air of real design to your newsletter, while a half-dozen tiny pieces of clip art will only make your newsletter look amateurish.

- Consider running clip art in a second color or screened as background to other elements.

Exhibit 7.7
Two newsletters from Weyerhaeuser show a heavy use of graphics, both original illustration and a creative application of clip art.

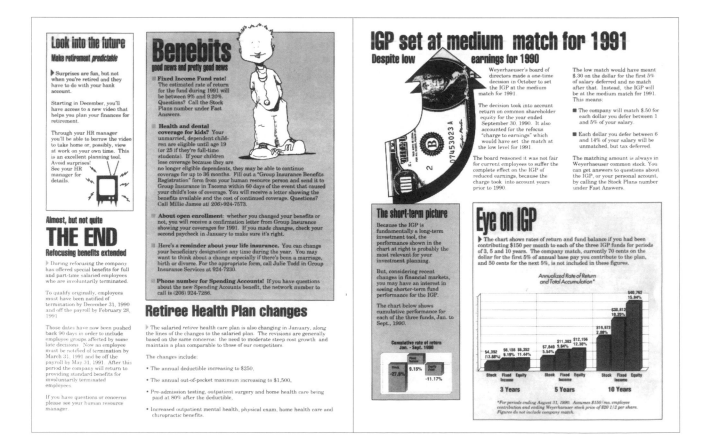

Clip art can impart a sophistication to your publication if used creatively in this way.

Hiring an Illustrator

Hiring an illustrator is a big step. It is going to cost money, so it better be worth it to you. For example, do you need to pay $300 for an illustration in a 200-copy newsletter? Probably not. Cost effectiveness is the real key to deciding on hiring outside help of any kind—especially illustration. On the other hand, the kind of originality a good illustrator can add to your newsletter may well be the deciding factor in who picks it up and reads it.

If you do decide to hire an illustrator, shop around. Talent and prices vary immensely. As with clip art, most good illustrators are going to charge you a rate equivalent to their abilities. Be aware that some will charge you a rate greater than their abilities. It's up to you to sort them out. Ask for samples of their work. Believe me, they'll be happy to show you their portfolios. Don't be afraid to ask for references either. If they have a reputation for meeting deadlines and satisfying their clients, they'll be more than willing to give references.

Try to locate an illustrator who will be able to provide you with the kind of art *you* want. Although a good artist will also be able to bring a new and creative point of view to your newsletter, don't be bullied by their opinions. Artists are also temperamental. You'll have to learn to deal with that. Generally, describe what you want and let them try it from several different perspectives, then pick the one you like.

Most importantly, set a deadline in advance and make them stick to it. If they are good illustrators, they'll meet your deadlines. Remember, you're paying them not only to produce art for you, but also to produce it on deadline.

Printing Your Art

Unless you have your original art executed to the exact size you need for your newsletter, you will probably have to have it reduced. Your printer is the place to go. The camera operator at your local print shop can shoot an extremely clean reproduction of your artwork, scaled to the exact size you need. The result is a PMT, or photo-mechanical transfer. This process darkens blacks to an intensity suitable for printing and reproduces even fine lines extremely well. In addition, if your graphic isn't just line art (simple black and white pen work), it may need to be screened. This process isn't usually any more expensive than having a PMT shot, but it is more complicated. See **Printing Your Photographs** below for details on screening.

Working with Computer Illustration

Illustration is one of the hardest publication elements to accomplish on computer. But the beauty of computer-generated illustration is that it can be manipulated at will and used over and over again. In essence, you create your own clip art each time you commit an illustration to computer.

Computer illustration can be broken into four categories:

- art created from scratch by an artist using computer software, or scanned art, or photos

manipulated in some way after scanning,
- scanned art used as-is after scanning,
- clip art (created in either of the above two ways),
- and technical illustration.

Let's look at these one at a time.

Illustration Programs

For artists or illustrators, the computer is just one more tool at their disposal. Earlier illustration programs were fun and easy to learn and use, took up very little file space, and looked just like computer-generated art when printed. For the non-artist, they were little more than toys; however, for the artist or illustrator, they opened new doors into the world of computers—a world heretofore left primarily to the number-crunchers and newly initiated word processors.

Programs like *MacPaint* and *MacDraw* (once put out by Apple and now by Claris) were pioneers in the field of computer illustration. *MacPaint*, a bit-mapped, freehand art program, allowed even the novice to play artist on the computer screen. The only problem with these programs was the final product. Unless severely reduced when printed, the bit maps showed the end product to be typical computer art.

Object-oriented illustration programs such as *MacDraw* were next on the scene. Object-oriented art used *PostScript* to create precise angles and straight lines for the printer. The result was illustration that had a "pen-drawn" rather than a computer-drawn appearance—sort of. Although newspaper illustrators took programs like *MacDraw* to their artistic limits, the flexibility wasn't there for the dyed-in-the-wool perfectionist or the technical illustrator.

Then, along came Adobe *Illustrator* from the people who had invented *PostScript*, the language that allowed object-oriented art and computer type-setting to enter a new age. Adobe *Illustrator* literally rocked the illustration and computer world. It could create lines, Bezier curves, geometric forms; and scale, distort, rotate and reflect any shape you created. *Illustrator* was to the graphic artist what *PageMaker* had been to the layout artist. It was based on a whole new technology and wasn't for the faint-hearted. Even those with previous computer-art experience were at first uncomfortable with *Illustrator*; however, once mastered, it became *the* computer tool for artists.

Exhibit 7.8

The sampling of computer-designed illustrations below were all created in Aldus *FreeHand*. (Clockwise from left) Leonardo DaVinci's famous self portrait, scanned, traced, then filled in *FreeHand*; dice created from scratch right on the screen; a photo scanned at high contrast, then traced and filled; and a cartoon drawn by hand, scanned, traced and filled in *FreeHand*.

Leonardo

Illustrator, and later its competitor Aldus *Free-Hand*, are still the preferred methods for creating computer-generated art that doesn't look like computer-generated art. The two basic methods for doing so are to scan an original and manipulate it in the illustration program, or draw it from scratch.

For the novice or non-artist, scanning and manipulating art may be the best approach, although learning a program as complex as *Illustrator* or *FreeHand* just to use scanned art is a bit like learning to fly a 747 just to use your family car on the weekends. In any event, the method is simple enough.

- Scan the art you wish to use as line art. If you are going to trace it in your illustration program

(a function now offered by both *Illustrator* and *FreeHand*), it's best to scan it as a TIFF file rather than a paint file. The jagged, bit-mapped lines of a paint file will trace out as jagged, bit-mapped lines as well. In addition, don't try to trace gray-scale scans. Neither illustration program distinguishes between the gray levels well. If you absolutely have to trace a gray-scale photo, make it as high contrast as possible by using a photo software program such as *Image Studio* or *FreeHand* itself, since it allows for image control much the same way *PageMaker* does.

- Once the image is scanned, you can work with it to make it look less like a computer-generated drawing. Unless you have one of the new trace programs designed for use in conjunction with an illustration program, doctoring your scanned image will be somewhat frustrating and time consuming.

Exhibit 7.9

Because computer illustration programs keep your lines perfectly straight and your curves perfectly curved, creating logos, standing heads and banners becomes much easier for the non-artist. The examples below were created right on the computer.

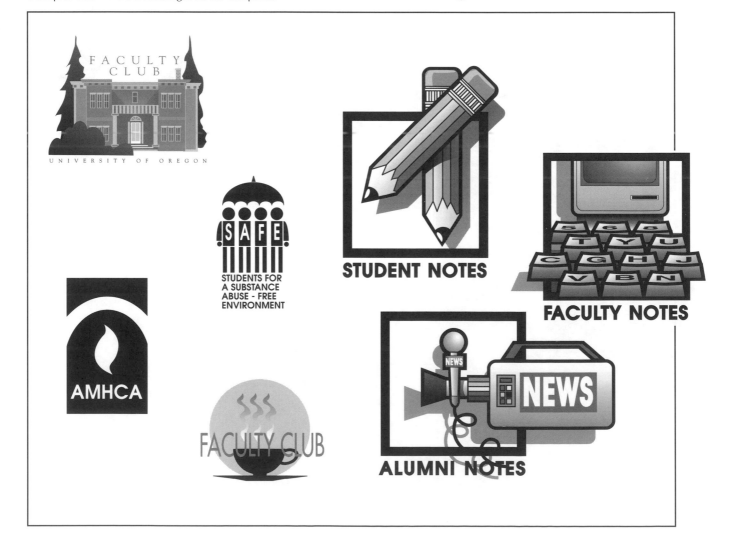

Exhibit 7.10

Above left is a scanned image traced in Adobe *Streamline*, as it appears when the traced image is opened into an illustration program such as Adobe *Illustrator* or Aldus *FreeHand* (center), and the final illustration complete with shading and highlights (right).

For the experienced graphic artist, drawing from scratch is always rewarding and instructional. The best way to learn an illustration program inside out is to experiment; and nothing tests your skills better than creating from scratch. Both *Illustrator* and *FreeHand* provide a great deal of guidance by way of manuals and tutorials.

Scanned Art

Reworking scanned art is one way of using an illustration program. However, you can also use scanned art as-is by scanning a piece of art directly into your page-makeup program for use as a locator for finished art or as finished art itself.

When using scanned art, keep a few guidelines in mind.

- When scanning anything other than pure line art, use as many gray scales as your scanner will produce and a 300 dpi resolution. This will allow you to reproduce any art with gradations of coloring or gray areas including pencil drawings, pastels, and paintings.

- For the best reproduction of lines, even in line art, scan to a TIFF or other photo format at a 300 dpi resolution. To eliminate any graying of background areas or lines, adjust your scanner (if it's adjustable) to a higher contrast or use your page-layout program to do it.

- Watch out for file size. A complex piece of line art (say, one with a lot of cross-hatching) can easily take up as much disk space as a large gray-scale photograph. Scaling during scanning, or reducing resolution at scanning or in a photo manipulation program can help.

- If disk space allows, scan at a larger size than your final artwork will be. Reducing scanned line art greatly enhances its crispness, although reducing fine lines will tend to muddy the image.

- Using scanned art and photos as place holders or locators for finished art lets the layout person fit copy and graphic elements exactly, leaving spaces for stripping in finished art. If you're using scanned art for this purpose, there is no need to take up valuable disk space with high-resolution gray-scale images. Unless you're fitting copy around art, scan at a low resolution (72 dpi *MacPaint* format is just fine) and import it into your page-makeup program for placement.

Clip Art

Dozens of manufacturers now offer computer-generated clip art services. Originally, these were based on the bit-mapped technology of the early paint programs or the clumsy but clean draw programs. Today

Exhibit 7.11

Don't blow up bit-mapped clip art. Enlarging the individual pixels (cells) makes them truly look "computerized." Avoid clip art of any kind that comes with several illustrations to a page or file. Instead, purchase bit-mapped clip art in large originals that you then scale down. The larger the original, the cleaner the art. *Encapsulated PostScript* art, on the other hand, can be enlarged many times its original size without any loss of definition.

you can purchase clip art in either bit-mapped format or object-oriented format (usually referred to as *PostScript* art) that can be placed directly into your page-makeup program or loaded and manipulated in either *Illustrator* or *FreeHand.* Clip art usually comes on disk or CD ROM (Compact Disk Read Only Memory), a compact disk that is accessed by your computer in order to retrieve information only. Because it can store millions of kilobytes of information, clip art that might fill twenty or thirty double-sided, double-density disks can be placed on one compact disk.

Much of what passes for clip art now, however, is a mixed blessing. In any given collection, you will find both superb and amateurish examples. The individual pieces may have been created by dozens

of artists using any number of methods ranging from scanning original clip art with little or no modification to art created from scratch on the computer. The latter is usually the preferred format for serious clip art users since it is usually divisible (ungrouped) into its various original components and thus highly manipulable using an illustration program. Scanned images don't ungroup because they were scanned as whole images instead of drawn from scratch.

When using clip art, consider the following rules of thumb.

- Decide in advance on the format you want to use. If your publication requires excellent and sharp reproduction, choose *PostScript* clip art. If you are publishing a daily or weekly newsletter that won't suffer from less than magazine-quality artwork, use bit-mapped clip art. It can be cheaper and often is available in greater variety than *PostScript* art because of the disk space requirements. Some very excellent bit-mapped clip art is available.

- Don't use it in its original size. Clip art isn't usually intended for use as a 3" x 4" or 1" x 2"

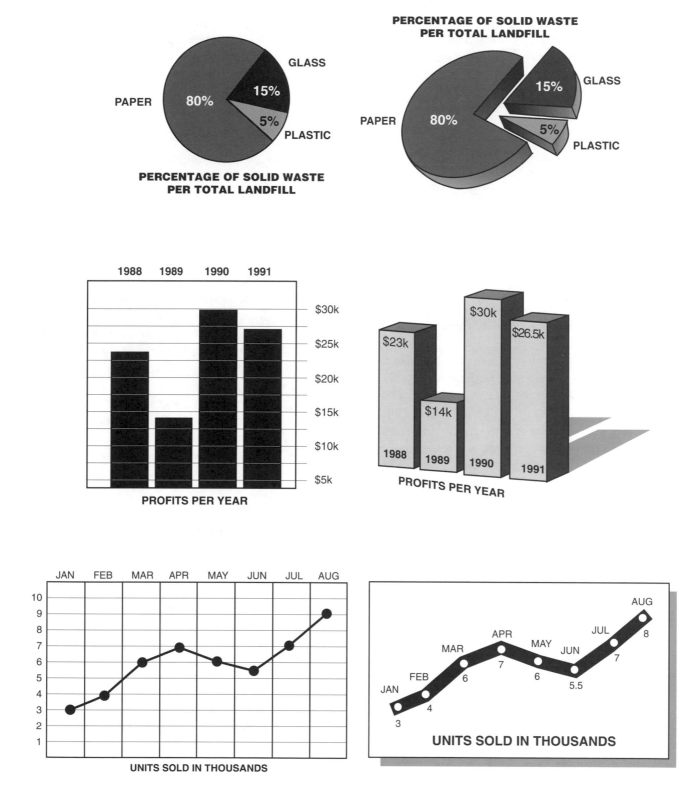

Exhibit 7.12

As you can see from the various types of charts and graphs pictured here, there is usually more than one way to depict information. Experiment with different approaches and use the one that presents the information in the clearest possible way—not the one that is the most creative or pretty.

piece of illustration. Nothing offends the artistic sensibilities more than a publication peppered with tiny illustrations. Experiment with sizes and different croppings. Make a number of thumbnails or quick layouts until you're satisfied with your illustrations.

Information Graphics

Information graphics are best left to technical artists. It is a highly specialized area and, like drafting, isn't usually the forum for the typical illustrator. But, as a publisher, you need to be aware of two approaches to technical art.

CAD (computer-assisted drawing) has become a buzzword in the desktop publishing business. Architects, designers, and drafting people alike sing its praises. Basically, CAD programs combine the precision of an illustration program with the needs of a designer to work in three dimensions. CAD software allows you to create three dimensional images, rotate them, enlarge or reduce them, and manipulate them in dozens of ways. For technical artists who have labored hundreds of hours recreating the same part of a complex machine over and over again for each individual version of a drawing, computer-assisted design is heaven sent.

But, unless you are an illustrator (technical or otherwise) you'd best stick to clip art or hire out.

Graphing programs (graphic spread sheets) have multiplied over the past few years. In the old days, you analyzed a pile of raw data, plotted it as a chart, and painstakingly drew it out to the exact dimensions needed. Now you can do it with a single key-stroke. Unfortunately, many of these programs are bit-mapped. The final printout is okay if it's going into a report, but if you want to wow your audience with this year's corporate earning's statement, you're going to have to find a flashier program. Fortunately, more programs are now available in a *PostScript* format that provide clean charts and graphs.

For the desktop publisher whose graphic needs are usually a lot less precise, it is often advisable to create the graphs in an illustration program or right in your page-makeup program. And don't forget freelancers. Hundreds of graphic artists around the country make a healthy living creating unusual ways to graph information. We see the creative results every day in our newspapers and magazines.

Finally, if you can't produce an instantly readable graph or chart, don't use one. It's self-defeating to muddle your message with an undecipherable chart,

and can be distracting as well. Although one picture can be worth 10,000 words, it may add more verbiage than you're looking for.

Photography

The bane or the savior of almost any newsletter is photography. Most newsletters are filled with photography—mug shots, group shots, awards photos, retirement photos, promotions, openings, tours, and nearly everything that can be captured on film. The problem is that most newsletter photography is done by the editor or by someone else with little or no experience. Now, as editor, you wouldn't attempt to illustrate your own newsletter with nifty pen drawings or beautiful watercolors—if you weren't an artist. Why then, do editors insist on taking their own photographs when they aren't photographers? The reason is that most people think of themselves as competent enough to take a photograph good enough for a newsletter. Unless you *are* a professional photographer (or a *really* good amateur), don't do it.

A well-written, well-designed newsletter can be literally destroyed by bad or even mediocre photography. As with clip art, if you have the choice between a bad photograph and no photograph at all, choose no photograph at all.

Hiring a Photographer

Your first consideration should be to hire a professional. The same guidelines used for hiring an illustrator apply here. Shop around, ask for samples and references, pick someone whose work matches your needs, and make sure they can meet your deadlines. Be aware that photographers specialize. Don't hire a wildlife photographer to shoot corporate photos for your newsletter. And, when you do hire a photographer, make sure they understand the nature and look of your newsletter as *you* conceive it. For every article they are going to illustrate with one of their photographs, make sure they have read the story, understand the points being made, have met the people central to the story and are familiar with the environment in which they will be shooting. If you have any specific needs (such as a shot of person *A* shaking hands with person *B*), tell them before they waste two rolls of film shooting *A* and *B* separately.

After they finish their assignment, have them develop a *proof* or *contact sheet*. A proof sheet is a single 8" x 10" print of all the shots in a roll of film, run

Exhibit 7.13

A proof or contact sheet is made by exposing your entire roll of film in its original size (33mm wide) on a single sheet of paper. Using a jeweler's loupe (a magnifying glass shaped like a small cup), you can then look carefully at each shot, and pick the ones you want to print without having to pay the price of printing the entire roll. You can also indicate cropping on a proof sheet.

in the actual size of the negative (very small). You will need a jeweler's loop to view them properly, but it saves having the entire roll developed just to pick one picture. Based on your choices from the proof sheet, then indicate how many prints you want and whether you want any special handling, such as cropping or enhancement of the contrast.

Doing It Yourself

So, what if you have to take your own photographs because it's just too costly to hire someone else to do it? First, get yourself a 35mm camera. Don't use your tiny snapshot camera for newsletter-quality photographs. Get something with an auto-focus lens of about 40mm, or a zoom with about a 40-80mm range. And don't shoot color film. Most newsletters don't publish color photos even if the newsletter is printed in color. The cost of printing full-color photographs is prohibitive for most newsletter publishing. If you anticipate shooting primarily indoors, get a flash attachment as well. And use a fairly standard, high-

speed film, such as Kodak Tri X 400 speed, and stick with it. Assume you are going to use lots of film. Buy 36-exposure rolls and expect to shoot a complete roll for each subject. It will probably take a whole roll to get a couple of useable prints.

Once you decide to use photography for a story, also decide what kind of photos you want to include. Try to come up with compositional ideas that exclude standard mug shots, or hand-shaking shots, or any of the other clichés you see in newsletters all the time. For example, instead of taking a photo of your company president sitting behind his desk (like a million other newsletter photos), have him sit on the window ledge, or shoot him getting out of his car, or walking down the hallway with his secretary. In other words, look for the out-of-the-ordinary.

Taking a photograph isn't like looking at something with the naked eye. The camera encloses what we normally see inside a rectangular frame, eliminating all peripheral information. That's why a scene shot for a movie in your hometown won't look the same when you see it on screen as it does to you when you look at that same scene every day as you walk to work. You view the scene complete with peripheral vision, taking in not only the center of your attention, but also the area surrounding that center. A camera effectively blocks that part out.

What this means is that you are going to have to choose very carefully exactly what you want in your

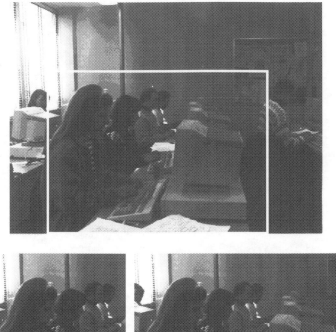

Exhibit 7.14

The original photo (top left) shows an off-center composition but too much room above the focal point of the photo. Cropping for a horizontal layout (top right) focuses attention of the central detail of the photo. Vertical cropping narrows the focus even further (bottom left). The results of cropping for both vertical and horizontal layout are shown bottom right.

photograph and what you want to leave out. The best way to compose a photograph is to conceive of your subject in ground thirds. Remember, layouts executed in ground thirds rely on asymmetric balance. In photographic composition this means to keep your subject slightly off center. The focal point of your photograph should be either to the right or left of your center line. The same rule applies to horizontal elements. Horizons and other strong horizontal lines should not cut through the center of your photograph.

You should know in advance whether you will need horizontal or vertical photos. If you are using a primarily vertical layout, don't compose your subjects horizontally. You don't literally have to turn your camera sideways (although it might help orient you vertically), but you do have to compose your shots so that the strongest vertical elements are near the center and extraneous elements are to the outside.

When composing horizontally, remember that the outside of any frame is *magnetic.* That is, elements not anchored near the center of your

composition will be attracted to the outside edges of your picture. For example, a studio interview shown on television between two seated people will have them seated much closer together than they would normally sit for a casual conversation. In fact, if you were in the studio you would probably notice that the two people were literally touching knees. If this closeness isn't exaggerated, the distance between the two people would seem much greater on the TV screen than it actually is. That's because the outside edges, free from peripheral elements, seem to draw the internal elements to them.

The only solution to a shot in which the primary elements haven't been consciously grouped near the center of the shot, is to crop the outside edges later. Most photos benefit immensely from tight cropping. In fact, a basic rule of thumb is to always crop your photographs as tightly as you can. Eliminate anything

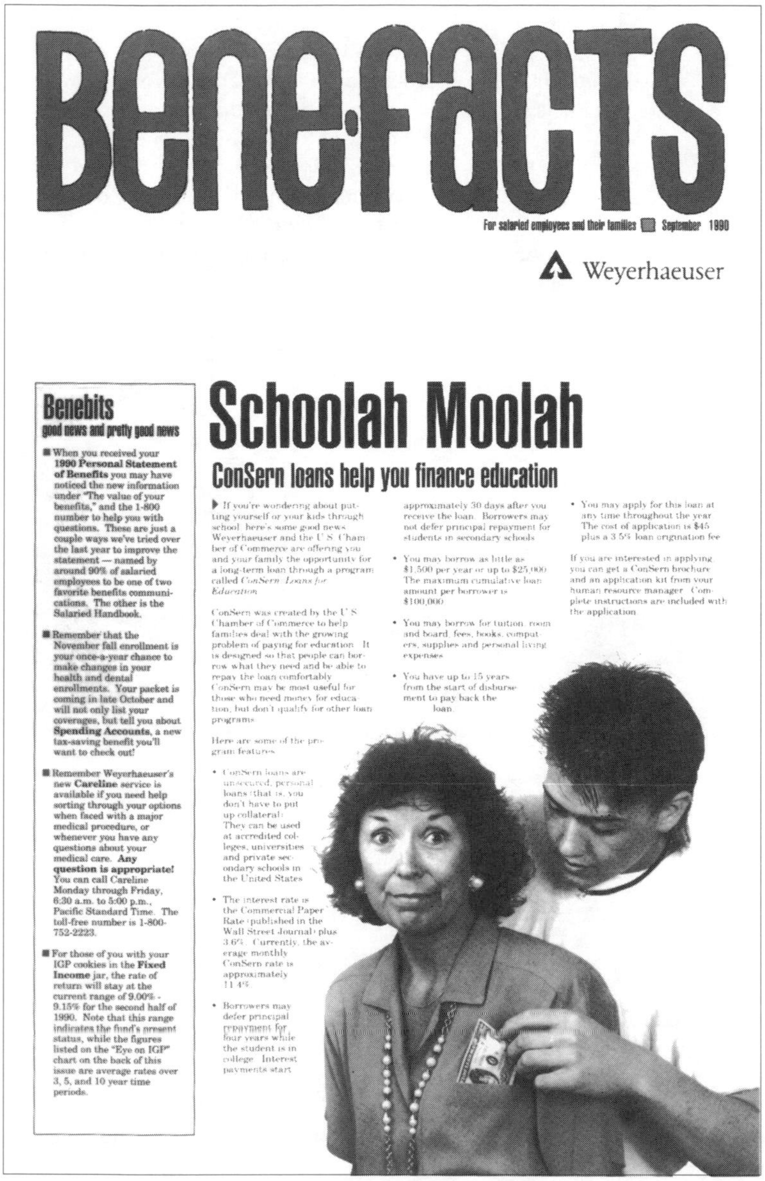

Bene·Facts

For salaried employees and their families ■ September 1990

Weyerhaeuser

Benebits

good news and pretty good news

- When you received your **1990 Personal Statement of Benefits** you may have noticed the new information under "The value of your benefits," and the 1-800 number to help you with questions. These are just a couple ways we've tried over the last year to improve the statement — named by around 90% of salaried employees to be one of two favorite benefits communications. The other is the Salaried Handbook.
- Remember that the November fall enrollment is your once-a-year chance to make changes in your health and dental enrollments. Your packet is coming in late October and will not only list your coverages, but tell you about **Spending Accounts**, a new tax-saving benefit you'll want to check out!
- Remember Weyerhaeuser's new **Careline** service is available if you need help sorting through your options when faced with a major medical procedure, or whenever you have any questions about your medical care. **Any question is appropriate!** You can call Careline Monday through Friday, 6:30 a.m. to 5:00 p.m., Pacific Standard Time. The toll-free number is 1-800-752-2223.
- For those of you with your IGP cookies in the **Fixed Income** jar, the rate of return will stay at the current range of 9.00% - 9.15% for the second half of 1990. Note that this range indicates the fund's present status, while the figures listed on the "Eye on IGP" chart on the back of this issue are average rates over 3, 5, and 10 year time periods.

Schoolah Moolah

ConSern loans help you finance education

If you're wondering about putting yourself or your kids through school, here's some good news. Weyerhaeuser and the U.S. Chamber of Commerce are offering you and your family the opportunity for a long-term loan through a program called *ConSern: Loans for Education*.

ConSern was created by the U.S. Chamber of Commerce to help families deal with the growing problem of paying for education. It is designed so that people can borrow what they need and be able to repay the loan comfortably. ConSern may be most useful for those who need money for education, but don't qualify for other loan programs.

Here are some of the program features.

- ConSern loans are unsecured, personal loans (that is, you don't have to put up collateral). They can be used at accredited colleges, universities and private secondary schools in the United States.
- The interest rate is the Commercial Paper Rate (published in the Wall Street Journal) plus 3.6%. Currently, the average monthly ConSern rate is approximately 11.4%.
- Borrowers may defer principal repayment for four years while the student is in college. Interest payments start approximately 30 days after you receive the loan. Borrowers may not defer principal repayment for students in secondary schools.
- You may borrow as little as $1,500 per year or up to $25,000. The maximum cumulative loan amount per borrower is $100,000.
- You may borrow for tuition, room and board, fees, books, computers, supplies and personal living expenses.
- You have up to 15 years from the start of disbursement to pay back the loan.
- You may apply for this loan at any time throughout the year. The cost of application is $45 plus a 3.5% loan origination fee.

If you are interested in applying, you can get a ConSern brochure and an application kit from your human resource manager. Complete instructions are included with the application.

Exhibit 7.15

Another option for cropping photographs involves creating a silhouette or outline crop. All you need to do is indicate to your printer what you want cropped out, and it can be accomplished easily during the normal screening process. However, unless you are typesetting on a computer layout program, copyfitting around the cropped photo will be difficult to achieve. Talk to your typesetter or printer about how to have your copy set to accommodate a silhouette photo.

unnecessary to your picture. Keep only the central idea intact, and even that can probably be cropped somewhat. You may also have to crop in order for your photograph to fit into the space you've allotted for it; however, many fine photos originally intended for a pre-designed space have benefitted from rearranging the page to fit the picture. If you've got that kind of photograph, don't ruin it with needless cropping.

Scaling goes hand in hand with cropping. Scaling refers to fitting the proportions of your photograph to the proportions of the space it will go into on your layout. You will rarely be using a photo full-sized for your layout. It will have to be scaled down in order to fit. For example, let's say you have a vertical photograph 5" x 7" and you need to fit it into a 3" x 4" space. Reducing the original to 60 percent of its size will make it fit the three-inch requirement, but the seven-inch side will be nearly one-fourth inch too tall. This is where cropping comes in. You can easily crop one-fourth inch from almost any photograph without harming the composition. Since you will probably be scaling nearly every photograph you put in your newsletter, you should buy yourself a *proportional wheel*. They can be found at almost any art store and only cost a few dollars. They are extremely easy to use and only take a few minutes to learn.

Once you have scaled your photographs and indicated cropping, you will need to have final prints made to your specifications. A final word of advice: have your photographs custom developed. Don't take them to a one-hour photo shop at the local mall. Most of these places don't do black and white anyway. If you use a custom-developing shop, you can probably rely on the

Exhibit 7.16

A proportion wheel is indispensable for sizing photos and artwork, and it's easy to use. Just line up one of the two dimensions of your original photograph (either length or width will do) on the inside wheel with the size you need to scale it to on the outside wheel. The percentage of your original size will appear under the arrow at the top of the window. The number times of reduction is above the arrow at the bottom of the window. In the example below, let's say we are reducing a 10" wide photo to 7⅞". The percentage reduction will be roughly 29 percent.

Exhibit 7.17

Another option for sizing is to use a calculator. The only disadvantage of this method is that you must work with decimels instead of fractions. To use your calculator to size artwork, you must first convert the measurement from fractions to decimals. For example, if you need to reduce 7⅜" to 3¹¹⁄₁₆", you derive a decimal equivalent of 7⅜ by dividing 8 into 3, or 7.375. Likewise, 3¹¹⁄₁₆ becomes 3.688. Next you divide 3.688 by 7.375 to get .5, or a reduction to 50% of your original size.

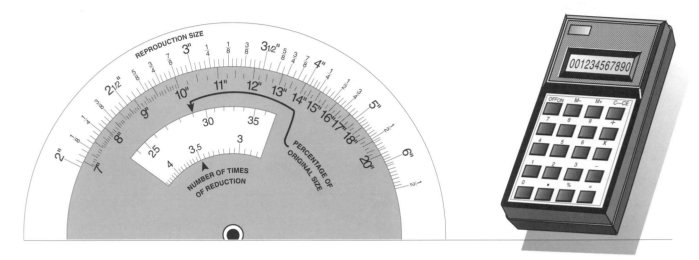

people there to help you determine cropping, sizing, and other photo enhancements that might help your newsletter. For instance, if your best photo looks a little underexposed, they can probably correct for that in the custom processing. Or, if it came out a bit too bright, that can be compensated for in processing as well. Just remember, what you see on your proof sheet isn't necessarily what you can get in the final processing. Tell your processor exactly what you want and how you're going to be using it. Don't pay for anything you don't need, but rely on expert advice when in doubt.

Grouping Photographs in Layouts

A special consideration in working with photography is the *photo spread*. Although, normally, you will be using one photo per story (if any at all), there are times when you will have more than one good photo you'd like to use. Creating a photo spread takes practice; however, here are a few guidelines to use when working on a layout with more than one photo in a single story.

- If you have an unusually long story, say more than a full page, consider spreading your photos

out to add interest to various sections of the article; especially if the photos relate to different parts of the story.

- Try to avoid using the same size photos. Varying the size, either through cropping or scaling, adds variety to your layout. However, be careful to adjust to the vertical or horizontal grid you are using.

- If the photos are related by subject but don't refer to different parts of the story (say there're all of the company picnic) consider grouping them. The trick to grouping photos is to vary sizes and balance them against each other and other weighted elements on the page. Keep grouped photos close together—usually no more than a pica apart. Farther apart, and they will lose their psychological relationship for the reader.

- Whether grouped or sprinkled throughout your layout, use captions as graphic elements as well. A lengthy caption can fill white space and help balance a page just like any other element.

Printing Your Photographs

Now that you have nice cropped and scaled photos to work from, there is one more important step you must take before they will be ready to print as part of your newsletter.

A black and white photograph is not just a black and white photograph. As the slogan for Hewlett Packard's *ScanJet Plus* says, "Between black and white, there's a lot of gray...." A photograph is what is known as a continuous-tone image. That is, it contains not only black and white, but a complete range of grays in between. Since printing presses only print in one density (either there is ink on the paper or there's not), you can't get gray without some

---

Exhibit 7.18

Notice in the photo spread layout below that the photos all share a common horizontal border that separates the top two from the bottom two photos. This enhances their relationship.

mechanical prestidigitation. This optical trickery is called *screening* or *halftoning*.

A halftone screen converts continuous tones to a series of dots of varying sizes and concentrations. The larger and closer together the dots, the blacker that portion of the image appears. The smaller and farther apart the dots, the lighter that portion of the image. Your printer's photographer will take your original photograph and literally take another picture of it through a wire screen. These screens come in varying densities and patterns. A 45-degree dot pattern is the most common, but density is a matter of what you're going to use your photo for. Screen density is based on how many lines of dots are in an inch. The more lines, the finer the screen. Generally speaking, the poorer the reproductive quality of your chosen printing process, the coarser the screen should be. So a newsletter that is going to be quick copied (a process that doesn't reproduce any nuances at all) would use a halftone screen of 65-85 lines per inch. A photograph being used in a newsletter that will be

---

Years of protest

The 60s were a time of campus unrest, soul searching, and fun.

Lorem ipsum dolor sit amet, consectetuer adipiscing elit, sed diam nonummy nibh euismod tincidunt ut laoreet dolore magna aliquam erat volutpat. Ut wisi enim ad minim veniam, quis nostrud exerci tation ullamcorper suscipit lobortis nisl ut aliquip ex ea commodo consequat. Duis autem vel eum iriure dolor in hendrerit in vulputate velit esse molestie consequat, vel illum dolore eu feugiat nulla facilisis at vero eros et accumsan et iusto odio dignissim qui blandit praesent luptatum zzril delenit augue duis dolore te feugait nulla facilisi. Lorem ipsum dolor sit amet, consectetuer adipiscing elit, sed diam nonummy nibh euismod tincidunt ut laoreet dolore magna aliquam erat volutpat. Ut wisi enim ad minim veniam, quis nostrud exerci tation ullamcorper suscipit lobortis nisl ut aliquip ex ea commodo consequat.

Duis autem vel eum iriure dolor in hendrerit in vulputate velit esse molestie consequat, vel illum dolore eu feugiat nulla facilisis at vero eros et accumsan et iusto odio dignissim qui blandit praesent luptatum zzril delenit augue duis

exerci tation ullamcorper suscipit lobortis nisl ut aliquip ex ea commodo consequat. Duis autem vel eum iriure dolor in hendrerit in vulputate

dolore te feugait nulla facilisi. Nam liber tempor cum soluta nobis eleifend option congue nihil imperdiet doming id quod mazim placerat facer possim assum.

Lorem ipsum dolor sit amet, consectetuer adipiscing elit, sed diam nonummy nibh euismod tincidunt ut laoreet dolore magna aliquam erat volutpat. Ut wisi enim ad minim veniam, quis nostrud exerci tation ullamcorper suscipit lobortis nisl ut aliquip ex ea commodo consequat. Duis autem vel eum iriure dolor in hendrerit in

vulputate velit esse molestie consequat, vel illum dolore eu feugiat nulla facilisis at vero eros et accumsan et iusto odio dignissim qui blandit praesent luptatum zzril delenit augue duis dolore te feugait nulla facilisi. Lorem ipsum dolor sit amet, consectetuer adipiscing elit, sed diam nonummy nibh euismod tincidunt ut laoreet dolore magna aliquam erat volutpat.

Ut wisi enim ad minim veniam, quis nostrud exerci tation

ullamcorper suscipit lobortis nisl ut aliquip ex ea commodo consequat. Duis autem vel eum iriure dolor in hendrerit in vulputate velit esse molestie consequat, vel illum dolore eu feugiat nulla facilisis at vero eros et accumsan et iusto odio dignissim qui blandit praesent luptatum zzril delenit augue duis dolore te feugait nulla facilisi. Lorem ipsum dolor sit amet, consectetuer adipiscing elit, sed diam nonummy nibh euismod tincidunt ut laoreet dolore magna aliquam erat volutpat.

Ut wisi enim ad minim veniam, quis nostrud exerci tation ullamcorper suscipit lobortis nisl ut aliquip ex ea commodo consequat. Duis autem vel eum iriure dolor in hendrerit in vulputate velit esse molestie consequat, vel illum dolore eu feugiat nulla facilisis at vero eros et accumsan et iusto odio dignissim qui blandit praesent luptatum zzril delenit augue duis dolore te feugait nulla facilisi.

Lorem ipsum dolor sit amet, consectetuer adipiscing elit, sed diam nonummy nibh euismod tincidunt ut laoreet dolore magna aliquam erat volutpat. Ut wisi enim ad minim veniam, quis nostrud exerci tation ullamcorper suscipit lobortis nisl ut aliquip ex ea commodo consequat. Duis autem vel eum iriure dolor in hendrerit in vulputate velit esse molestie consequat, vel illum dolore eu feugiat nulla facilisis at.

offset printed on a white, coated paper could use a much finer screen—say, 120-130 lines or better. Magazine photos are typically 133-line screens.

If you are in doubt as to what line screen to use when having your photos halftoned, ask your printer.

Exhibit 7.19
The top blowup of a halftoned photograph shows the composition of dots that literally fool the eye into seeing a complete range of grays. (Clockwise below) Photos screened at 65 lpi, 85 lpi, 100 lpi, and 120 lpi.

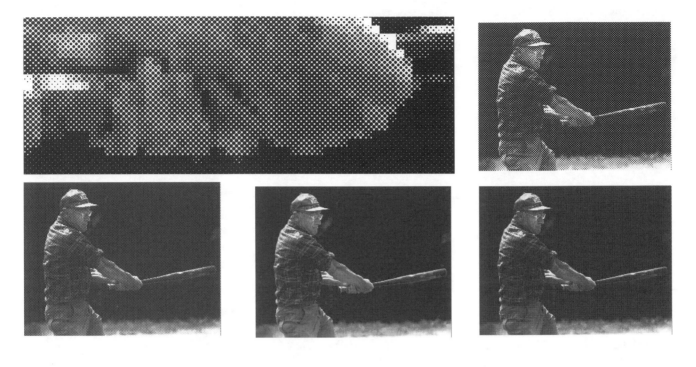

Working with Computer Photography

Until recently, even if you created your entire publication on computer, you still had to convert your photographs to halftones before they could be printed. Then along came *scanning*. Scanning is a term loosely used to describe a process whereby a continuous-tone photograph (or any artwork for that matter) is "scanned" electronically and transferred into information that is readable by various computer software programs.

There are basically two types of scanners: *bi-level* and *gray-scale*. Bi-level scanners save information as bit maps like those a computer "paint" program produces and work fine if you just want a bit-mapped reproduction of line art. But, if you want to produce a photograph with a simulation of grays, you're going to have to use a gray-scale scanner. Gray-scale scanners run the gamut from expensive to cheap, from "this is okay for layout" to "this is almost magazine-quality."

If you're serious about getting some functional mileage out of a scanner, buy one that will give you at least 64 levels of gray. You can get by on 16 levels of gray, but only if you're producing a low-grade newsletter or if you're just using your scanned images as "locators" for final artwork in your mechanical. If you ever plan to use your scanned photos for a higher-quality publication, you might as well start with a higher-quality scanner. Don't assume that higher quality means higher price. You'll be surprised at what you can get for under $2000.

Even if you pay a fortune for your scanner, you're still only going to get a maximum of 256 levels of gray out of it. The only real difference between full gray-scale scanners is in the way they compute the levels of gray—a subject we don't need to get into here. However, you do need to understand something of how a scanner, computer, and printer produce those "miracle" halftones.

The Process

Let's suppose you have a scanner or access to one. Here's how the process works, in a nutshell.

1. Place your original photograph on the scanner. You should start with a good original. Here's why.

   - When you scan photos that have already been published or printed, you are laying one dot pattern over another. There is literally no way you can align your scanner so that your scanning pattern will match the original halftone screen. You'll often get a disturbing *moire* effect—the result of superimposing two incompatible patterns on each other—usually most noticeable in backgrounds and solid gray areas where it will give your image a sort of mottled look.

   - Since a typical halftone darkens with each generation it goes through in the publication process, it is best to start with a low-contrast (flat) photo. Printers and lithographers will tell you that the best results are obtained from a scanned photo in which the lightest areas are at least 10 percent gray and the darkest areas are no more than 90 percent gray.

     Few scanners allow you to set this kind of detailed assignment of light versus dark areas. However, photo retouching and manipulation programs such as *Digital Darkroom* and *Image Studio* now include techniques for making these adjustments once you import the scanned image. See below for more on these programs.

2. Set the *sampling rate* for your scan. Most of the better scanners let you indicate how many dots per inch you want to store from your photograph as information in your computer. Current wisdom recommends scanning at a rate roughly analogous to the line-screen density or lpi you plan to use when you print. Both *PageMaker* and *Image Studio* recommend scanning at 150 dpi. When you scan at 150 to 300 dpi, you're really covering your bases pretty well. If you're using a scanner capable of recording 256 levels of gray to scan a photo at 150 dpi, you're creating an image that will give you at least 72 gray levels on a Linotronic 100 and more than 256 levels on a Linotronic 300. If you print to a LaserWriter, use the default setting. You're not going to get any better image than that produced with a 53-line screen at 300 dpi. Keep the following guidelines in mind when determining sampling rate.

   - *PageMaker* recommends scanning any images for use in its program at 150 dpi, regardless of the output device. This is good advice. This dpi is high enough to give you excellent resolution off both the Linotronic 100 and 300 and won't hurt your output to the LaserWriter if you use its default screen.

   - In some cases—photos with sharp diagonal angles for instance—scanning at a higher dpi can *help* final resolution since at a lower dpi these edges appear jagged. Don't scan any higher than twice the final screen lpi, however. You're wasting disk space after that. But remember, if you designate a lower screen value in your output program, you void the higher sampling rate. That is, if you print to a Linotronic with a designated screen of 150 lpi and you scanned at 300 dpi, you're only going to get one dot every $1/150$ inch—no matter what. This means that you effectively lose 150 dots, or half your stored information.

   - Use a higher resolution sampling rate such as 300 dpi to scan black-and-white line art. It will take up more space, but it will give you much cleaner images.

   - If you plan to enlarge your scanned image after you place it in your page-layout program, use a higher sampling rate. For instance, if you scan at 100 dpi and enlarge 200 percent, your dpi drops to half the original or 50 dpi. The reverse is also true. If you plan to reduce, you can scan at a much lower dpi. A 100 dpi scan reduced 50 percent will give you a 200 dpi image.

   - Some photo software programs like *Image Studio* will allow you to scale your image by lowering the resolution as you load it into the program for touch-up or manipulation. For example, if you are importing an image scanned at 300 dpi, you can lower the resolution to 150 (50 percent) as you load it into *Image Studio*. This also shrinks the size of the image file.

3. Choose the proper format for saving your image. Most scanner software allows you to save into the most common photo formats: TIFF (*Tagged Image File Format*), EPS (*Encapsulated Postscript*), and *MacPaint*. Both TIFF and EPS files take up a lot of space. In fact, a complex 8½" x 11" photo scanned

at 300 dpi could take up over 1 megabyte of space! Unless you've got a lot of memory, you're going to be concerned about file size. Here are some ways to save space.

- Saving to RIFF (*Raster Image File Format*) can cut your file size by 30 or 40 percent. Programs such as *Image Studio* use RIFF as an operating format (even though you can still save in TIFF, EPS, and *MacPaint*), but unless your layout software accepts RIFF, you're not going to be able to use it.

- As mentioned above, you can open your file into *Image Studio* at a reduced resolution, say 150 dpi instead of 300 dpi. This will seriously cut down the amount of file space your photo will take up. I've found, for instance, that TIFF files created at even 150 dpi can be formidable in size. But, when opened at a reduced resolution of as much as 50 percent, the original loses very little when run on a Linotronic 300. Most photos will be reduced or cropped when placed in the final publication layout. An 8" x 10" photo scanned at 150 dpi, reduced 50 percent to 75 dpi, then reduced in physical size to 2¼" x 3" (70 percent reduction) will still give you a 127 dpi image and a potential Linotronic output of up to 250 lpi screen.

- Scale your image as you scan it. If you know that you're not going to use an 8" x 10" full size

but rather at 50 percent, scan it at 50 percent and save half the disk space.

- Reduce the sampling rate. Remember, you rarely have to sample any higher than 150 dpi for any gray-scale image.

- If your scanned images will only be used for placement or rough layout, scan them at a very low resolution such as a 72 dpi *MacPaint* file. This saves you space and makes manipulating the images in your page-layout program faster.

4. Use a photo software program such as *Image Studio* or *Digital Darkroom* to edit, crop, touch up, and do virtually anything to a photo that a trained darkroom specialist can to.

5. Use a page-layout software that allows you to manipulate your scanned images further. *Page-Maker*, for instance, has an image control menu that allows you to set line screen and angle (best stick with 45 degrees) brightness and contrast. In fact, if you don't set your line screen in your page-layout program, it will default to the printer settings automatically.

Be aware, however, that in order to save file space, *PageMaker* only stores a screen image of your photograph. It won't look very good, but it will give you a good idea of how to place it, adjust it, and crop it. When printing, you'll have to "link" the photos to the file in which the original resides. *PageMaker* documents will ask you for this information each time you open them. Once you've linked the photos, however, *PageMaker* will remember where they are unless you move them to another folder or disk.

6. Once you've placed your image into your page-layout program, you can make a number of adjustments. Some programs allow gray-scale image adjustments to brightness or contrast. Most programs allow for cropping and scaling. The adjustments you make depend on whether you're going to be using your placed image as final art or just for placement. Here are some things to keep in mind.

   • Cropping can be done in any one of the several stages prior to placement in your page-layout program. Some scanners allow for cropping before you scan; however, cropping as you scan prevents you from changing your mind later on. Although you can further crop the photo, what you crop out as you scan is gone until you scan it again. Photo software programs such as *Image Studio* allow cropping as well as many other subtle adjustments. Using this type of program also finalizes your cropping once your image is placed in your page-layout program. You should always save your original photo as well as your adjusted version just in case.

   The beauty of cropping in your page-layout program is that you can crop your whole photo to your heart's content. If you don't like it, just uncrop it. The adjustment isn't cut in stone. The only problem is that the original size of your image is always resident in the page-layout program file, whereas a precropped image only uses the memory it needs to represent that size.

   • Scaling is the single most attractive feature of using a computer to generate photos for your layouts. In the traditional layout approach you had to measure the exact amount of space you allowed for your photo, measure your photo, scale it using a proportional wheel or calculator, indicate cropping to your printer or lithographer, and have your photo shot and screened in the appropriate size.

   Now, all you do is place it, and scale it until you get it the way you want it. If it won't fit proportionally, crop it to the proper proportions and then scale it again.

Remember, if you know in advance that you are going to scale a photo down, say 50 percent, either scan it at 50 percent its original size and at the resolution (sampling rate) you intend to use for your final printout, or scan it at a lower sampling rate in its original size, since resolution will double when you scale the photo in your page-layout program.

• Take advantage of any fancy layout techniques your software allows. For example, *PageMaker* has a text-wrap function that allows you to literally wrap your text around your photos or other scanned images. This is very helpful if you are using silhouette photos that you have cropped in a photo-manipulation program.

One reminder, however: don't get carried away. Just because your program allows you to wrap text (or something else) doesn't mean your message supports that sort of look. Be sure of your intended message and its "look" before you experiment too much.

One of the great benefits of computer layout is the ability to make changes, change the changes, change them back again, and make some more. If you're careful and systematic, you won't lose any of your best ideas.

• Save frequently! Although some programs save automatically, don't rely on them too much. After each major change or addition, save your file. And, if you aren't sure of which page arrangement you like, save each version under a slightly different name using a "save as" function.

7. Don't take what you see on the screen at face value. Most Macintosh screens only show a 75 dpi *dithered* image. Dithering refers to reproducing an image on the screen in pure black and white, with no shades of gray. This means that you're not going to see a real gray-scale image until you print it out. And, if you're viewing a 300 dpi image on a 75 dpi screen, it's going to look much larger than it actually is. Both of these conditions will lead you to make a number of sample copies of scanned photos before you get them just right.

And, even if you do get them to your satisfaction off the laser printer, they won't come close to what they'll look like off the Linotronic. Using a high-resolution monitor will help. The Mac II monitor or one of the larger layout monitors such as *Radius* will give you a complete range of grays. In fact, the monitor image will often be better than even Linotronic output. Here are some things to consider when preparing for your final output.

- If you're using your scanned photos for a simple, not too flashy newsletter, scan at 150 dpi or lower and use laser-printer output as your final image. You'll be surprised at how clear it really is.

- If you're looking for a more sophisticated, near-magazine quality look, scan at 150 dpi or greater (depending on whether you plan to enlarge or reduce the final image) and run it on a Linotronic with a 100- to 133-line screen.

- Bottom-of-the-line 256-level gray-scale scanners will produce a very good image, but it will darken considerably when it's run on a phototypesetter like the Linotronic.

The solution is to learn to manipulate your images with the software so that your final product will match your desired product. This may require setting density ranges at 10 and 90 as mentioned above, altering brightness and contrast, or changing screen resolution. The trick is to experiment. Some scanners, such as the Apple Scanner, produce test strips using various settings. You can produce a test strip of your own by varying the settings on a page full of the same photo (or section of a photo with the most representative contrast) and having it run on the Linotronic. Be sure to indicate the exact settings above each photo.

- Don't fall for what you've read about it taking 30 minutes or an hour to run one scanned photograph on a Linotronic. Sure it will if you run an 8" x 10" photo scanned at 300 dpi unaltered. If it takes up 2 MGB of disk space, it's going to take forever to print out. But, if you reduce the file size by one of the methods cited above, you won't lose any noticeable resolution and it won't take much time at all to run a photo. My experience has been that a photo scanned at 150 dpi, manipulated in *Image Studio* to reduce file size, physically reduced to the final placement size, and printed on a Linotronic 300 along with a complete 8 1/2" x 11" page of copy only takes from 4 to 6 minutes. In fact, we've run tabloid-sized pages with as many as five photos in 6 to 7 minutes per page. Remember, the size of the image file affects how long it will take to run the scanned image. And, unless you are certain your final product will come out right the first time, keep experimentation to a minimum. Experimenting on the Linotronic can be expensive, and every test photo you run will decrease the cost effectiveness of the process.

Exhibit 7.21

All of the variations you see here were accomplished in about 45 seconds on this page layout. You can see how versatile computer cropping and scaling is. Please avoid the temptation to distort photos just because you can. At least don't print them that way. Your subjects won't think it's nearly as funny as you do.

- If your final product will be offset printed, consider running your pages directly off a Linotronic as negatives. Although most of us are most familiar with Linotronic-paper positives (very much like PMTs) it also produces negatives that can then be used to make the plates.

If your Linotronic service doesn't charge any more for negatives than positives, this alone can save you money by eliminating a step in the printing process—shooting the negatives from your camera-ready mechanicals.

Another reason for going with negatives is that the photos produced on a Linotronic positive at anything over 100 lines-per-inch screen will be too fine a halftone to be re-shot as a negative. The result will be a "muddy" image. Printing directly to negative film will save this step and maintain clarity.

Writing

Although it may be the design of your newsletter that draws reader attention initially, it's your writing that will bring them back for more. Good writing doesn't just happen—it takes practice, practice, practice.

Most newsletters are journalistic in style. They usually include both straight news and feature stories and range from informal to formal depending on the organization and its audience. Usually, the smaller the organization, the less formal the newsletter. Large corporations, on the other hand, often have a very formal newsletter with a very slick format combining employee-centered news with company news.

The responsibility for writing the newsletter is almost always handled in-house, although some agencies do produce newsletters on contract for organizations. In-house personnel tend to be more in tune with company employees and activities. Sometimes the writing is done in-house and the production, including design, layout, and printing, is done by an agency.

Length of articles varies. Some newsletters contain only one article, while others include several. An average, four-page newsletter uses about 2,000 words of copy. Depending on the focus of the newsletter, articles can range in length from "digest" articles of less than 100 words to longer articles of 600 words for newsletters that cover only one or two topics per issue. The trend today is toward shorter articles, especially for the newsletter aimed at the businessperson or corporate executive. Even for the average employee, newsletter articles usually need to be brief. Most newsletters make use of simple graphics or photographs. While most are typeset (or, increasingly, desktop published), many are simply typed.

Regardless of how your newsletter is published, someone has to gather the information for the articles, write them, edit them, and get them into print. This is probably the most important job associated with newsletter publishing, since it is *what* you put in a newsletter that will keep your readers coming back for more.

Where Do Stories Come From?

No one can tell you where or how to come up with acceptable ideas for articles. Sometimes you might receive ideas from employees or management. Sometimes a news release or a short piece done for another publication will spark enough interest to warrant a full-blown newsletter article. Whatever the source of the idea, you must next evaluate the topic based on reader interest and reader consequence.

If you're familiar with your audience's tastes, you can quickly determine their interest. To evaluate consequence, ask yourself whether they will learn something from the article. Although light reading is fun for some, an organizational publication isn't usually the place to engage in it.

Every newsletter editor will tell you that getting story ideas isn't all that hard. Finding someone to write them is. There are a couple of methods for enlisting writers. If you are putting out an in-house publication, try assigning "beats" just like a newspaper. If you're lucky enough to have a staff, assign them to different types of stories—perhaps by department or division, or by product or service. If you don't have a staff, rely on certain people in each department or division to submit stories to you. Sometimes the simple promise of seeing their name in print is enough inducement.

You can also send employees a simple request form, spelling out exactly what you are looking for. The return information will be sketchy, but you can flesh it out with a few phone calls. This is an especially good method of gathering employee-related tidbits that don't deserve an entire story but should still be mentioned. Another method for organizing your shorter stories is to group them according to topic. For example, group all stories relating to employee sports, or all stories about employee community involvement, or promotions, or extramarital affairs, and so on.

Of course, if your publication is a narrowly focused horizontal publication, you may end up doing most of the research and writing yourself. Many such newsletters are truly one-person operations. Because desktop publishing allows an individual to act as reporter, editor, typesetter, and printer, this type of publication is enjoying a rebirth.

Whatever system you use to gather stories, as editor you will probably be doing most of the writing as well as the editing.

Researching Stories

If you write most of your own stories, you know that every topic must be researched thoroughly. The first step in a normal research process is to do a "literature search" to determine whether your article has already been written. If it has, but you still want to explore the topic for your specific audience, then try another angle.

Next, gather background information. Try to get specifics. You can't write about something you don't know a lot about personally. It also pays to get firsthand information. Interview people who know something about your topic. Not only will you get up-to-date information, but you may end up with some usable quotes and some new leads.

Don't forget the library. Many a fine article has been written based on a library visit. Library research is among the most valuable, and one of the cheapest, forms of research. In any event, most articles will be fairly complete and accurate if you do a little background research and conduct an interview or two.

Since newsletter articles are usually short, this is about all the information you can use.

Interviews

For many articles, human interest is important. This is where interviews come in. Firsthand information is always best when you can get it. Interview those intimately involved with your topic and use their information when you write. Interviewing is a special skill and it takes a lot of practice. Who you interview will have a great deal to do with how informative or interesting your interview will be. Although you can't always control who you interview, you can prepare so that you can make the most out of your meeting.

The Basics of Effective Writing

Not many of us learned to write the way we do in school—instead, we learned on the job, picking up bad habits and having those habits further ingrained by people who couldn't put it down much better than we could. That's why it's important to pause for a few moments and check our writing style to see if we have acquired any bad habits that might be corrected, even at this late date.

That's the purpose of this section—to help you understand some of the accepted methods of good writing and to apply these methods to your personal style. You need to be aware of how to change those things that you would like to change while leaving the good parts intact.

Using Effective Words

All of us think we know how to use a dictionary. It's part of every writer's library. The problem is that a lot of people don't *use* their dictionaries and assume rather than check the meanings and spellings of words. This leads, of course, to misinterpretation of written materials by readers.

One of the biggest problems in using dictionaries is deciding whether or not a word is appropriate in context. For instance, a word that might be entirely appropriate in informal English might not be appropriate in formal English. Dictionaries can be of some help. Most provide guidance in selecting the right word. For instance, a dictionary might label the word *swipe* as a colloquial or informal alternative to mean for to *steal* or *plagiarize*. You wouldn't want to use it in a formal, business letter. This brings us to our first

How To Conduct a Successful Interview

Following are some tips to help you through a successful interview.

- Do your homework. Collect background information on the people you're going to interview, as well as the topics. Don't be embarrassed by your own ignorance of the topics; however, the better you know the topics, the more time you can save by asking for confirmation or denial of specifics, rather than asking for in-depth explanations.

- Prepare your interviewees in advance of the interviews. Contact them well in advance, set a convenient time for the interview (convenient for them, not you), and make sure they know exactly what you are going to cover and why. That way, they can also prepare for the interview by gathering pertinent information—or, at the very least—their thoughts. Ask if you can talk with them, not interview them. A talk puts people at ease—an interview can make them tense and formal.

- Write down a list of questions that you want answered, working from the general to the specific. But be prepared to let the interview range according to the interviewee's responses. Often, an answer will open new areas of inquiry or suggest an angle you hadn't thought of before. Be ready to explore these new avenues as they come up.

  Ken Metzler, journalist, educator, and author of *Creative Interviewing* claims that the best interviewers should not only expect surprises, but should ask for surprises in their willingness to explore rather than follow a strict set of questions.

- If you are going to use a tape recorder, check to make sure that your interviewee is comfortable with being taped, and that you have fresh batteries or that an electrical outlet is available. And, even though you are taping, always take notes. This physical activity usually puts the interviewee at ease by showing that you are listening, and it serves as a good backup if your recorder stops functioning or your tape runs out.

  Your recorder should not occupy the space between you and your subject. Move it a little to the side, but make sure the microphone isn't obstructed. The space between you and your subject should be free of any object that may be a source of distraction. (You should also keep your note pad in your lap, if possible, or simply hold it.)

- Break the ice. Open your interview with small talk. Try a comfortable topic, such as the weather, or, if you know something about your interviewee, a familiar topic that is nonthreatening. For example, if you know your interviewee is an avid golfer, ask if he or she has had a chance to play much lately. Almost any topic will do—in fact, most of the time, something will suggest itself naturally.

- As your interview progresses, don't be afraid to range freely, but return occasionally to your pre-set questions. Although the information you gather exploring other avenues may add greatly to your collection of relevant facts, remember to cover all the ground necessary for your article.

- If you are ever unsure of a quote or think you might have misunderstood it, ask your subject to repeat it. Even if you are taping the interview, accuracy on paper and in your own mind is worth the slight pause.

- Finally, be prepared to have to remember some key conversation after your interview is officially over. Most of us are aware of the phenomenon that Ken Metzler calls the "afterglow effect," when dinner guests, for example, stand at the door with their coats on ready to go and talk for another 30 minutes. The same thing usually happens in an interview. You've turned your recorder off and put your pad away, and on your way out the door, you have another ten minutes of conversation. In this relaxed atmosphere, important comments are often made. Remember them. As soon as you leave, take out your pad and write the comments down or turn on your recorder and repeat the information into it. However, always make sure that your interviewee is aware that you are going to use this information as well. Don't violate any assumed "off the record" confidences.

Remember, get as much as you can the first time out. Most interviews range from 30 minutes to two hours. A follow-up interview, providing you can get one, will never be as fruitful or relaxed as the first one.

rule: Avoid using informal words in formal writing.

Informal:
It seems that Mr. Jordan swiped the information on the new plastic widget from a brochure he found in his files.

Formal:
It seems that Mr. Jordan plagiarized the information on the new plastic widget from a brochure he found in his files.

It's usually safe to assume that if a word is unlabeled in your dictionary, it is considered to be in general usage and therefore formal.

For the newsletter writer, contractions (which are usually considered informal usage) can be useful. Frequently, you can take on a familiar tone with your target audience by using contractions.

Slang and jargon

All industries have their jargon. Banks call Certificates of Deposit "CDs," journalists call paragraphs "graphs," police call a record of arrests a "rap sheet," and highly technical industries develop entire dictionaries of shorthand notations. Reserve jargon for external information pieces only if they are to be read by experts in the field. For internal pieces, jargon is usually acceptable. For the lay reader, use jargon only if you are able to explain its usage in lay terms. It is wise to follow this procedure unless you are sure that your jargon has become accepted general usage.

When jargon becomes cumbersome, it overrides meaning. What we commonly refer to as "legalese" and "bureaucratese" are really overuse of jargon. The result is ambiguity. For example, words like *impact* and *input* have now become jargon to many industries. They sound "trendy" to many people and give them a false sense of belonging to a select group of "experts."

Jargon:
Most of the time is taken up *inputting* data into the computer. (A noun misused as a verb.)

General:
Most of the time is taken up *entering* data into the computer. (A verb used correctly.)

Jargon:
The severe downturn in the economy has negatively *impacted* our industry. (A noun misused as a verb.)

General:
The severe downturn in the economy has negatively *affected* our industry. (A verb used correctly.)

In your efforts to write clearly and concisely, remember that the object of written communication is to communicate. In other words—don't "fuzzify."

Exactness

Exactness is an art. Most of us tend to "write up" when we assume a formal style. But when we "write up," we lose precision. What we should strive for is clarity, and clarity can be achieved most easily by using exact words. Most of our writing is read by people who know something about us and what we do, but we cannot always assume that to be the case.

Denotative and Connotative Meanings

One way to avoid confusion is always to use words whose denotative meanings most closely match those understood by our audience. The *denotative* meaning of a word is its "dictionary" meaning and, of course, the best way to determine that is to look the word up. The first example following uses the wrong word.

Wrong:
The employees were visibly *effected* by the president's speech on benefits. (*Effect* means result.)

Right:
The employees were visibly *affected* by the president's speech on benefits. (*Affect* means influenced.)

Connotative meanings are those your audience may associate with words in addition to or instead of their dictionary meaning. Connotation is the result of automatic associations your audience makes when interpreting some words. For example, you may intend the word *dog* to mean a four-footed, warm-blooded animal of the canine species. To audience members whose past associations with dogs has been positive, a picture of a particularly friendly dog may pop into mind. For some who may have had negative experiences—such as being bitten by a dog—the association may be entirely the opposite of what you intend. Although there is no way to guard against all such associations, there are certain words or phrases that you should avoid as being *too* vague in connotation to be useful to you as a communicator.

Think of the different connotative meanings for words such as *liberal, conservative, freedom, democracy, communism,* and *patriotism.* Words with multiple connotations may not be the best words to select if you are striving for exactness.

Some words or phrases may have little or no connotation, such as *place of birth*. The denotative meaning of this phrase is clear, but there is little connotative meaning. However, if we replace the phrase with the word, *hometown*, not only does the denotative meaning become clear, but the word also gains a definite connotative meaning—usually a positive one.

Specific Words vs. General and Abstract

Exactness requires that you be specific. Writing in generalities is even worse. When we read something which has been written in general, nonspecific terms, we can't help but feel that something is being left out—perhaps on purpose.

General words are indefinite and cover too many possible meanings, both denotatively and connotatively. Specific words are precise and limited in definition.

General	Specific
car	Honda, Accord LX
people	Delawareans
animal	cat
precipitation	rain

Abstract words deal with concepts or ideas which are intangible, such as *freedom* or *love*. Use these words, but make sure that they are not open to misinterpretation.

Walters finds that the *freedom* he experiences at his new job is the key asset of working for Traxton. (Does *freedom* mean Walters can come and go as he pleases? Perform only the work he wants? Talk back to the boss? What, exactly?)

One of the parts of speech (remember those?) affected the most by inexactness is the adjective. A number of adjectives are extremely general in nature and impart little or no additional meaning to a noun, thus negating their function.

General:
Marisa, please take this report to word processing and tell them it's a rush job. (Show me something that isn't a rush job!)

Specific:
Marisa, please take this report to word processing, and tell them we need it by 3:00 this afternoon. (Now, word processing has a specific deadline.)

Avoiding clichés

At one time, all expressions were original; however, that was probably a long, long time ago. Today,

we're frequently stuck with trite or overworked expressions or clichés. The problem with these is that they may be entirely overlooked by your reader who has probably seen them a thousand times.

Trite:
Nine out of ten times Harcourt is wrong in his instant analysis of a problem.

Better:
Most of the time Harcourt is wrong in his instant analysis of a problem.

Trite:
Harcourt is claiming his latest plan is a *viable option* in controlling employee absences.

Better:
Harcourt is claiming his latest plan is a *solution* to the problem of employee absences.

Stock expressions are viewed by many writers as acceptable shortcuts that aid understanding.

John Smith, *a native of* Chicago... *or*

Chicago *native* John Smith...

Generally, these semantic shortcuts impart the correct meaning without being vague or appearing trite. Other phrases have become clichéd through overuse, and have subsequently lost their meaning.

The head of programming says this new product will keep APC *on the cutting edge*.

James Sutton, president of Associated Products Corporation, *announced today* (May 25) the release of a new line of plastic widgets.

The key is to recognize trite, overused expressions and clichés and understand when they can be useful and when they can hurt your message. Remember, good writers avoid worn out words and opt instead for fresh usage.

Wordiness

Being too "wordy" is a habit that most of us fall into at one time or another. Perhaps, as was mentioned above, we once thought it meant we were writing in a formal style. Actually, the opposite is true. Formal English should be no more wordy than informal English. In fact, it should be even more precise because it is formal. As a writer, you will find that the best way to eliminate wordiness is through editing. You probably already have more editors than you need, but your best editor is still you. You can eliminate a lot of shuffling of papers up and down the channels of communication for approvals if you perform some surgery early on. When you edit, strike out the needless phrases and words that add no additional information to your work, and clarify with precise words.

First draft:
Bowler says he would like to attempt to schedule our very next company picnic to be held in or around the city of Wilmington in order to facilitate transportation by employees to the site.

Revised draft:
Bowler intends to schedule our company picnic in Wilmington to make it easier for employees to get to.

Naturally, you don't want to be brief to the point of abruptness, but you can see what exactness can do in the editing process. The key is to make sure that all important information is covered in enough detail to be useful to the reader.

Unfortunately, we often over-clarify in an attempt to make our messages understood; however, much of what we write is simply redundant or not needed for clarification.

The in-basket is completely full. (How can it be incompletely full?)

Johnson has come up with a most unique design for dismantling the employee pension fund. (It's either unique or it's not.)

The meeting date has been set for March 31, the last day of the month.

Emphasis

Organization of words within a sentence, sentences within a paragraph and paragraphs within a larger work are key to clear writing style. We typically organize based on the importance or weight assigned to these words, paragraphs or larger elements. By placing them in a prescribed order, we give the thoughts they represent emphasis.

Following are some of the standard methods for gaining emphasis.

- Place the most important words at the beginning or end of the sentence.

  Unemphatic:
  There was a terrific explosion in the Xerox room that shook the whole building. (There is an unemphatic word in an emphatic position.)

  Emphatic:
  A terrific explosion in the Xerox room shook the whole building.

- The end of a sentence is also a strong position for emphasis.

  Unemphatic:
  I know Tom was the one who stole the stapler.

  Emphatic:
  I know who stole the stapler—Tom.

- Increase emphasis by arranging ideas in the order of climax. Rank items in a series by order of importance, building from the least important to the most important.

  Jill was abrasive, lazy, undedicated, and basically ill-equipped to deal with her co-workers. (In this case, *ill-equipped* is used to sum up Jill's other attributes.)

  Watch out for an illogical ranking of ideas. If done unintentionally, this could cause some unwelcome hilarity.

  Because of his brief exploration of the casinos, Jerry became morose, despondent, melancholic, and lost twelve dollars.

- Gain emphasis by using the active rather than the passive voice.
  The active voice indicates that the "doer" of the action is the most important element in the sentence; the passive indicates the "receiver" is the most important.

  Unemphatic:
  Not much is being done to defray health benefit costs by the employer.

  Emphatic:
  The employer is not doing much to defray health benefit costs.

  Unemphatic:
  The study, accomplished by the Financial Department, showed a sharp decline in quarterly earnings.

  Emphatic:
  The Financial Department's study showed a sharp decline in quarterly earnings.

- Add emphasis by repeating key words or phrases. Such repetition not only adds emphasis, but often serves as a memory stimulant.

  False hopes were raised by these negotiations, false indications of changes which may not occur, and false expectations on the part of management as to its ability to fulfill false promises.

Don't mistake repetition for emphasis with redundancy. The difference is in the added strength of the statement.

- Add emphasis by balancing sentence construction. Balanced structure occurs when grammatically equal elements are used to point to differences or similarities. The usual construction is one in which two clauses indicate parallel elements.

  Knowing the health hazards and still smoking is freedom of choice; not knowing and smoking is victimization. Working here is boring; not working here is unemployment.

- Increase emphasis by varying sentence length. Constant sentence length creates monotony, and monotony creates disinterested readers. Although this rightly belongs under the longer elements we will cover next, you should consider the value of varying sentence length within the space of two or three sentences viewed as a unit.

  Content employees are dedicated, remain on the job longer, suffer fewer illnesses, create fewer problems, and rarely complain. In short, they are productive.

  I understand. You have a number of assignments due simultaneously, your secretary is out sick, your copier is broken, and you cannot get an outside line. I still need it now.

Writing Effective Sentences

Generally speaking, newsletter sentences are fairly short—for a couple of reasons. First, most readers find short sentences easier to understand. Second, the column width of most newsletters restricts sentence length somewhat. For example, a compound-complex sentence of 30 words might take up several inches of column space. A good rule of thumb for determining proper sentence length is to keep sentences at about 16 words long. Naturally, you're not going to count each word you write, but you get the idea. Short sentences are easier to read. This is also the case with word length. Nobody wants to stop and ponder a beautifully constructed word of eight syllables. On the other hand, too much of anything can lead to monotony. The key to effective sentences,

then, is to vary sentence length. Don't string together short, choppy sentences if they can be joined to form more interesting, compound sentences.

Monotonous:
The day begins when Harvey walks into the office. He sits down. He begins to type on his 1923 Underwood. It is the typewriter with the black, metal carriage. Harvey hates typing this early in the morning. He is never fully awake until at least 10 o'clock.

Varied:
The day begins when Harvey walks into the office, sits down and begins to type on his 1923 Underwood with the black, metal carriage. He hates typing this early in the morning, since he is never fully awake until at least 10 o'clock.

Notice that related ideas are linked as compound sentences. Linking unrelated ideas is an easy mistake, and sounds silly.

The day begins when Harvey walks into the office, sits down and begins to type on his 1923 Underwood. It is the typewriter with the black, metal carriage, and he hates typing this early in the morning.

(What does his typewriter having a black, metal carriage have to do with Harvey's dislike for early-morning typing?)

Another easy method of preventing monotony is to alter the beginnings of your sentences. In other words, don't always write in the subject-verb-object order. One of the best ways to vary this order is to use a subordinate clause first.

Because of his dislike for early-morning typing, Harvey never showed up at work prior to 10 o'clock.

Starting out early, Harvey walked two blocks at a brisk pace, then collapsed.

And don't forget—beginning a sentence with a conjunction is perfectly acceptable. Remember, though, that even conjunctions have meanings and usually infer that a thought is being carried over from a previous sentence.

Not only was Harvey later than usual, he was downright tardy. And I wasn't the only one to notice. (Implies that the information is being added to the previous thought.)

Not only was Harvey later than usual, he was downright tardy. But I was probably the only one who noticed. (Implies a contrast with the previous thought.)

With a little reworking, even a series of clauses strung together because they are related can be fixed up. Remember, conjunctions can be useful but overused.

Clauses strung-together:
Francine is always on time, and she frequently comes in before regular office hours, and she never leaves before quitting time.

Reworked into a complex sentence:
Francine is always on time, frequently coming in before regular office hours and never leaving before quitting time.

Clauses strung-together:
He ran down the street, and then he stopped at the main entrance, and he took a deep breath, and then he went inside.

Reworked into a compound predicate:
He ran down the street, stopped at the main entrance, took a deep breath, and went inside.

Creating Effective Paragraphs

As the sentence represents a single thought, so the paragraph represents a series of related sentences. There is no set number of sentences you should include in a paragraph; however, paragraph length is shorter today than in the past. Short paragraphs invite readership while long paragraphs "put off" the reader. The key, of course, is coherence which means that ideas must be unified. You can give unity to your paragraphs in several ways.

Make each sentence contribute to the central thought

The first sentence should generally express the theme of the paragraph. Although the thematic statement may actually appear anywhere in the paragraph, the strongest positions are at the beginning or the end; and the end is usually reserved for a transitional lead into the following paragraph.

Our annual operating budget is somewhat higher than expected due to the increase in state allocations to higher education this fiscal year. The result will probably be an increase in departmental allowances with the bulk of the increase showing up in the applied sciences. Although Arts and Sciences have been "holding up" well, we don't expect that they will be able to maintain this independence for long. As a result, their departmental budgets will also reflect this positive financial shift. Next year's outlook is a different story.

The lead sentence sets the theme for the entire paragraph, which is this year's budget. The final sentence indicates that the next paragraph will probably deal with next year's budget. What you want to avoid are unrelated sentences. If they are truly unrelated, then they deserve a paragraph of their own. If they are slightly related, then the relationship needs to be pointed out.

Arrange sentences in a logical order

Placing your sentences in logical order also implies that you must provide smooth transitions between them indicating their relationship. There are several ways to group sentences to show ranking.

* *Time order* and *chronological order* are sometimes synonymous, although chronological order often implies a direct mention of time or dates.

   The growth of communication in the northernmost regions of America was rapid and coincided roughly with the development of the land itself. In 1867, shortly following the Civil War, the first telegraph line was strung between Dawson Creek and Whitehorse. By the turn of the century, the lines had been extended through to Seattle, on the Southeastern coast, and Anchorage, along Prince William Sound. The First World War saw a flurry of development as military involvement increased in the region. And with this involvement, came a windfall of communication development which lasted until 1959.

   Time order is appropriate when explaining the steps involved in an action.

   Changing a printer ribbon is a relatively easy task, even for an office executive on a Saturday afternoon. First, push the ribbon-release button, and remove the old ribbon. Throw it away. Remove the new ribbon from its box, insert it into the slots provided for it and snap it down. Next comes the hard part. Pull out enough ribbon to place around the ribbon guides against the platen and thread it through the "slots" in the guides. You are now ready to print.

* *Space order* implies movement from one location to another: right to left, up to down, east to west, high to low, and so on.

   It rained all day yesterday. The weatherman had shown in glaring detail how the jet stream would carry the warm, moist low front from the snow-filled Cascades of the Northwest, over the Rockies, onto the plains, and finally into my backyard on the Atlantic coast. Apparently, it hadn't lost anything in the transition.

- *Order of climax* means that arrangement follows from the least important element to the most important element in the paragraph, or in ascending order of importance. Most of the time, the climax is the concluding sentence .

> If the clerical staff is uncomfortable with the workload, their immediate supervisors are the first to know. Middle managers are often reluctant to act on "workload" problems, but if pressured, will pass on complaints to executive officers. If the problem isn't handled to the satisfaction of all the parties involved by the time it reaches the executive level, a vice president may have to intervene; but pity the poor vice president who can't handle the problem. The president's office is a bastion of corporate sanctuary. Woe to him who would invade it.

When arranging sentences in order of climax, consider moving from the general to the specific or vice versa. Sometimes, moving from the familiar to the unfamiliar will soften the blow of dealing with a new idea.

> When we view each member of our office staff as an individual, we sometimes develop tunnel vision. We have to understand the larger picture in order to alleviate this problem. They are all a part of a much larger organism. Together they form departments. Departments form divisions. The larger company is composed of these divisions and the company is part of a much larger conglomerate. To take the analogy further, the conglomerate is only one of the hundreds of such groupings which help make our system of economics one of the most successful in the world.

Make logical transitions between sentences

Related ideas are given further unity by the use of logical transitions between sentences. A good transition usually refers to the sentences preceding it. Remember that a transitional word or phrase also has a meaning. Make sure the meaning adds to the understanding of the sentences or phrases preceding the transition.

> The floor plan was completely haphazard; furthermore, it appeared to crowd an already crowded office area. (Furthermore indicates an addition to the thought begun in the first clause.)

> Don Johnson was the first to try the new water fountain. On the other hand, he was the last to try

the potato salad at the last company picnic. (The phrase indicates contrast.)

> Fourteen employees were found to be in violation of company policies forbidding alcohol on the premises. Consequently, inspection of employee lockers will probably become commonplace. (Indicates that the second sentence is a result of actions in the first.)

> The rate of consumption has tripled over the past 18 months. In short, we have a severe problem. (Indicates a summary or explanation.)

> Jeremy covered the news desk. Meanwhile, Judy was busy copying the report before Wally returned and discovered it was missing. (An indication of time placement.)

One of the major problems with the use of transitional words and phrases is the reliance on a very few common groupings. Many people tend to use words like *however* to bridge every transitional creek. After a while, its use becomes monotonous. The answer? Vary transitional phrases. There's always another word you can use. Think about it.

The same applies to transitions between paragraphs. Use words and meanings which tie the thoughts together and form a smooth bridge between subject changes. After all, even dissimilar ideas need to be linked. If they were so dissimilar that you couldn't link them logically, they wouldn't belong in the same document.

Paragraph Development

There are a number of ways to develop your paragraphs to show unity and coherence. Notice that all of the examples below supply relevant details in support of a main idea.

You will often find that *developing a definition* will add unity to a paragraph.

> There are a number of ways of viewing the office water cooler; however, to a social scientist, it is a communal gathering place at which ideas and information are freely disseminated. It is an informal location, usually outside the territorial boundaries of any one employee and therefore accessible to all on an equal footing. It is the traditional "oasis," shared by any who are in need of water and at which all are free to share. To imply that this communal ground is the "property" of any one individual or department is to negate its real value. At it, we not only quench our thirsts for liquid, but also for information outside the formal boundaries of protocol.

Frequently, *classification* will serve to relate like ideas in a paragraph.

> There are three categories of clerical aid within the company. At the lowest rung of the pay scale is the clerk. A clerk's job includes light typing, no shorthand, much filing, and a tremendous amount of running around. Next up on the scale is the secretary. More typing is involved (at a much faster speed and with more accuracy), much filing, some shorthand, and a great deal of running around. At the top is the executive secretary. Typing is a must (at great speeds and accuracy), good shorthand, much filing, and more running around than the Stanford University track team.

The main idea can be made more coherent by *comparing* or *contrasting* it with a like idea.

> *Comparison:*
> A committee meeting is like a football game. The chair is the quarterback, and so is the directing force; however, the members are the players without whom no goal can be obtained. The key to the game plan, then, is to coordinate the players into a single unit with a single goal. The players must be made aware that a unified, or team, effort is integral to the accomplishment of that goal and that the quarterback is the director—not the coach. The director recommends; he does not command.

> *Contrast:*
> The typical office environment is orderly. Without order, little can be accomplished. Remember the recess periods of your school days? You were able to act freely, without consideration of the restrictive environment of the classroom. You were free to explore your voice, your agility, and your mastery of fast-paced games not suited to the indoors. Once inside, however, you were required to conform to the needs of the classroom—quiet, and order. Within these confines, work can be accomplished with a minimum of disturbance; and the accomplishment of that work is as important in an office environment as in a classroom.

One of the best ways to develop a paragraph and its central idea is to show cause and effect. Most things in life are a result of something else. For most of us, though, it takes some thought to trace that development.

> The so-called "open office" environment popular in newer buildings today has its roots in several trends. Since the mid-1970s, energy conservation has been a major concern in the United States. The open office requires less heat in the winter and less cooling in the summer, due mainly to the lack of walls. In the place of these walls, we now have "dividers" which, although they serve to mask sound, allow for the free circulation of air throughout an entire floor. In addition to conservation, open offices serve to homogenize workers by removing the traditional boundaries of high walls and closed doors. Employees now have access to each other through a network of openings, yet maintain the margin of privacy needed for individual productivity.

Obviously, a paragraph need not be restricted to any single method of development but can benefit from a combination approach. The key, of course, is to be clear, and any method which promotes clarity is a good one.

Unity and Logical Thinking

We've already learned something of unity by studying the placement of ideas in a logical order within sentences, paragraphs and whole compositions. Now, let's turn to logic itself. In writing, we should try to present our ideas as logically as possible so that our message seems as coherent and reasonable as possible to enhance understanding.

A major problem hindering understanding is semantics. Semantics involves the meanings of words individually and as they appear in a context. We should be extremely careful to select words that hold the same meaning for the reader as for us. One way to do this is to define terms which are likely to be either misunderstood or not understood at all.

> The major cause of antenna malfunction is the lack of foundation stability. The antenna cannot be properly anchored due to permafrost, a permanently frozen layer of ice and soil some three feet below the surface.

> All copy to be printed by the in-house print facility should be camera ready (properly sized, clean, and pasted in place).

Often a word can be defined by inserting a synonym.

> The altercation, or fight, lasted only three minutes.

> Sled dogs are not only used to running over muskeg—boggy terrain—but often relish the softness of the ground.

Generalizations

A generalization is an assumption based on insufficient evidence. It is a belief that what is true of a few members of a group (regardless of how you categorize that group or what it composes) is true of the entire group.

Women are lousy drivers.

Asians are inscrutable.

Blacks are great dancers.

Tall people are good basketball players.

Generalizations can be harmless or they can be dangerous. In writing, generalizations such as these should be avoided. If you do make a generalization, you must support it. This means that you must present adequate evidence that what you are saying is true for most of a particular group.

> The most striking figure given out at today's press conference indicates that four out of every five workers take some kind of drug on the job. A recent survey conducted by a Chicago-based firm within the various divisions of Associated Products Corporation shows that out of the 500 employees questioned, at least 400 indicated that they had taken drugs on the job. According to an Associated Products spokesman, the term *drugs* is defined to include prescription medicine, coffee, liquor, and the less traditional (and more notorious) illegal compounds.

In this paragraph, the writer has made a generalization, given supporting information, and defined terms. This would certainly be considered adequate support.

Cause and effect relationships

Logic is simply reason. What most people see as reasonable, they also assume is logical. It seems reasonable to assert that you *seldom* fall asleep before midnight, but any reasonable person would detect the unreasonableness in "I *never* fall asleep before midnight."

Illogical statements often result when the writer fails to set up adequately a *cause-and-effect* relationship. We can construct such a relationship based on either *inductive* or *deductive* reasoning. Inductive reasoning proceeds from the particular to the general. It implies a kind of generalization, in that generalizations are made based on specific evidence. That evidence is usually deemed sufficient to support a generalization. The results of scientific experimentation, for instance, are based on induction.

> A recent study by the Association for Scholastic Testing shows that school children between the ages of 7 and 14 learn quicker and absorb more knowledge when the lesson is interactive. Additional studies by National Employment Associates indicate that high school students with computer skills attain higher-paying jobs upon graduation. It is clear that computer training is fast becoming a necessary component in the education process.

The deductive process involves working from the general to the specific. Specifics are usually determined from generalizations. If you know, for instance, that a high fever usually accompanies influenza—and you have a high fever during the flu season—then you might seek a doctor's care. You have deduced a specific need from a generalization. You may not, in fact, have influenza, but you have made a valid decision based on deduction. The basic assumption, however, must be sound for our deductions to be valid.

> It is clear that computer training is fast becoming a necessary component in the education process. Through this training, students will become better equipped to deal with a burgeoning technology. Teachers will be eased of the responsibility to be all things to all students because of the interactive nature of computer learning. And students will ultimately benefit through higher-paying jobs.

As you can see, this deductive process was based on a previous inductive process. Most deductions are, in fact, based on previously collected information from which generalizations are made.

The inductive-deductive processes are prone to problems in construction. The following are the most common:

1. Because one item follows another chronologically, don't assume that the latter is a result of the former.

   > Helen came in late this morning, and everything has been going downhill since then.

   > Fred wouldn't be seeing Marge "on the side" if everything was all right at home.

2. Because one thing is true doesn't mean that you can infer another truth from it. This is commonly called a *non sequitur.*

   > The recent, sharp upturn in the economy will certainly result in lower unemployment.

   > Liz is something of an "air head." She'll never make it in the business world.

3. Don't beg the question. Sports interviewers frequently do this.

Champ? Was that the greatest match you ever fought or what? (Implies that the match *was* the greatest, thus biasing the response.)

Begging the question assumes the truth of a statement you are trying to verify.

Janice snuck in at half past eight this morning. What do you suppose she's up to? (Maybe she slept late and isn't up to anything.)

4. Don't set up an either/or situation unless it really is one.

Either you're going with me to the meeting or you're not. (Obviously a reasonable statement.)

Either you're on my side or you're not. (Why can't I see the value in two different arguments without being on anyone's side?)

This is often called the all-or-nothing fallacy because it sets up a false dilemma ignoring the fact that other variables or possibilities exist.

Dedicated employees either come to work on time or they're simply not dedicated.

School systems are either innovators, because they acquire and use computers, or they're traditional-ists who choose to ignore the future.

Finally, never argue a point that you can't back up with facts simply because you believe it to be true. Although much of what we believe is based on personal predispositions formed throughout our life-times, it is never too late to learn something new or to add facts to our existing knowledge.

If you are to be a good, persuasive writer, you must learn to be objective. For most writers, subjec-tivity indicates that you have a stake in what is being argued or, at least, a personal opinion. Opinions are best left for newspaper columnists or editors who are paid to express their opinions. Objective writing is the hallmark of the logical (reasonable) writer. If you present the facts objectively, and they support your argument or point of view (whether that point of view is one which is personally held or not) your argument will be logically sound.

Planning and Writing Effective Articles

A sentence usually contains a single idea. A para-graph contains a number of sentences related by a single theme. So too, an article for a newsletter contains a series of paragraphs unified by a single theme and related by logical transitions.

For many of us, the writing is the easy part—planning is the snag. And the toughest part of planning is deciding exactly what to say and what to leave out. Most of us tend to overwrite. In the words of one observer: "Writing is like summer clothing—it should be long enough to cover the subject, but brief enough to be interesting."

The first task in writing, then, is to choose your subject and limit yourself to the information needed to cover it. There are several ways to accomplish this. One of the easiest ways is to work from a very general topic to a specific topic.

banking ➔ withdrawing and making deposits ➔ avoiding waiting in lines ➔ using automatic tellers ➔ using automatic tellers in the lobby

This may seem simple, but it does help clear your thoughts and crystallize your ideas through the act of putting them on paper. Naturally, the theme of any piece is intimately tied to its purpose. If, for instance, your purpose is to encourage patrons to use the automatic tellers in the banking lobby, it may be necessary to come directly to the point in your pitch. However, in doing so, you will probably use one of the traditional writing approaches.

Most of us remember our high school English classes in which we were taught to write various papers for different purposes. Among the most common approaches were:

Exposition—used to inform or explain

Argumentation—used to convince or persuade

Narration—used mostly for entertainment value

Description—used to explain through verbal "pictures"

In newsletter writing, narration is the least fre-quently used except in feature-type stories. The other methods are often used and combined to present information to readers. A lot depends on whether you are trying to be persuasive, or are simply presenting information—the two most common goals of news-letter writing.

The Central Idea

Once you have decided on the purpose of a particular piece, you should try to write down a central idea in a single sentence or *thesis statement*. Suppose, for instance, that your goal is to convince employees to come to work on time each day. This will be a persuasive piece. The method you have chosen to use might be exposition, which will inform your employees. What is your thesis statement? It might be something like this:

> Coming to work on time puts you in step with the other employees who work with you, gives you time to adjust to your daily environment, allows you the leisure of some pre-work interaction with others, and impresses your employer.

So, in a single sentence, you have set down several controlling ideas which can now be elaborated upon. The next step is to develop a working plan or rough outline.

The Outline

Before you begin an outline, it helps to put down some ideas which are appropriate to the topic. These can be in the form of a simple list. For instance, to continue the previous example, perhaps you have decided to stress promptness by comparing the benefits of being on time with the disadvantages of coming in late.

Advantages of coming to work on time

— Allows time to adjust to daily routine
— Allows time for interaction with fellow workers
— Impresses employer
— Allows time to eat breakfast or have coffee
— Allows time to read through the paper

Disadvantages of coming in late

— You are rushed into daily routine without adjustment period
— You have no time to interact informally with fellow workers
— You do not impress employer
— You have no time for breakfast or coffee
— You have no time to read the paper

Now you have a starting point. It might be that you want to address the points one by one, covering the advantages first, then the disadvantages. Or perhaps you want to compare the advantages with the disadvantages one at a time.

Outline Organization

Outlines are extremely useful as a checklist of key points. You may use the outline simply to check your final written piece against to make sure you have covered all points (regardless of final order), or you may have each point represent a complete paragraph

or section of your finished document in the order presented in the outline.

In either case, make sure that your ideas are related within each paragraph and that each paragraph follows logically from the previous one. The same methods you used to arrange your sentences within the paragraph can be used to arrange your paragraphs within a larger composition: time order, space order, or order of climax.

Newsletter Style

Because newsletters inform and entertain, articles should be written in an entertaining way. Usually, news about the company or strictly informational pieces utilize the standard news story style. Employee-interest pieces tend to use the feature story style. Feature-type articles for newsletters should be complete, with a beginning and an ending.

Straight News Style

Before we get into a discussion of how to *write* straight news, let's look at exactly what news *is*.

A journalistic definition of news can be very useful if you're attempting to provide pure information to a target public. Journalists all seem to agree on several major criteria for judging whether something is news or not.

- Consequence. Does it educate or inform? Is it important to lifestyle or the readers' understanding or ability to cope with current events? Does it have any moral or social importance? Basically, is it something your readers would want to know?

- Interest. Is it unusual, entertaining information? Does it arouse emotions? Does it have human interest value? People like to read about other people like themselves.

- Timeliness. Ever wonder why news is called news instead of olds? People like to read about topics with currency. If it isn't new itself, it should take a new angle on an old topic or, at the very least, add something to a current issue.

- Proximity. Does it have a local interest angle? This is especially important for in-house newsletters. The information presented should usually pertain to events affecting the employees and occurring locally (i.e., within the organization).

- Prominence. Does it concern people or events well known by the readers? Like it or not, readers respond to celebrities or events that are already in the news. Focusing on a prominent person or event can serve as an angle to call attention to other news.

If your stories contain any of the above elements, they are probably newsworthy (at least from a journalistic perspective), which means they will stand a good chance of interesting your target audience. Once you have determined that you have something newsworthy to say to your readers, the next decision has to do with how you say it.

A great many writers are unfamiliar with what journalists call "straight news." More than anything else, this phrase refers to a style of writing, common to newspapers, known as the *inverted pyramid.* Technically, this means putting all the pertinent information needed for a cursory understanding of the story theme in the opening paragraph, then working in a descending order of importance through to the end of the story.

There are several reasons for the growth of this fairly peculiar style of writing. First, it allows busy editors to cut a story from the bottom up without having to worry about eliminating any critical information. Because newspaper stories are measured in column inches, every inch counts. An editor in a hurry, and with only six inches of space to fill, can safely cut a story written in inverted pyramid from the bottom up until it fits. The other reason most cited is the penchant of newspaper readers to read *only* the first couple of paragraphs of any given story. If you are able to pack most of the pertinent information into the first few paragraphs, then readers are able to scan stories (which most do anyway).

Whatever the reason, the inverted pyramid makes sense for shorter, straight news stories. *Straight news* also implies that the story is free of embellishment and bias and comes straight to the point. It doesn't require a fancy lead-in or an elaborate close. Consider the following straight news story that appeared in a student newsletter.

Counselors' Association 'hires' PRSSA

The American Mental Health Counselors Association (AMHCA), a representative association for community counselors, has hired PRSSA to develop and implement a series of communication projects. The projects began last spring when a committee of five PRSSA members developed a PR plan for AMHCA. The comprehensive plan is targeted at present and potential members. The two main objectives of the plan are to strengthen AMHCA as a membership organization and to create awareness of AMHCA among its target audiences.

After receiving approval for the plan from AMHCA board members, PRSSA was asked to develop more specific projects. This fall, a committee of eight PRSSA members worked on two projects. The first was to develop a logo and slogan for AMHCA to be used on all informational materials. The logo, now finished, symbolically represents the safety and shelter of a hearth, utilizing a stylized Hebrew symbol for home and well being.

The second project involved redesigning an existing AMHCA brochure. The committee developed a whole new layout and cover design.

The committee will also continue to develop projects during winter and spring terms. The main project will be a series of brochures for AMHCA. The brochures will range from information on membership to information on mental health counseling. Other upcoming projects include writing a series of public service announcements to be broadcast nationally for Mental Health Week in March.

"Overall, the project has been a great experience for all of us involved," said committee chairperson, Wendy Wintrode.

Notice that the story opens with what journalists refer to as a lead. The most common type of lead found in a straight news story is known as a *summary lead;* it answers several important questions about the story: who, what, when, where, why, and how. Most journalists know that it is almost impossible, and unnecessary, to try to include all of these elements; however, the most germane points should be covered. Remember, that although a lead is typically the first paragraph of a story, it sometimes continues into the second paragraph as well. Look again at the lead (first two paragraphs) in the preceding story.

Who? The American Mental Health Counselors Association.

What? Has hired PRSSA to develop and implement a series of communication projects.

When? The projects began last spring.

Where? Unless there is a specific need to pinpoint the place, this element isn't needed.

Why? This is usually the most difficult to explain and least often appears in the lead, but is expanded upon as the story progresses. In this case, however, the answer is the final sentence in the second paragraph.

How? The answer to this one, like the answer to "why," is usually found later in the story. In this case, it is developed throughout the remainder of the piece.

Although the most common straight news lead is the summary lead, other types are also used—the delayed lead for example. In this type of lead, the point of the story is delayed slightly while an interesting angle is developed or a character is set up through a quote, or a scene is set through description. For example:

> School children all over the country will soon be learning the three *R*'s on a *C* thanks to a $1 million grant from Associated Products Corporation (APC). APC has recently donated the money to set up a fund for the purchase of educational computers that, when combined with APC's newest software, will teach reading, 'riting and 'rithmetic in a whole new way—on computers.

If this reads less like straight news than the preceding story's lead, then you've discovered why straight news rarely uses a delayed lead. Delayed leads most often appear in feature-type stories because they are excellent ways to set a scene, introduce a character or simply attract and hold attention.

Feature style

The feature story produces what the name implies—a feature. Its style is more relaxed, takes a point of view, discusses issues, people, and places. It creates ambience by using "color"; that is, it uses words creatively to describe what is happening. In a straight news story, the focus is on an unbiased presentation of facts; in a feature story, the emphasis is on description. Consider the following feature story based on the straight news story above. Only the first few paragraphs and the closing are included here.

> ### Clearing up the confusion over mental health
> What's the difference between a therapist, psychologist, psycho-therapist, psychiatrist, and a counselor? If you don't know, you're among the millions of people who are confused about the multi-tiered mental health counseling field.
>
> In an effort to clear up some of the confusion, the American Mental Health Counselors Association (AMHCA) has "hired" a university student group to produce a public information campaign for them. The Public Relations Student Society of America (PRSSA) at the University of Oregon has been retained by the Association to develop a program of information that will better define the various roles contained under the umbrella term "mental health counselor." Jane Weiskoff, regional director of AMHCA says that the confusion seems to stem from a misconception over what constitutes a "counselor."
>
> "In the mental health profession, there is a perceived hierarchy," she says. "Psychiatrists are seen as being at the apex of the field with psychologists, therapists, and other counselors falling into place under them. We'd like to clarify and possibly alter that perception."
>
> Part of the plan, which has already been produced and approved, is to establish and maintain contact with current AMHCA members through a series of brochures and an updated and redesigned association newsletter. These informational pieces will carry the message that mental health counselors come in a variety of forms with a variety of educational and training backgrounds, and that each of these levels is suited to certain types of counseling. The goal is to establish credibility for certain of the counseling functions not fully recognized at this time by the general public and the mental health profession....
>
> ... If committee chairperson Wendy Wintrode has her way, the term "mental health counseling" will soon have a completely different, and definitely more expanded, definition. "We want everyone to know that professionalism doesn't begin and end with a small clique at the top—it is the guiding force behind the entire field of mental health counseling."

As you can see, this story is considerably different from the straight news version. The facts are still here, but the focus is on creative information presentation. The lead is a question (a typical delayed lead strategy). Answering that question becomes part of the story itself. Quotes are used liberally. They not only validate and lend credibility to the subject being discussed, they add *human interest*. Human interest is rather loosely referred to as anything that highlights the human element in a story. We too often associate it with syrupy stories about children or animals; however, human interest ranges from simple inclusion of the human "voice" in a story to an entire profile featuring a single person. The following lead is from a profile on a corporate legal department and its head. Notice how the scene is set before the subject is introduced.

Sitting behind a cluttered desk, boxes scattered around the office—some still unopened—is the new head of Associated Products Corporation's Law Department, Ed Bennett. Ed is a neat man, both in appearance and in speech. As he speaks about the "new" Law Department, he grins occasionally as though to say, "Why take the time to interview someone as unimportant as a lawyer?" That grin is deceiving because, to Ed and the other attorneys who work for Associated Products Corporation, law is serious business.

The profile

The profile is most typically a feature story written specifically about a person, a product or service, or an organization or some part of it. It literally profiles the subject, listing facts, highlighting points of interest, and—most importantly—tying them to the organization. Regardless of the subject of your article, you are writing for a specific organization and the article must have some bearing on it—direct or indirect.

The personality profile

Personality profiles are popular because people still like to read about other people, whether these people are just like them (so they can easily relate) or very different (so they can aspire or admire). Of course, a personality profile should do more than just satisfy human curiosity, it should inform the reader of something important about the organization itself by putting it in the context of a biographical sketch. For example, this lead was written for a brief profile on an award-winning engineer:

When Francis Langly receives the Goodyear Medal this spring, it will represent the symbolic crowning of a lifetime of dedication to the field of chemistry. Awarded by the Rubber Division of the American Chemical Society, the Goodyear medal is the premier award for work in the field of specialty elastomers—an area that Langly helped pioneer. When Langly makes his medalist's address to the gathering in Indianapolis in May, his comments will be a reflection of almost 50 years of innovation and development which began in 1938 when he joined Rogers Experimental Plastics Company as a research chemist.

What does this say about the organization? It implies, for one thing, that the company is obviously a good one to have such a well-respected person work for it for so long. A profile like this calls attention to the merits of the organization by calling attention to someone who has something to do with it—or, in

some cases, to someone who benefits from its services or products. Consider the following lead:

Guy Exton is a superb artist. His oils have hung in galleries all over the country. But, for nearly five years, he couldn't paint anything. In order to paint, you typically need fingers and a hand, and Guy lost his right hand in an auto accident in 1983. But now, thanks to a revolutionary new elastomer product developed by Rogers Experimental Plastics Company, Guy is painting again. He can grip even the smallest of his paint brushes and control the tiniest nuance through the use of a special prosthetic device designed by Medical Help, Inc. of Franklin, New York. The device, which uses REP's "Elastoflex" membrane as a flexible covering, provides minute control of digits through an electro-mechanical power pack embedded in the wrist.

One of the most common types of personality profiles is the Q & A (question-and-answer format). This style typically begins with a brief biographical sketch of the person being interviewed, hints at the reason for the interview, and sets the scene by describing the surroundings in which the interview took place. For the remainder of the piece, speakers are tagged Q or A. Sometimes, the interviewer is designated with the magazine's name (for example, *The Corporate Connection* might be shortened to *CC.*). Likewise, the interviewee might be designated by her or his last name.

The descriptive narrative tells the story of the individual being profiled from a second-person point of view. Naturally, quotes from the subject may be included, but sometimes a successful profile is simply a biographical sketch, and won't necessarily need them.

The product or service profile

Profiling a product or service means describing it in a way that is unusual in order to draw attention to the product and the organization. This is often done in subtle ways. For example, the personality profile lead on the artist Guy Exton is really a way of mentioning a product. Clearly this doesn't detract from the human interest angle, but it does accomplish a second purpose (probably the primary purpose) which is publicity. The same techniques you use in other article types can be used in profiling products. The Q & A, most typically used for personality profiles, can often double as a way to profile a new product through a personal interview.

The organizational profile

In the organizational profile, an entire organization or some part of it is profiled. The organizational profile and the personality profile are accomplished much the same way, except that you need to interview a number of key people in the unit you are profiling in order to obtain a complete picture of that unit.

The Details of Writing

The Lead

A good lead is just as important to a newsletter piece as to a news story. It's still the hook that entices the reader into reading the complete piece.

Although to a great extent newsletters depend on design to attract readers, the well-written article is what draws them back. Like any good story, the newsletter article should have a definite beginning, middle, and end. Of course, if the article is written like a straight news story (inverted pyramid) it will begin with a tight lead and taper off as it progresses. In both cases, the lead is the key.

Your lead must tell the reader what the story is about. It is not necessary to cram everything into the lead; however, you must include enough information so that the reader doesn't have to search for your topic. For straight news articles, the lead needs to come right to the point with the facts up front. For a feature, the delayed lead may be used. In this type of lead you create ambience, then place your story within the environment you have created. Other techniques include leading with a quote and placing it in context, or using metaphor, simile, analogy, anecdote, or other interest-getting devices. Although most of us forgot these literary tools the minute we left freshman composition, we shouldn't assume that good writing can get along without them. Look over the following literary uses of metaphor, simile, and analogy and then compare them with the newsletter article leads that follow them.

- A **metaphor** literally says that one thing *is* another:

  ...cauliflower is nothing but a cabbage with a college education. (Mark Twain)

  Tree you are,
  Moss you are,
  You are violets with wind above them. (Ezra Pound)

- A **simile** says that one thing is *like* another:

  Though I must go, endure not yet
  A breach, but an expansion,
  Like gold to airy thinness beat. (John Donne)

  In time of peril, like the needle to the lodestone, obedience, irrespective of rank, generally flies to him who is best fitted to command. (Herman Melville)

- An **analogy** makes hard-to-understand ideas easier to grasp by placing them in reader context; or, in the following example, by making a point of view more understandable through humor:

  Soap and education are not as sudden as a massacre, but they are more deadly in the long run. (Mark Twain)

The following leads show even the most mundane subject is of interest to someone and deserves the most interesting treatment possible. Pay particular attention to the number of scene-setting or descriptive words used in these leads.

Leading with a quote:

"Steelhead trout are an elitist fish; they're scarce, big, beautiful, and they're good fighters," says Bob Hooton, Fish and Wildlife biologist responsible for steelhead on Vancouver Island. (*Salmonid*, newsletter of the Canadian Dept. of Fisheries and Oceans)

Leading with an anecdote:

When teachers, lawyers and other well-seasoned professionals tell you to leave work at the office, take their advice. If you don't, you will end up sleeping with your work—and only with your work—every night. (*PReview*, newsletter of the University of Delaware PRSSA)

If past experience is an indication, the telephones at our Client Services Center in Laurel, Maryland, will rarely stop ringing on December 16. That day the Center begins accepting calls for appointments to review diaries from the Fall 1982 radio survey. (*Beyond the Ratings*, national newsletter of Arbitron)

April 1st marks the beginning of a new era in banking—and a new dawn of satellite communications. On that day a clerk in Citicorp's Long Island, N.Y. office will make history by picking up the phone and dialing a Citicorp office in California. (*Telecommunications Week*, national newsletter published by Business Research Publications, Inc.)

Leading with an analogy:

Your living room may be a high-crime area—if that's where you watch TV. A study to be published in October by The Media Institute finds that TV crime is far more violent than real life crime…. (*Business and the Media*, national newsletter published by The Media Institute)

You've heard the adage "two heads are better than one." What about 40? The Division's plants, more than 40 of them, are "putting their heads together" in the form of a Division-wide information sharing project recently released. (*Action Connection*, employee newsletter of Weyerhaeuser Packaging Division)

Like almost everything else, the image of the chemist is changing. Once thought of by many as a world of burbling test tubes and vials of questionable looking liquids, chemistry is changing to meet the technical and environmental needs of the microchip age. (*Current News*, employee newsletter of Delmarva Power)

Setting the scene:

It's 5:30 on a Monday afternoon and you've just finished one of *those* days. Not only did the never-ending pile of work on your desk cease to go away, but you just received two additional "A" priority assignments. On top of that, the phones wouldn't stop ringing and the air conditioning wouldn't start working, even though the temperature hit 95. (*Spectra*, employee newsletter of the SAIF Corporation)

It's pretty quiet at Merwin Dam in southwest Washington. Two generators are running. The water level is down a little so folks along the reservoir can repair some docks while the weather stays nice. For the 21 people working at the dam, it's business as usual. But, there is a subtle change. There's no longer a threat hanging over their heads that Pacific might not own or operate the dam. The court case that could have forced Pacific to give it up was finally resolved at the end of February. (*Pacific Power Bulletin*, employee newsletter of Pacific Power)

Cramming Mom, Dad, the kids and perhaps a pet together in a car, camper, cabin or hotel for a two-week vacation will either bring day-to-day tensions to a boil—or draw everyone wonderfully closer. The key to a successful vacation is preparation. With adequate planning, you can return home a stronger family—not a carload of bitter enemies. (*Bottom Line/Personal*, a digest-type newsletter for subscribers published by Boardroom Reports, Inc.)

Leading with a metaphor/simile:

Recession fears faded like Presidential Candidates this spring. Markets were jolted by the February employment release which showed an increase in employment of over 500,000…. The mood has gone full circle as there is renewed focus on the strength of the economy with its 5.4 percent unemployment rate, and the whiff of higher inflation in the air. (*Northwest Business Barometer*, a quarterly economic review for customers from U.S. Bank)

The Body

Once the lead is conceived and written, the story must elaborate on it. If possible, make points one by one, explaining each as you go. Get the who, what, when, where, and how down in the most interesting way possible—but get to the point early.

The clearest way to write an article is to work from the general to the specific. Begin with general descriptions of your subject and work to specific information one point at a time. This approach is legitimate regardless of the level of your point. For example, it holds for the overall theme of your article, and it holds for each subpoint supporting your overall theme.

Let's say, for instance, that you are writing about a new line of software. You might begin by introducing the software in general terms.

> Traxton Electronics newest software package isn't aimed at the busy executive looking for a faster method of dictation. Nor is it aimed at the average, desk-bound office worker seeking increased productivity. The new software is aimed directly at someone about four feet tall, who spends up to seven hours a day staring at a blackboard and listening to a grownup expound the virtures of everything from math to history. In short, it is designed specifically for seventh graders.

From this general introduction, you move to a still general but slightly more specific description.

> Traxton's "New Classroom" software has been developed to provide a complete curriculum package for junior high school students, covering subjects in six areas.

As you progress through the article, specifics should develop gradually until the general topic has been completely fleshed out.

> All of the primary subject areas are covered, including math, history and science. The level of each

subject area ranges from beginning to advanced and allows both problem learners and faster learners an opportunity to learn and develop at their own pace....

The History package includes a series of interactive programs that lead students through simulated conversations with important historical personalities. For example, "Talking with the President," allows students to carry on an interactive discussion with seven presidents of the United States whose policies or actions helped shape the future of the country.

As already mentioned, one of the best ways to develop a coherent feature article is to work from an outline. An outline lists your main points and supporting subpoints, and allows you to organize them into a coherent whole with a logical progression from general to specific.

Remember, the body of the article must support your main point, hopefully already made in the lead, and elaborate on it. Anticipate questions your reader might have, and answer them satisfactorily. Remember to utilize logical transitional devices when moving from one point to another. Subheads, while technically sound, don't alleviate the need for thoughtful transitions.

Back up your statements with facts and support your generalizations with specifics. Although newsletter articles seldom use footnotes, they are not completely inappropriate. Usually, however, citation can be taken care of in the body of the text. If, however, you are quoting someone, be sure to use attribution. Don't just give the person's name. A person's title or job may lend your quote authority if that person is considered knowledgeable or an expert on your subject.

In a feature, cover the news angle in a more people-oriented way. Use color, paint word pictures to help readers hear, smell, and feel the story. If your story has a possible human-interest angle, use it. It helps your readers relate to the message through other human beings. Above all, don't be afraid to experiment with different approaches to the same topic. Try a straight news approach, then a human-interest angle or maybe a dramatic dialogue. In every case, try to make your story specific to your audience. Remember, they are major players in your scripts, in reality or vicariously.

The Close

The most powerful and most remembered parts of your article will be the beginning and the end. Good endings are as difficult to write as good beginnings. However, there are only a few ways to wrap up an article and bring your readers to closure (a sense that they are satisfactorily finished): summarize your main points (summary ending), refer back to the beginning in some way (referral ending), or call for action (response ending), although this last is rarely used in magazine article writing. Consider the following leads with their respective endings.

Posing a question in the lead/summary ending

Lead:
Name the oldest civilization in North America. If your anthropological information is such that you pinpointed the Aleut peoples of Alaska, you are both well-informed and correct.

Ending:
"Intellect and knowledge, technical skills, helpfulness, and concern for the truth are still the hallmarks of Aleut culture," observes the Connecticut anthropologist, Laughlin. Such virtues are valuable assets, ever more useful as the 21st century approaches, and the bedrock on which the best that is Aleut may find permanence and continuity. (Richard C. Davids for *Exxon USA*)

Setting the scene in the lead/referral ending

Lead:
For one emotion-filled moment on July 28, when the Olympic torch is lit atop the Los Angeles Memorial Coliseum, this sprawling California city will be transformed into an arena of challenges and champions. But that magic event, shared with two billion television viewers around the world, will mark more than the beginning of the XXIII Summer Olympic Games.

Ending:
For GTE employees worldwide, perhaps some of that special thrill can be shared by just watching the Games on television, and knowing that whenever gymnastics, fencing, water polo, volleyball, yachting or tennis are televised, those images and sounds will have passed through the hands of 425 fellow employees—GTE's Team at the Olympics. (Bill Ferree for *GTE Together*)

An anecdotal lead/summary and referral ending

Lead:
In 1737, Benjamin Franklin wrote in the *Pennsylvania Gazette* of an auroral display so red and vivid that some people thought it was a fire and ran to help put it out.

Ending:

Although the effects of auroral activity on the lower levels of the earth's atmosphere are more apparent, the effects on the upper atmosphere are not, and we are only now beginning to understand them. With more understanding, we may eventually view the aurora with a more scientific eye, but until that day comes, it still remains the greatest light show on earth.

Editing Your Articles

The primary reason for editing newsletter articles is lack of space. Since newsletters are typically small-format publications, you never seem to have enough space to fit the amount of information you have gathered. Of course, the opposite is true, too. If you haven't gathered enough information to fill out your newsletter, you run the risk of creating a spotty publication full of empty space. Larger-than-normal graphics can help here, but the best solution is to make sure you have enough story ideas to fill your newsletter with written information, not just pretty pictures.

The freewheeling attitude of some article writers (especially novices) also contributes to the need to edit. Since many writers of basic company publications end up dealing with pretty dry topics, an assignment to do an article for the house newsletter might be seen as an invitation to creativity. This usually leads, in turn, to a looser style, wordiness, and lack of organization. Whatever the reason, even the best-written article can benefit from intelligent editing.

A quick word here about the term "intelligent editing." This implies that you are being edited by (or are yourself, if you're doing the editing) someone who knows something about writing—both grammar and style. Unfortunately, as many of us who have worked on newsletters for years know, editors are often chosen because of their position within the organizational hierarchy (or the obligatory approval chain) and not for their literary talents.

One of the best (if perhaps a bit cynical) rules of thumb for dealing with "inexpert" editing is to ignore about 80 percent of it. You quickly get to recognize what is useful to you and what is not. Basically, editing that deals with content balance and accuracy is usable. Most strictly "editorial" comment is not. A vice president's penchant for ellipses or a manager's predilection for using *which* instead of *that* are strictly stylistic preferences (and often ungrammatical).

In many cases, even if you do ignore these obligatory edits, these same "editors" won't remember what they said when the final piece comes out. A rule-of-thumb for most experienced writers is to try to avoid being edited by non-editors. If you can't, at least see how much you can safely ignore.

As for editing yourself, there are several methods for cutting a story that is too long, even if you don't think you can possibly do without a single word.

- Look at your beginning and end to see if they can be shortened. Often we write more than we need by way of introduction or closing when the real meat is in the body of the article.

- If you used a lot of quotes, cut the ones that are even remotely "fluff." Keep only those that contribute directly to the understanding of your story.

- Are there any general descriptions that, given later details, may be redundant? Cut them.

- Are there any details that are unnecessary given earlier general descriptions? Cut them. (Be careful not to cut both the general description and the details.)

- Are there any people who can be left out? For instance, will one expert and her comments be enough or do you really need that second opinion?

- Finally, look for wordiness—instances in which you used more words than you needed. This type of editing hurts the most since you probably struggled over that wording for an hour and went through your thesaurus twenty times.

Your goal is to get the article into the size you need without losing its best parts or compromising your writing style. Good luck.

(Text continues on page 130.)

Exhibit 8.1

Take a close look at the article on these two pages and notice to what degree the edited sections add to the article. If they add indispensable information, they shouldn't be edited out.

These four paragraphs, although adding additional information, can be cut without loss to the overall information impact of the story since they deal with details that we can actually get along without. Naturally, given enough space, we would opt to leave the story intact.

Whatever you do, don't edit out the purpose for writing the article in the first place. In this case, it's mention of a product.

DGA Wins UL Certificate

The sign on the door reads "Grade 'A' UL Central Station." To the people at Dallas General Alarm (DGA) and to the hundreds of businesses and homes they protect, this means the availability of some of the best alarm and intrusion detection systems in the country. In fact, almost every improvement made at DGA over the past few years has had as its goal the attainment of UL certification.

In 1924, Underwriters Laboratories, Inc. began offering a means of identifying burglar alarm systems that met acceptable minimum standards. The installing company can apply for investigation of their services and, if found qualified, may be issued UL certification.

To the customer, this certification can mean a large reduction (sometimes up to 70 percent) in insurance premiums, depending on the exact grade and extent of the UL-approved service used.

However, Dallas General Alarm doesn't sell only UL service. "We sell and lease our systems on the merit of the system and the particular need of the customer," says Dave Michaels, Director of Quality Control for DGA. "Of course, those who do have the UL Grade 'A' system installed can usually pay the extra cost entailed with the savings they make on insurance alone."

What makes this Grade "A" system so effective that insurance companies charging sometimes thousands of dollars a year in coverage are willing to cut 40, 60 or even 70 percent off their premiums?

"The UL people are really tight on their standards," says Michaels. "They conduct a number of 'surprise' inspections of DGA on a regular basis. If we fall down in any of their requirements, we get our certification cancelled."

DGA has its own tight security system consisting of television monitors on all doors and verbal contact with people entering their offices. The central control room is always manned and locked. A thick, glass window allows the operators on duty to check personally all people entering the premises. Other UL requirements are extra fire proofing for the building itself and a buried cable containing the thousands of telephone lines used to monitor the various alarm systems which run out of the building. The cable is unmarked, preventing the adventurous burglar from cutting it and thus disabling the hundreds of systems served by DGA.

The over-a-thousand customers who either lease or buy alarm or detection systems from DGA range from some of the biggest businesses in Dallas to private residences. In addition, all of the schools in the Dallas area are monitored from the DGA central station against break-in and vandalism.

The monitoring devices, located at the DGA central control, vary from a simple paper tape printout to actual voice communication with the premises being protected. For instance, the card-key system used by Atlantic Richfield Company allows access to certain areas through the use of a magnetic card inserted into a slot in the door. Access is forbidden to those lacking the proper clearance and the number and time of the attempted access are printed out at the DGA central station.

By far the most impressive system is the *Hyper Guard Sound System* which allows the central station operators actually to listen into a building or home once the system is activated. If the building is entered, the sound sensitive system is activated, causing an alarm to go off at the DGA central station. By the use of microphones installed on the premises, the DGA operators can then determine the presence of an intruder. The owners, of course, sign in and out verbally when they open and close. Most of these customers also carry the special "holdup" feature of this system which allows them to trigger, unnoticed, an alarm in the event of a robbery.

"We tried out a lot of other sound-activated systems," says Michaels, "but the 'Hyper Guard' made by Associated Products Corporation is the best I've ever seen." Michaels says that the Hyper Guard system is probably 20 times more sensitive than most other brands DGA has tried. "And, in our business, sensitivity is a key component of a successful detection."

Once an alarm is received from any of the hundreds of points serviced by DGA, it is only a matter of seconds before security guards, police, ambulance or fire department are notified and on their way. DGA maintains direct, no-dial lines to all of these agencies.

DGA currently contracts with Smith-Loomis which dispatches two or three security guards to each of DGA's calls. "Our average response time is under 4 1/2 minutes," says Dave Michaels. "Of course, we often have to wait on the owner to show up to let us in." Michaels says that if DGA keeps a key to the premises, another 10 percent often can be taken off on insurance premiums because it allows a faster response time and a higher apprehension rate. "Recently, we got two apprehensions in three alarms at a local pharmacy," he says. "We roll on every suspicious alarm. UL only allows one opening and one closing time per business unless prearranged," says Michaels. "This way, we know exactly when there should be nobody on the premises."

DGA offers a number of different systems. Some respond to motion, and some to sound. There are systems with silent alarms and systems with on-sight alarms fit to frighten the toughest intruder. DGA also handles smoke and heat detection systems. But, the key to a UL Grade "A" certified system, says Michaels, is the central control. "That's the added factor in a Grade 'A' system," he says. "We know immediately when something has occurred, and we respond."

Frank Collins, president of Southwestern Gemstones, Inc., has had his Grade "A" system since September. "I was robbed last year of over $400,000 worth of merchandise," he says, "and I was uninsured. That won't happen again." Collins is impressed with his system.

From his office in the Calais Building, Collins can watch everyone who enters his showroom via television monitor. A telephone allows visitors to identify themselves from outside the front door before entry. The showroom has an impressive array of precious gems and gold and a great many antique art objects, frequently hand-made turquoise and silver pieces. "I got the complete works," Collins says, "audio sensors, motion sensors, TV monitor, everything," resulting in a good-sized cut in his necessarily high insurance premiums.

For the many high-risk businesses served by Dallas General Alarm, the UL Grade "A" system seems to be the answer.

"We don't expect more than a couple of hundred customers for the UL system over the next few years," says Dave Michaels, "but that's all right. Our customers know their needs and they know that they can't get a better system for the price." Collins smiles. "For the three or four dollars a day this system costs, they couldn't even afford a guard dog."

Here is a good example of an extra character who can be deleted without substantial loss to the story. Although this kind of testimony adds credibility to any story, in this case, the story is about DGA, and their spokesperson actually provides the first-person credibility needed for the purpose—which is to get one of the products mentioned.

Exhibit 8.2

As you can see from these layouts, the unedited version of the DGA story (opposite) takes up approximately one and a half pages including pull quote, photo and caption. The edited version takes up only a single page including a reduced photo, edited caption, and the full-sized pull quote.

Exhibit 8.3

On the next three pages are two lists. The first (page 128) is a standard list of copy-editing markes to be used if you edit your copy before delivering it to the printer or typesetter for typesetting. Use a red pencil to make these marks in the text of your original manuscript. The second list (pages 129 and 130) comprises proofreader's marks. These are for use on typeset copy you receive from your printer or typesetter to make corrections you will have reset. Again, use a red pencil or pen. Because the typesetter looks only for changes rather than reading through the entire proof, you need to place your corrections in the right or left margin next to the line of type to be corrected. Then indicate the place in the text where the correction is to be made. It often helps to draw a line from the marginal instruction to the mark in the text.

Copy-editing marks

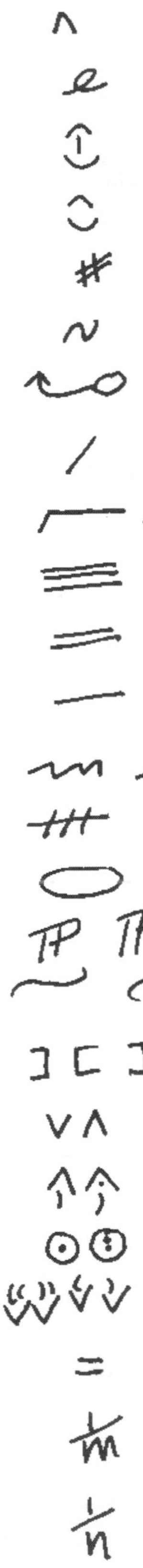

insert in the text

delete, a punctuation, word, or letter

delete and close up space

close up space

add a space

transpose; change order the

move word or a phrase

set in lower-case [lower-case]

LOWER CASE a series of capital letters [lowercase]

set in capitals [CAPITALS]

set in small capitals [450 B.C.]

italics [*italics*]

boldface [**boldface**]

remove an underline

spell out abbrev or number [set 1 hr as one hour]

indicate a paragraph

run in; no paragraph

center

superscript or subscript [πr^2 or H_2O]

comma or semicolon

period or colon

double or single quotation marks or an apostrophe

hyphen [vice-president]

em dash
[typewritten as two hyphens—without spaces]

en dash [1:00–3:00 p.m.

To change other marks of punctuation, either cross out the wrong one and write the correct one beside it or alter the existing one

Proofreader's marks

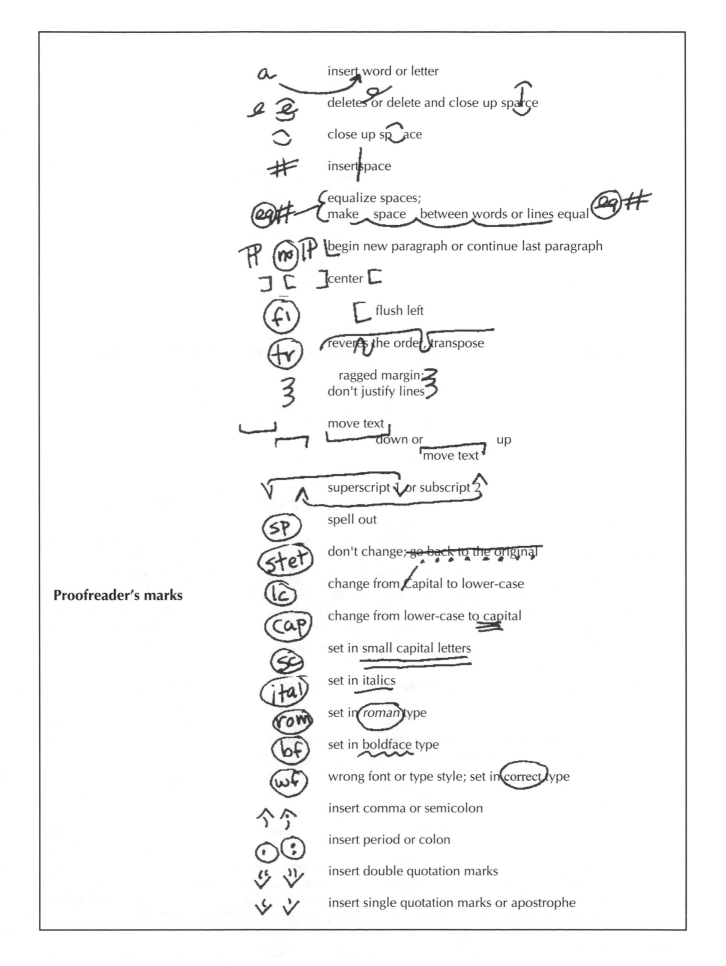

a — insert word or letter

deletes or delete and close up space

close up space

insert space

equalize spaces; make space between words or lines equal

begin new paragraph or continue last paragraph

center

flush left

reverse the order, transpose

ragged margin; don't justify lines

move text down or up; move text

superscript 1 or subscript 2

spell out

don't change; go back to the original

change from Capital to lower-case

change from lower-case to capital

set in small capital letters

set in italics

set in roman type

set in boldface type

wrong font or type style; set in correct type

insert comma or semicolon

insert period or colon

insert double quotation marks

insert single quotation marks or apostrophe

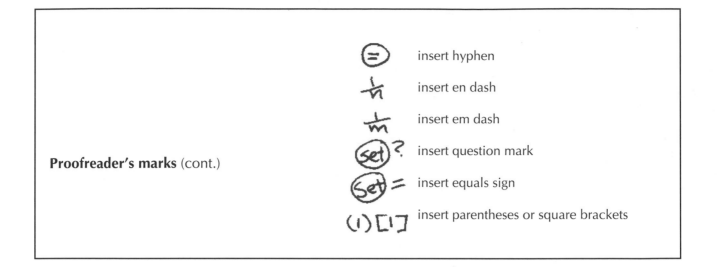

Proofreader's marks (cont.)

insert hyphen

insert en dash

insert em dash

insert question mark

insert equals sign

insert parentheses or square brackets

Writing Headlines

Headlines are important to any publication, but especially so for newsletters. Headlines should grab the readers' attention and make them want to read the article. They should be informative and brief. Here are some guidelines that should help you in constructing good headlines.

- Keep them short. Space is always a problem in newsletters. Be aware of column widths and how much space that sentence-long headline you are proposing will take up. Every column inch you devote to your headline will have to be subtracted somewhere else. Headlines don't have to be complete sentences, nor do they have to be punctuated unless they are complete.

- Avoid vague words or phrases. Your headline should contribute to the article, not detract from it. Cute or vague headlines that play on words should be left for entertainment publications like *Variety* (famous for its convoluted headlines). If possible, avoid standing heads for recurring articles such as "President's Message" or "Employee Recognition." It is better to mention something of the article's content in the headline, such as "Packaging Division wins company-wide contest."

- Use short words. Nothing is worse than a long word in a headline that has to be hyphenated or left on a line by itself. You can always come up with an alternative that is shorter.

Writing Kickers, Deckheads and Crossheads

Kickers are explanatory heads, usually set in a smaller type (or italics), that appear above the headline, typically underlined to further separate them visually from the headline. For example:

'ACME buyout impending,' says President Smith
Statewide Telecom makes takeover bid

In most cases, a headline is sufficient; however, there are times when a rather lengthy deckhead is necessary, especially if the headline is brief or cryptic. *Deckheads* can be as long as a complete sentence, and, like kickers, are usually italicized and sometimes of a larger point size than the following body copy. Deckheads appear below the headline.

'A drama of national failure'
A best-selling author says that AIDS reporting has been short-changed in the media, sometimes consciously.

Deckheads should be used only for clarity's sake. They are most effective graphically when you can devote more than a single column width to them.

Crossheads are the smaller, transitional heads within an article. You shouldn't need them in a typical newsletter article. About the only time they might be useful is in a longer article—perhaps a newsletter devoted to a single subject. Crossheads should be very short and should simply indicate a change in

President asks for employee vote of confidence

President asks for employee vote of confidence

Employee vote of confidence asked for

Employee vote of confidence asked for

President seeks employee support

Exhibit 8.4

Headlines have to be written to fit the available width in which you intend to fit them. Editing a headline to fit requires some creative thought. As you can see from this example, headline 1 will fit three columns well, but when stacked to fit two columns, it leaves an awkward orphan (a single word left on a bottom line). Headline 2 is a rewritten version of 1 designed to fit two columns. You can see that when stacked for one column, however, the same problem occurs. Headline 3 is a rewrite designed for a one-column stack. Try to keep approximately the same width in each line of a stacked headline.

subject or direction. Most writers use crossheads in place of elaborate transitional devices. Since space is always a consideration, using a crosshead instead of a longer transitional device will save you several column inches.

However, if you do use crossheads, make sure that more than one is warranted. Like subpoints in an outline, crossheads don't come solo. Either delete a single crosshead, or expand your points to include another one.

Writing Captions

Captions, or cutlines, are the informational blurbs that appear below or next to photographs or other illustrations. They are usually set in a smaller point size. Like headlines, they should contribute to the overall information of an article, not detract from it.

Keep captions brief. Make sure they relate directly to the photograph. (The best captions also add information that may not be included in the article itself.) Captions for mug shots should be the name of the person only.

If your caption is necessarily long, make sure it is clear. If you are naming a number of people in a photo, for example, establish a recognizable order (*clockwise from the top, right to left, from the top, from the left*, etc.).

Captions, like headlines, should not be vague or cute. You simply don't have enough space to waste developing that groaner of a pun you've been dying to try out.

Writing Pull Quotes

Pull quotes are relatively new to newsletters. Traditionally a magazine device, they draw a reader's attention to a point within an article. They almost always appear close to the place in the article from which the quote is taken.

Pull quotes don't have to be actual quotes, but they should at least be an edited version of the article copy. Pull quotes usually suggest themselves. If you have a number of good quotes from an interviewee, you can always find a good one to use as a pull quote. Or, if you simply want to stress an important point in an article, use it as a pull quote.

Pull quotes can also create white space or fill up unused space left over from a short article. A good pull quote can be as long or as short as you want and still make sense. They can span several columns, be constrained to a single column, head the page, appear in the center of a copy-heavy page, or help balance some other graphic element on the page.

Remember, good pull quotes reflect the best your article has to offer. A mundane pull quote is wasted space.

The Legal Aspects of Writing

All those who deal in public communication are bound by certain laws. For the most part, these laws protect others. We are all familiar with the First Amendment rights allowed the press in this country. To a certain degree, some of those rights transfer to all writers. For example, corporations now enjoy a limited First Amendment protection under what is known as *commercial speech*. Commercial speech, as defined by the Supreme Court, allows a corporation to state publicly its position on controversial issues. The Court's interpretation of this concept also allows for political activity through lobbying and political action committees.

But, as with most rights, there are concomitant obligations—chief among them is the obligation not to harm others through your communication. The most important "don'ts" for newsletter writers concern slander or libel (defamation), invasion of privacy, and infringement of copyrights or trademarks.

Defamation

Defamation is the area of infringement with which writers are most familiar. Although it is variously defined (each case seems to bring a new definition), defamation can be said to be any communication that holds a person up to contempt, hatred, ridicule, or scorn. One problem in defending against accusations of defamation is that there are different rules for different people. It is generally easier for private individuals to prove defamation than it is for those in the public eye. Celebrities and politicians, for example, open themselves to a certain amount of publicity and, therefore, criticism. While a private individual suing for libel must only prove negligence, a public figure must prove malice. In order for defamation to be actionable, five elements must be present.

- There must be communication of a statement that harms a person's reputation in some way—even if it only lowers that person's esteem in another's eyes.

- The communication must have been published or communicated to a third party. The difference here is that between *slander* and *libel*. Slander is oral defamation and might arise, for example, in a public speech. *Libel* is written defamation, though it also includes broadcast communication.

- The person defamed must have been identified in the communication, either by name or by direct inference. This is the toughest to prove if the person's name hasn't been used directly.

- The person defamed must be able to prove that the communication caused damage to his or her reputation.

- Negligence must also be shown. In other words, the source of the communication must be proved to have been negligent during research or writing. Negligence can be the fault of poor information gathering. Public figures must prove malice—that is, the communication was made with knowing falsehood or reckless disregard for the truth.

There are defenses against defamation. The most obvious is that the communication is the truth, regardless of whether the information harmed someone's reputation or not.

The second defense is *privilege*. Privilege applies to statements made during public, official, or judicial proceedings. For example, if something normally libelous is reported accurately on the basis of a public meeting, the reporter cannot be held responsible. Privilege is a tricky concept, however, and care must be taken that privileged information be given only to those who have right to it. Public meetings are public information. Only concerned individuals only have a right to privileged information released at private meetings.

The third most common defense is fair comment. This concept applies primarily to the right to criticize, as in theater or book critiques, and must be restricted to the public-interest aspects of that which is under discussion. However, it also can be construed to apply to such communications as comparative advertising.

Privacy

Most of us are familiar with the term *invasion of privacy*. For newsletter writers, infringing on privacy is a serious concern. It can happen very easily. For example, your position as editor of the house magazine doesn't automatically give you the right to use any employee picture you might have on file, or divulge personal information about an employee without their prior written permission.

Invasion of privacy falls roughly into the following categories.

- Appropriation is the commercial use of a person's name or picture without permission. For instance, you can't say that one of your employees supports the company's position on nuclear energy if that employee hasn't given you permission to do so—even if they do support that position and have said so to you.

   Private facts about individuals are also protected. Information about a person's lifestyle, family situation, personal health, etc., is considered to be strictly private and may not be disclosed without permission.

- Intrusion involves literally spying on another. Obtaining information by bugging, filming, or recording in any way another's private affairs is cause for a lawsuit.

Copyright

Most of us understand that we can't quote freely from a book without giving credit, photocopy entire publications to avoid buying copies, or reprint a cartoon strip in our corporate magazine without permission. Most forms of published communication are protected by copyright laws.

The reasons for copyright protection are fairly clear. Those who create original work, such as novels, songs, articles, and advertisements, lose the very means to their livelihood each time that novel, song, or advertisement is used without payment.

All writers need to be aware that copyrighted information is not theirs to use free of charge, without permission. Always check for copyright ownership on anything you plan to use, in any way. You may want to rewrite information, or paraphrase it, and think that as long as you don't use the original wording you are exempt from copyright violation. Not so. There are prescribed guidelines for use of copyrighted information without permission. You may use a portion of copyrighted information if:

1. It is not taken out of context.

2. Credit is given to the source.

3. Your usage doesn't affect the market for the material.

4. You are using the information for scholastic or research purposes.

5. The material used doesn't exceed a certain percentage of the total work.

Never use another's work without permission.

Trademarks

Trademarks are typically given for the protection of product names or, in certain cases, images, phrases, or slogans. For example, several years ago, Anheuser-Busch sued a florist for calling a flower shop "This Bud's For You." The reason, of course, is that the slogan was commonly recognized as referring to Budweiser beer. The Disney studios have jealously guarded their trademarked cartoon characters for over fifty years and their trademark appears on thousands of items. Charles Schulz' Peanuts' characters are also used for hundreds of purposes, all with permission. Even advertisments that mention other product names are careful to footnote trademark information.

One of the main reasons for trademark protection is to prevent someone not associated with the trademarked product, image, or slogan from using it for monetary gain without a portion of that gain (or at least recognition) going to the originator. Another important concern is that the trademarked product, image, or slogan be used correctly and under the direction of the originator. Certain trademarked names, such as *Xerox, Kleenex,* and *BandAid,* have for years been in danger of passing into common usage as synonyms for the generic product lines they are part of.

The companies that manufacture these brand names are zealous in their efforts to ensure that others don't refer, for example, to photocopying as "xeroxing," or to facial tissue as "kleenex." In fact, one of the legal tests for determining whether a brand name has

---

© **Copyright**—Used to protect copy of any length. Can be either "noticed"—or marked—without actual federal registration (which limits protection under the law) or with registration (which expands the degree of legal protection).

 Registered Trademark—Used to protect any word, name, symbol, or device used by a manufacturer or merchant to identify and distinguish his goods from those of others. This mark indicates that the user has actually registered the item with the federal government, allowing maximum legal protection.

 Trademark—Similarly used, but as a "common law" notice. In other words, material marked this way is not necessarily registered with the government and thus has limited and not full protection.

Exhibit 8.5

become a synonym for a generic product line is whether it is now included in the dictionary as a synonym for that product.

As harmless as it may seem, using the term "xeroxing" in a written piece to refer to photocopying, or the simple use of a cartoon character on a poster announcing a holiday party may be a trademark violation. The easiest thing to do is to check with the originator before using any trademarked element. Often, the only requirement will be either to use the true generic word (in the case of a brand name), or mention that the image, slogan, or name is a trademarked element and give the source's name.

Layout

Traditional layout requires a great deal of patience and accuracy, and can be the most frustrating part of newsletter publication for the beginner. However, computer layout has made this job one of the easiest in the production process.

Design is the conceptualization of a particular look for your newsletter. *Layout* refers to the actual bringing together of the various elements into a complete newsletter. The process includes several stages, culminating in a camera-ready layout ready for printing. Not all of these stages are necessary all of the time; however, the more you work on a preliminary layout, the better your final product is going to be.

Types of Layouts

The traditional layout stages are:

- **Thumbnails**. Small sketches of a number of different possibilities, usually viewed as a group for quick, visual comparison.

- **Rough**. Usually a full-size version of the thumbnail you've selected as your format, including more detail, yet still literally hand drawn.

- **Comprehensive**. Once you've decided on a basic layout, a comprehensive is built with representations of all the elements in place where they would fit on the final layout.

- **Mechanical**. This is the final, camera-ready layout with all of the actual elements pasted in place, ready for printing.

Thumbnails

Thumbnails aren't absolutely necessary, but they are an important first step if you are conceptualizing a newsletter for the first time. Several sketches of possible layout options can help you eliminate the least desirable fairly quickly. The term thumbnail implies that the sketches are quite a bit smaller than the ultimate format of your newsletter. How small depends on how much detail you need to make a preliminary decision. Some graphic designers make dozens of thumbnails before making a decision. Others make only one or two.

Rough

A rough is still a sketch, but in the full-size format you will be using. A rough allows you to add detail to your layout that you might have missed in a thumbnail. Working full size also helps you to begin to determine space requirements for articles and graphic elements.

Comprehensive

This is what most layout people refer to as the *dummy*. A dummy is an actual mock-up of the finished newsletter, complete with greeked copy, windows for photographs, headlines, and other elements indicated and in place. *Greeking* refers to copy that is nonsense or unintelligible. On handmade layouts, greeking is indicated by ruled lines or lines of squiggles made to look like columns of copy. *Windows* are empty boxes, usually with an X drawn through them, indicating photo placement. Designing a dummy by hand is a tedious job, but the result is a layout that resembles, as exactly as possible, what the final publication will look like. Most comprehensives also include any second color you plan to use. This color can be added with pencil, marker, rub-down acetate cut with a matt knife, or any other method that will give you a suitable representation of your second color.

Mechanical

The mechanical is your camera-ready layout and should be based on your dummy. Everything you want to appear on your printed newsletter should be on your mechanical. A little later, I will talk about what you should include versus what you might have to have someone else provide for you, such as typesetting and photographic halftones.

Camera-ready Layout: Your Job vs. Their Job

Even if you've decided to lay out your own mechanical for printing, there are a number of elements that you will have to obtain from others—usually your printer and/or typesetter. First, unless you are typewriting your newsletter or using a word processor to produce copy ready to paste in place, you will have to copyfit your stories and send them out for typesetting. And if you are using photographs, you will have to send your originals, scaled and with cropping indicated, to a printer for screening. In addition, any other artwork will have to be shot to size as either a screen or line art. Make sure you have given yourself enough turnaround time to have this outside work done. Once you have assembled all the elements in their final, camera-ready formats, you are ready to begin.

The Tools of Layout

Hot wax and razor blades. That's the way old-timers describe traditional *paste-up* (a term indicating that you put your layout together by hand). If you *are* laying out your newsletter by hand, there are some simple tools you will need to make your job easier. Trying to do a paste-up without these tools is like trying to fly without wings—you'll be engaged in a lot of useless motion, and never really get off the ground.

- A sturdy layout surface. A drafting table or some other flat surface large enough to accommodate your complete layout is a must. Drafting tables are excellent work surfaces since they can be tilted to give you the proper perspective while working. A completely flat surface will distort your perspective if you sit while working on it. In fact, if I do work on a normal desktop (which I've done thousands of times), I prefer to stand so that I can get a straight-on view of my layout. Pick something with a smooth surface that you can tape down the edges of your layout paper to. Never work on a layout that is not taped down.

- Layout paper. You can use two different approaches here. You can lay out your newsletter on a fairly heavy paper (preferably with a slick surface so you can move pasted elements around without tearing the paper), or you can choose a pre-printed paper with non-photo blue grids. If you go with plain paper, you'll have to draw your own grids in non-photo blue pencil so that they don't show up when photographed by the printer.

- Rulers. You'll need at least two types, probably three. A T-square is imperative for aligning horizontal elements properly with the edge of your layout surface. T-squares come in various sizes. Pick one that will reach from the edge of your layout surface to the farthest corner of your layout paper. You'll also need a triangle for aligning vertical elements on your layout. Choose one that is at least eight inches on its longest side. Finally, you'll need a metal ruler for cutting. Using a razor blade or matt knife to cut along a plastic-edged ruler can be a disaster. As long as you're going to need a metal ruler, you might as well buy one with inches, picas, and points on it. Many artists and designers run a strip of masking tape along the center line of their rulers and triangles with about a quarter of an inch clearance between the tape and the outside edges. This will help your ruler slide better, and if you use an ink pen to draw lines on your layout, the ink will not bleed (seep) under the edges of your ruler.

- Artist's tape. This is a type of masking tape that is easily removed from layout surfaces. If you use regular masking tape, it will remove the surface of anything you attach it to. The same with cellophane tape. Artist's tape can also be used to attach overlays, which we'll talk about later.

- Matt knife. Don't use regular razor blades or box knives. These are clumsy and dangerous.

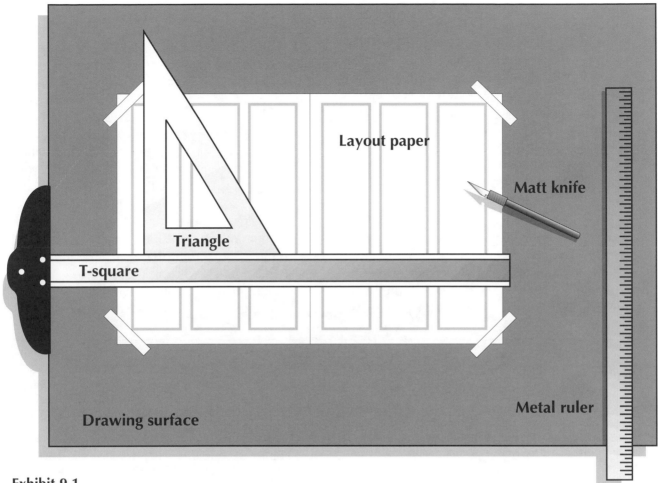

Exhibit 9.1
This illustration shows the proper placement of the triangle against the T-square for vertical alignment of elements.

Pick an artist's knife (X-Acto is probably the best known) and buy an extra pack of blades. The triangular blades of these knives dull fairly quickly and can shred your paper. Cutting with a matt knife takes a little practice. Ideally, you should hold the knife at about a 45-degree angle and cut along the edge of your metal ruler. Cut *slowly* and keep the knife blade firmly against the ruler edge. If you get off a straight line, stop, realign your ruler, and commence just above the point where you veered off the straight line. If your knife blade begins to snag your paper, tilt it to a lower angle to present more of the cutting surface of the blade and less of the point.

- Cutting surface. Don't cut on your layout paper or your layout surface. If possible, obtain a piece of glass large enough to accommodate your largest paper and cut everything on the glass. Don't use wood or cardboard surfaces as they quickly become marred and will snag your knife blade. Some synthetic surfaces are specifically designed as desk mats that allow cutting with no permanent damage to the mat. They usually come with a standard grid pattern for easier alignment; however, the larger sizes can be very expensive.

- Adhesive. What you choose to affix your elements to your layout paper is a matter of personal preference. Most professional layout artists use hot wax. Waxers come in a variety of sizes ranging from hand-held models like small irons that you use to coat the back of your paste-up elements, to larger models that you literally feed your elements through. They then come out the other side completely waxed. The beauty of hot wax is that a piece of paste-up that is waxed can be placed, removed, and placed again—over and over without rewaxing. Other options include rubber cement—an inexpensive but messy method. Rubber cement tends to pick up any dirt from your hands and working surfaces and leave it along the edges of your layout. Spray adhesive provides better coverage than rubber cement, but requires large sheets of surface paper to spray against. Every time you spray a portion of your paste-up, you have to replace the surface paper against which you sprayed it. Whatever method you choose, don't use glue sticks. They tend to lump up when applied and dry to an irremovable finish. And keep the spot where you apply adhesive away from your layout surface.

- Tissue paper. Buy it in sheets large enough to cover your whole layout for protection when it's ready for the printer, and for pasting up elements that will be in a second color over the place on your base layout where they will appear. This *flap* will indicate to the printer that whatever is on the tissue paper is to be in a second color.

- Press-down elements. These vary from press-type for headlines (purchased in sheets of complete alphabets), to shading film (also in sheets of differing densities or line screens), to border tape in varying thicknesses (purchased on rolls like any other tape). If possible, have your printer or typesetter provide headlines, boxes, screens, and rules already fit to your typesetting. Applying these elements by hand is tedious and fraught with complications. Applying border tape in hairline widths for column rules can be a nightmare. Placing and trimming something that is as thin as thread and twice as fragile will quickly convince you to put a little more money into your typesetting or printing costs.

Exhibit 9.2—The 1,2,3 of Layout

Once you've assembled all your materials, you're ready to lay out your newsletter. The following steps are typical of traditional paste-up, although, after some trial and error, you will probably develop your own special methods.

1. Paste your dummy layout where you can see the entire newsletter. If your layout surface is large enough, tape it down just above your layout paper. If not, tape it on the wall above your layout surface. Refer to it frequently as you work through your layout.

2. Use your T-square to align your layout paper to your layout surface, and when it is set, tape your paper down at each corner. Now when you place your T-square along the outside edge of your drafting table or desk and rest your triangle along its edge, you should be able to inscribe a perfect 90-degree angle on your layout.

3. Lay out one page at a time, in order, beginning with the front page. If you are using more than one color, paste-up everything that will be in your base color (usually black) first. Second-color elements will be placed later on tissue or acetate. If you have done your copyfitting properly, you should already know that all your elements will fit into your layout. However, even the best-planned publications sometimes surprise you. Be prepared for last-minute adjustments and don't get frustrated. Remember, with patience and a sharp matt knife, you can make anything fit.

4. Cut out all your typeset articles at once and keep them in separate piles—one pile for each story. Before you apply any adhesive, lay out your stories, photos, and other graphic elements in the spots you have designated for them on your layout according to your dummy.

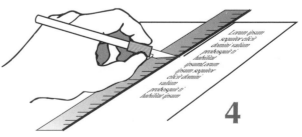

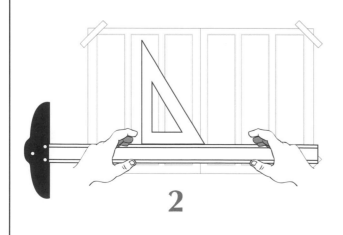

5. Once you are sure they will all fit properly in the space you have allotted, apply adhesive to one element at a time. If you apply adhesive to more than one at a time, you will have pieces of paper sticking to everything in sight. Beginning on the left of each page, paste down the elements one after the other until each page is complete.

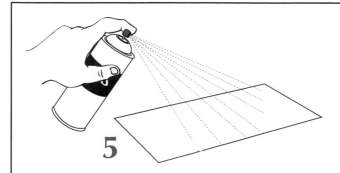

5

6. As you paste down your various elements, use your T-square and triangle to align them properly with the edge and margins of your layout. Wipe your rulers occasionally to keep them clean so that they don't smudge your layout.

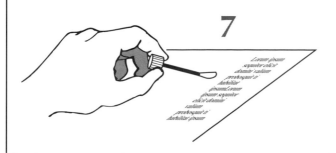

6

7. Since it's nearly impossible to keep a layout completely clean, keep a brush handy to sweep off dust, eraser residue, and paper trimmings. A bottle of white correction fluid can come in handy if you need to touch up a smudge or errant ink mark. Remember, *anything* black will print out.

7

8. Once you have placed everything that will be printed in your base color, paste-up your second-color overlays. Use either tissue (tracing) paper or clear acetate (which is much easier to see through) for second-color elements. The advantage of using tissue is that you can write your second-color instructions to the printer in non-photo blue pencil. You can't use a pencil on acetate.

There are two ways to handle this *flap*. You can cut your tissue or acetate to fit only the area in which the second color will appear, or you can cut it to fit the entire page size. In either event, the overlay should be the full width of a single page. If, for example, the second color will appear only in the banner, all you really need is a piece of overlay cut to the width of the page, extending to just below the banner. Lay your overlay down where you want, and tape it to your layout at the top only so that you can flip it up to see what's underneath. This is why it's called a *flap*.

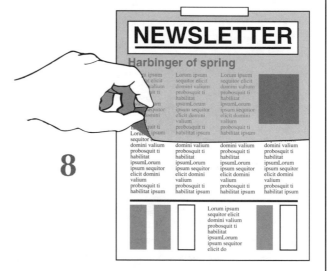

8

9. Once your paste-up is complete, cover the entire layout with a large sheet of tissue paper and tape it down at the top to form a large flap. This will keep your layout clean during transport to the printer. If you used a fairly light paper for your layout, you might want to tape it down to a stiff piece of matt board.

9

Working with Computer Layout

One of the key changes desktop publishing has brought about is the speed with which any publication can be laid out. That's because in computer layout, all your tools are in your computer and your drafting or layout table and paste-up board are on your computer screen.

The techniques described here are based primarily on Apple *Macintosh* hardware and Aldus *PageMaker* 4.0 page composition program, but may be roughly transferrable to other systems and software. However, my point is not to detail the use of one system over another, but to demonstrate the versatility of the computer in newsletter layout.

There are a number of basic advantages to computer page layout that you need to be aware of before you plunge into designing and formatting newsletters on your computer.

Placing Text and Graphics

The primary advantage of computer page layout is the ability to place text and graphics right on the page from word processing or illustration programs. Although other page-layout programs require you to create a frame in which you then place text or graphics, *PageMaker* allows you to place these items directly on the page, anywhere you want them. Once there, they can be manipulated in a number of ways. You can also place text one column at a time or in *PageMaker's* textflow mode which allows it to flow uninterrupted from page to page until it is completely placed. Text can be confined to any size column or stretched across columns by a simple movement of the mouse. Once on the page, text can be made longer or wider by manipulating the *handles* that are part of each *PageMaker* element.

Graphics, such as those imported from Aldus *FreeHand*, are placed in roughly the same way. By moving the mouse pointer to the position on the page where you want the graphic to appear and holding down the mouse button while dragging diagonally, you may designate the size you want the graphic to be when it is placed. This will then constrain the placed element to that area (in the case of text) or size (in the case of a graphic).

Once placed, the graphic may be sized, cropped, or otherwise adjusted depending on the software used to produce it. Graphics placed from PICT or EPS formats can be sized proportionally in *PageMaker* by simply holding down the *shift* key while dragging a corner handle. Paint-type graphics can also be sized without loss or compression of shading patterns if you hold down both the *command* and *shift* keys as you drag. If you don't hold down the *shift* key or *command* and *shift* keys while executing these maneuvers, the images will distort. Many programs now also include a text-wrap function that allows you to literally wrap text around a placed graphic.

Using Boxes and Lines

Today, even word processing programs allow you to create boxes and lines, but not all that long ago this was one of the primary selling points of a page-layout program.

Boxes

Although it is possible to import or place boxes and other such simple patterns from other programs, it is easier to create them in the page-layout program. Boxes do have to be moved each time you make an adjustment to type or format, but it's easier to move them in a computer program than on a pasted-up piece of paper.

Drop shadows are easy to create and can be effective if they are not overused. In *PageMaker*, drop shadows are produced by adding a darker-shaded

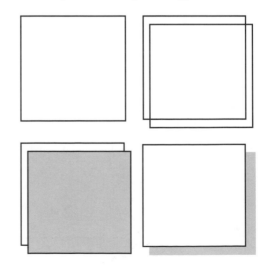

Exhibit 9.3

In creating a drop shadow, make sure your primary block is filled with white, then draw a second block over it, fill it with a screen (in this case, 20 percent), delete the outside line and send it to the back.

Exhibit 9.4

The beauty of computer layout is the ease with which you can manipulate the various elements on the page. Placing graphics and text in most layout programs is as easy as designating the space and importing the existing graphic or text. In *PageMaker*, you don't even have to designate the space in advance. All you have to do is place either the text or graphic icon and let it flow onto the page. In the case of text, it will either conform to the column into which you place it, or you can stretch it across as many columns as you like. Graphics can be sized as you place them by simply holding down the mouse button and dragging to designate the space you require the graphic to fit into.

He who permits himself to tell a lie once, finds it much easier to do it a second and third time, till at length it becomes habitual; he tells lies without attending to it, and truths without the world's believing him. This falsehood of the tongue leads to that of the heart, and in time depraves all its good dispositions.

Thomas Jefferson

He who permits himself to tell a lie once, finds it much easier to do it a second and third time, till at length it becomes habitual; he tells lies without attending to it, and truths without the world's believing him. This falsehood of the tongue leads to that of the heart, and in time depraves all its good dispositions.

Thomas Jefferson

box slightly diagonally and to the rear of your original box. Be sure your top box is not transparent, and delete the line around the shadow. Experiment with different shades and don't assume that black is the best for a drop shadow.

Tint blocks, boxes that are filled or shaded, should also be used with care. Very small type or type with thin serifs won't print well over a tint block, especially on a laser printer. Use a light shade (no more than 20 or 30 percent) and a type size of at least 12 point. If your final product will run on a Linotronic, be aware that fills or shades will appear darker than on a laser-printed copy. A 40 percent fill that looks fine on a LaserWriter will be too dark for a copy block on a Linotronic.

Lines

Like type size, line thickness is usually given in points. This is convenient since line width is much narrower than you would want to measure in inches. The standard seems to be 1 point; however, experiment with line thickness and use what seems most appropriate to your purpose. For example, some programs designate "hairline" as well as .05- and 1-point line thicknesses at the narrower end of the range. Hairlines are excellent for the lines used in coupons or fill-in-the-blanks forms. You'd be surprised how thick a 1-point line looks in these forms. On the other hand, a 2-, 4-, or 6-point line is quite a bit thicker *looking* than a 1-point line. Use the thicker settings sparingly.

Grids, Master Pages, and Templates

Once you're familiar with your page-layout program, you can experiment with actual newsletters. You can be producing simple newsletters in no time once you've mastered three devices that can be used to add consistency to your newsletters page by page and issue by issue: *grids, master pages,* and *templates.* The creative use of these devices can save you time and frustration and further streamline a process already greatly speeded up by the computer.

Grids

Grids are guides around which you build your newsletter. Their importance to layout can't be over stressed. Grids are not, as some graphic artists will tell you, confining. They do not stifle creativity or limit your imagination. They do aid you in balancing your newsletter page by page or from spread to spread.

A grid is composed of a series of non-printing horizontal and vertical lines. They can appear directly on the page you are working on or remain invisible until you call them up. They are variably adjustable and can be moved about to suit your needs.

For longer or regularly produced publications such as a weekly newsletter or monthly house magazine, grids are indispensable. Even for smaller publications such as brochures, grids keep your margins consistent and your layout balanced.

Master pages

Master pages are created (on *PageMaker*) at the beginning of your layout process and consist of any

---

Exhibit 9.5

On most screens, lines below 1 point don't show any smaller than the 1-point line. Sometimes, blowing the page up to 200 or 400 percent shows the difference. The best way to judge the differences, however, is to print out a proof sheet and look for yourself.

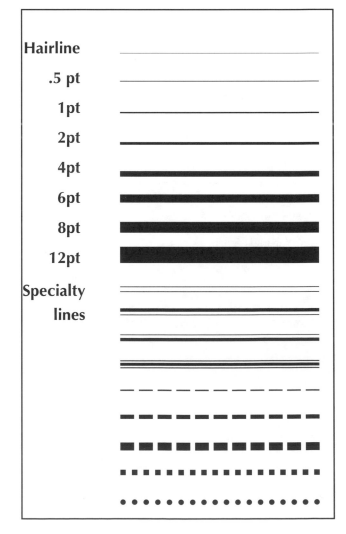

elements you want to repeat from page to page—not just grids, but also page headers, numbers, rules, and other graphic elements. Every page is then overlaid by the master-page elements unless otherwise over-ridden.

Master pages also hold the basic grid on which each page is built, including columns, margins and other space dividers. Some programs, such as Letraset's *ReadySetGo*, set up grids as a series of vertical and horizontal rectangles instead of columns.

Templates

Templates are probably the most useful tool for the newsletter editor. Templates allow you to save all of the grid elements, master pages, and style elements that will be reused each time, saving you hours of frustration. Templates were originally developed as tutorials for page-layout programs and later as specialty offerings packaged as guidelines for certain types of publications such as memos, newsletters, brochures, etc. Aldus packaged several early sets for newsletters and business publications and now includes a number of these with their *PageMaker* program.

Pre-packaged templates

For the less-experienced newsletter editor, pre-packaged templates can be a great help if they are designed for the program you are using or have access to. The key to making the most of a template is to decide in advance whether you are going to use it as-is or only as a base from which to experiment. Not every template is flexible enough for experimentation, but if you are aware of the limitations of the templates you are using and comfortable enough with your own skills, you can work both within and outside the established format.

A template includes the basic grid for the newsletter and a number of *place holders* and *spacers*. Place holders are usually samples of display or body type executed in the face, style, and size pre-set for that template. They appear exactly or approximately in the location on the page in which you would use them if you made absolutely no format changes. Again, the flexibility of your prepackaged templates depends a lot on your abilities and willingness to experiment.

Creating your own templates

Once you have the experience, creating your own custom templates is simple enough. The more you know about your page-makeup program, the easier it will be. Although your program will dictate the exact way in which you build your template, the following process—based on *PageMaker*—can be transposed to other software programs.

1. Establish page size, orientation, and margins in your *page setup* function. For example, if you are developing a template for a tabloid-sized newsletter, indicate *tabloid*, margins, number of pages, and beginning page number. Most templates are composed of two or three pages—a cover page and sample inside pages. If you have certain sections or departments with special heads or boxes, you can include these as well; however, try to keep your template to as few pages as possible and add special features when you begin to construct your actual issue. Normally you'll want to set up your front page separately from the inside pages with masthead and other recurring elements already in place.

2. Set the measurement system you wish to use. Most prepackaged templates and most professional layout artists use points and picas. You may use whatever you are most comfortable with; however, since you will undoubtedly be working with printers and typesetters, you might as well get used to their measurement system.

3. On your *master pages,* establish column number and width as well as any recurring elements that you want to appear on succeeding pages. For example, if you establish a 3-column format, it will repeat on every page thereafter unless suppressed on a page-by-page basis. In addition, most programs, including *PageMaker,* also allow you to indicate page number placement which then automatically numbers your pages. Other elements, such as boxes or rules, can be included here as well. You may either lock these elements, including margins and column guides, or leave them and adjust them on a page-by-page basis. Remember, what you put on your master pages will appear on every page after that, but it isn't carved in stone and can be either suppressed, altered, or changed at any time.

4. Create your *style sheet.* Establish all of the parameters for each of the type styles you will

be using and that you want to remain consistent from issue to issue. For instance, you might set your body text style at 10-point Times, justified with auto leading; your headline style at 24-point Avant Garde bold, centered with 25-point leading; your pull quotes at 14-point Avant Garde bold italic, centered with auto leading; and your captions 10-point Times italic, flush left with auto leading. You may also set such parameters as tabs, indents (both for paragraphs and whole subsections), hyphenation, and so on. The beauty of a style sheet has already been explained, but when combined with a template, it becomes an indispensable tool for the newsletter's editor or designer.

5. Create *place holders*. Place holders combine the advantages of a style sheet with a visual representation of where elements are usually placed in a given newsletter. For example, to create a headline place holder, simply type in the word "Headline" in the size and style that you wish your finished headline to be. To insert your finished headline, just place your text cursor, highlight the place holder word, and type in your headline. It will appear in the size and style of the place holder. Place holders can be used in place of or in conjunction with a style sheet. Some people prefer just to use a style sheet because of the flexibility. Place holders tend to pre-establish a design in your mind and are better for those who *need* a design pre-established.

6. Certain graphic elements such as imported art or special boxes can sometimes be placed on the *desktop* beyond the edges of the pages, cut and placed in the *clipboard* file (held only so long as your computer is on), or placed in a *scrapbook* for later use. Admittedly, elements saved this way take up more disk space; but if you use them a lot, yet don't want to lock them into any particular place on your layout, try "putting them to the side."

7. Once you have constructed your template, be sure to save it as a template. If you save it as a regular *publication*, any subsequent changes you make to it while laying out an issue will remain. If saved as a *template*, it will open only an untitled copy each time. Changes made to

that copy can then be saved as a separate issue of your newsletter.

Remember, templates aren't cut in stone—they're only etched on your computer's memory. But the templates exist to bring continuity and consistency to a newsletter. One of the pitfalls of computer layout is the ease with which changes can be made. *Resist the urge to change your newsletter just because it's easy.* Make changes infrequently. Make sure each change has a legitimate rationale, and then make sure you can live with the change once you've made it.

Laying Out a Dummy Newsletter on Computer

During the early stages of newsletter development, you will want to experiment with several layouts until you come up with one that you like and that fits your needs exactly. The computer allows you to lay out as many dummies as you need to make your decision. Remember, a *dummy* is a full-sized layout with all the elements to be included in your final layout mocked up—that is, indicated by shapes and lines rather than the real copy and graphics.

Text is typically greeked. Where you were forced to use lines or squiggles for greeked copy on a dummy executed by hand, with *PageMaker* you can represent greeked copy with actual lettering. If you have the actual copy written—great. If not, use the greeking that comes with *PageMaker*. Aldus refers to it as *Lorem ipsum* after the first two words of the greeked copy. For years, the only way to get this type of greeked body copy was to buy it as rub-down lettering in the size and font that represented what your real copy would look like or cut it out of magazines and glue it in place. Now, with a computer, you can make your own or, if you use *PageMaker*, use *Lorem ipsum*.

You can place your greeked copy directly onto the dummy page. You can also set columns (justified or unjustified, flush right or left, or centered). In fact, you can replicate any style or experiment with any alignment you would use in the finished product— as many times as you want.

Headlines can also be greeked in or written in a shorthand form until you develop the exact heads you will use for your articles. For example, if you have a story on an upcoming benefits package for employees, you might simply indicate where that article will go with a temporary head such as "benefits package." As with greeked body copy, headlines should be in the size and style of your finished newsletter.

Exhibit 9.6

The template (below) is representative of the basic template found accompanying programs such as *PageMaker*. Using this template, the newsletter page (inset) was created. You will find that adjustments will usually have to be made to type face and size.

Masthea

36pt. headline placeholder

18pt. subhead placeholder

24pt. column headline placeholder

This is a 12pt. bold byline placeholder

This is a 12pt. body text placeholder composed of Times Roman set flush left

This is a 12pt. caption placeholder of Times Roman italic

A spacer allows you to place a predetermined amount of space (in this case, 1 pica) at even intervals between elements on your page. Here, the body copy is placed 1 pica beneath a graphic element.

APC Action

A revolution in the making

New software may turn the tide in education

Lorem ipsum dolor sit amet, consectetuer adipiscing elit, sed diam nonummy nibh euismod tincidunt ut laoreet dolore magna aliquam erat volutpat.

Ut wisi enim ad minim veniam, quis nostrud exerci tation ullamcorper suscipit lobortis nisl ut aliquip ex ea commodo consequat.

Duis autem vel eum iriure dolor in hendrerit in vulputate velit esse molestie consequat, vel illum dolore eu feugiat nulla facilisis at vero eros et accumsan et iusto odio dignissim qui blandit praesent luptatum zzril delenit augue duis dolore te feugait nulla facilisi. Lorem ipsum dolor sit amet, consectetuer adipiscing elit, sed diam nonummy nibh euismod tincidunt ut laoreet dolore magna aliquam erat volutpat.

Ut wisi enim ad minim veniam, quis nostrud exerci tation ullamcorper suscipit lobortis nisl ut aliquip ex ea commodo consequat.

Duis autem vel eum iriure dolor in hendrerit in vulputate velit esse molestie consequat, vel illum dolore eu feugiat nulla facilisis at vero eros et accumsan et iusto odio dignissim qui blandit praesent luptatum zzril delenit augue duis dolore te feugait nulla facilisi. Nam liber tempor cum soluta nobis eleifend option congue nihil imperdiet doming id quod mazim placerat facer possim assum.

Lorem ipsum dolor sit amet, consectetuer adipiscing elit, sed diam

nonummy nibh euismod tincidunt ut laoreet dolore magna aliquam erat volutpat.

Ut wisi enim ad minim veniam, quis nostrud exerci tation ullamcorper suscipit lobortis nisl ut aliquip ex ea commodo consequat.

Duis autem vel eum iriure dolor in hendrerit in vulputate velit esse molestie consequat, vel illum dolore eu feugiat nulla facilisis at vero eros et accumsan et iusto odio dignissim qui blandit praesent luptatum zzril delenit augue duis dolore te feugait nulla facilisi. Lorem ipsum dolor sit amet, consectetuer adipiscing elit, sed diam nonummy nibh euismod tincidunt ut laoreet dolore magna aliquam erat volutpat.

Ut wisi enim ad minim veniam, quis nostrud exerci tation ullamcorper suscipit lobortis nisl ut aliquip ex ea commodo consequat. Duis autem vel eum iriure dolor in hendrerit in vulputate velit esse molestie consequat, vel illum dolore eu feugiat nulla facilisis at vero eros et accumsan et

APC moves up	**Page 2**
A penny for your thoughts	**Page 3**
Software	**Page 4**

Using finished graphics for dummies is a matter of taste. Some designers don't care to mess with detail on a dummy and simply use boxes to indicate where the graphics will go. However, if you have scanned photographs (usually at low resolution to save space on your disk) or computer-generated art, you can place your graphics over and over again with little or no trouble.

Preparing the Mechanical

The final stage of layout is the mechanical, the finished layout that goes to the printer. Again, the computer has revolutionized this process. If you are diligent, exact, and working with a limited range of graphics, you can literally present your printer with a mechanical in one piece—*with no pasted-up parts!* I have, in fact, sent whole newsletters directly to our printer's Linotronic 300 typesetter via our computer network and had the camera-ready mechanical handed back to me for inspection within a few hours. You can even go directly to negative film from a Linotronic, saving the cost of shooting negatives from a positive mechanical—but only if you are completely satisfied with your layout.

Assuming you are working in black and white, there are several ways to construct your mechanical.

1. You can have it run *entirely* off a Linotronic either from your computer disks or through a network or phone-line hookup. This implies that all of the elements on your mechanical are computer generated—word-processed text and display type; borders, boxes, and rules produced in your page-makeup program; photos scanned, cropped, and sized in either a photo-manipulation program—such as *Image Studio*—or right in your layout program; illustrations created in a paint, draw, or illustration program and imported or placed in your layout program; and any color separations already accounted for by your software.

2. You can run the basic mechanical (text, display type, rules, and boxes) on a Linotronic and have photos and art shot separately and stripped into the negative before the printing plate is made. If you don't have a scanner or access to electronic clip art, this is probably the closest you'll get to having the whole thing done in one step. Even at this level, the savings in typesetting and paste-up alone are worth it.

3. You can run your mechanical on a laser printer at either of the above two levels. This assumes you either don't have access to a Linotronic, or you don't feel that the extra quality is needed for your particular newsletter. Some very nice newsletters and brochures can be offset printed directly from laser-printed mechanicals. The difference to the trained eye (or anyone with a magnifying glass) is the type. It bleeds badly at larger point sizes and can even look fuzzy at smaller sizes. But if you're on a shoestring budget, this is a great compromise.

Adding Color

Today, full color on the computer is tedious and fairly imprecise. Although there are color monitors, full-color scanners, and photo programs to work with them, and processes to make and print the requisite separations—the end results are not as satisfying as the mechanical process now used. At the speed at which computer technology is advancing, however, it won't be long before full-color photography can be handled cost-effectively and with good results.

Many page-layout programs support spot color, and many more are developing color capabilities. Both page-layout programs like *PageMaker* and illustration programs like *FreeHand* have the ability to add color and make separations for printing. In fact, at this writing, both *PageMaker* and *FreeHand* contain a complete *Pantone* library of colors as well as the ability to mix your own.

If all you're doing is adding a spot color (using a second color only in certain areas of your layout), both programs, and many others, will do just fine. Just remember, working with color has always been a difficult proposition. Working with it on a computer can be rewarding and exciting, but it is also confusing and occasionally frustrating.

One final word of warning. If you are thinking of investing in color capabilities for your computer be aware of the WYSIWYG problem (what you see is what you get). Color monitors are the greatest thing since sliced bread, but they're hardly accurate. Don't expect the color you see on the screen to replicate on your new $8,000 color printer or look the same in your finished job hot off the press. One problem is that color monitors use light-mixed colors that just don't look the same as colors mixed with real ink. What can you do?

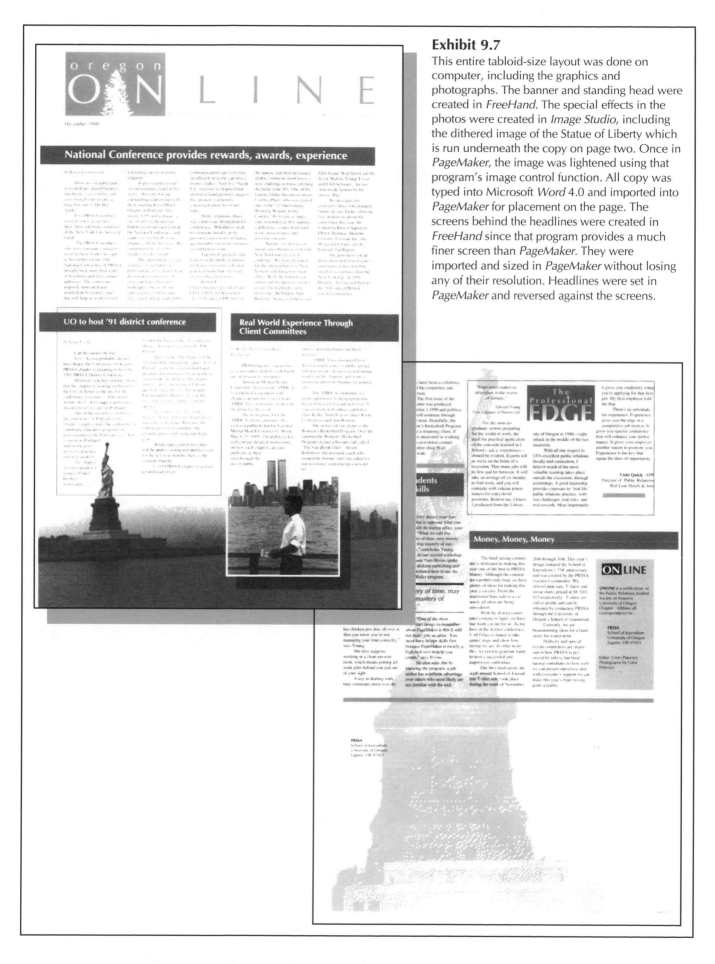

Exhibit 9.7

This entire tabloid-size layout was done on computer, including the graphics and photographs. The banner and standing head were created in *FreeHand*. The special effects in the photos were created in *Image Studio*, including the dithered image of the Statue of Liberty which is run underneath the copy on page two. Once in *PageMaker*, the image was lightened using that program's image control function. All copy was typed into Microsoft *Word* 4.0 and imported into *PageMaker* for placement on the page. The screens behind the headlines were created in *FreeHand* since that program provides a much finer screen than *PageMaker*. They were imported and sized in *PageMaker* without losing any of their resolution. Headlines were set in *PageMaker* and reversed against the screens.

1. First, set up your monitor with a color card. They are usually provided with the monitor. Some software programs, such as Aldus *FreeHand*, provide a color card based on the *Pantone* system. Get as close as you can to these color cards and check the adjustment every so often to make sure it hasn't wandered.

2. Once you have set up color in a newsletter, check it against what your printer is using. Don't expect a color-comp run on a color printer to match anything the printer has. Be ready to get a close match, or re-spec your color based on printer samples. If you use *Pantone* or another coded system, you can easily check out what you thought was Reflex Blue on your screen by taking a quick look at your printer's Pantone book.

3. Finally, be prepared for disappointment if you rely too heavily on your color screen for the final word. Use your monitor and software programs to their fullest, but be sensible and talk over your choices with your printer and *look at samples*.

Remember, the closer you can get to a finished mechanical on a computer, the more cost effective your production process is going to become. With the possible exception of scanned photos, the rest of the process saves money. Once scanned photos reach the quality of photographic halftones and the printing process quickens, prices will drop. Then you won't see any more traditionally done photos in newsletters.

Printing

How your newsletter ultimately looks depends as much on the printing process you use as on your abilities as a layout artist. As with other elements of production, you get what you pay for. However, you are not alone in this endeavor. The key is to know your printer.

The most beautiful layout in the world isn't effective until it's printed and distributed. And there is many a possible slip between what you laid out and what comes off the press—unless you do some necessary front work.

The trick to working successfully with printers is to know what you are talking about. There's no substitute for knowledge. The key is to try out several printers and work with those who not only give you the best deal, but who also are willing to give you guidance. This is not an easy process, but it does pay off in a lower frustration factor in the long run. You simply have to learn a bit about the printing process if you're going to get along with your printer. Every writer can tell you horror stories about printers who, after seemingly understanding exactly what *you* want, proceed to print exactly what *they* want. This is not to say that it is hard to get along with printers. It simply means that you have to know what you want and be able to explain it to someone who knows printing inside-out.

Printers can be an invaluable aid in selecting papers, inks, printing methods, folding, and so on. You *can* get what you want if you know how to ask for it.

Printing Processes

Many writers simply entrust the choice of printing methods to the printer. Most collateral pieces and many newsletters are simply offset printed, which is one of the fastest and cheapest methods to get good quality printing today. Other, quick-print methods will usually result in a loss of quality. If you want to impress your readers, use a quality offset technique. Other, more detailed printing jobs, such as embossing or special paper shapes, may require specialty printing. Be advised that specialty printing is costly. Make sure that you are willing to bear the extra cost before you decide on that gold-foil stamp on the cover of your new brochure. Although there are a number of printing processes available to you, probably the two you will have most contact with will be *offset lithography* and *quick printing*.

Offset Lithography

The most common printing process used today is offset lithography. The process is based on the principle that oil and water don't mix. In offset lithography, the nonprinting area of the printing plate accepts water but not ink, while the image, or printing, area accepts ink but not water. During the printing process, both water and ink are applied to the plate as it revolves. It is named *offset* printing because the plate isn't a reverse image as in most printing processes. Instead, the plate transfers its positive image to an offset cylinder made of rubber (which reverses the image), and from there to the paper (see **Exhibit 10.1**). Because the plate never comes in contact with the paper, it can be saved and used again and again, saving costs on projects that have to be reprinted periodically—unless, of course, you make changes.

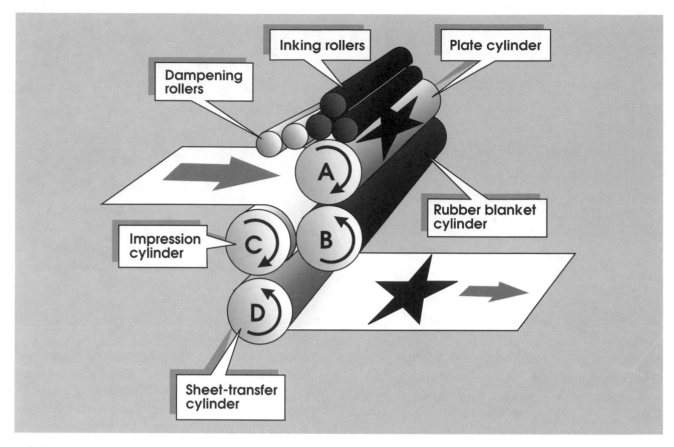

Exhibit 10.1
Offset printing gets its name from the indirect, "offsetting" printing process, in which the printing plate's image is "offset" to a rubber blanket which puts the ink on the paper. Notice how the type and image go from positive to negative to positive again.

Most newsletters will be printed this way. It is relatively inexpensive, compared to other processes, and it results in a high-quality image. Although small press runs of 1,000 or less can be made using offset lithography, it is especially cost-effective for larger runs, since presses are capable of cranking out hundreds of copies a minute.

Quick Copy/Print

The so-called *quick copy* or *quick print* process involves two methods of reproduction.

Quick print involves a small cylinder press using paper printing plates. The plates are created using a photo-electrostatic process that results in a raised image created with toner (much like the toner used in photocopy machines). This raised image takes the ink and is imprinted directly onto the paper.

Quick copy is really xerography, and has made tremendous inroads into the quick print area. The

larger model photocopiers used in this process can crank out multiple copies, collate, and often staple them.

Neither of these processes is useful for two-color work, but both are cheap and fast. If you are going to use quick copy, reserve it for rush projects or those that won't suffer from single-color xerography. Be aware, also, that there can be major differences between photocopiers, and even between copies run on the same machine. A copier that ran your last job beautifully may not repeat the same quality the next time if the toner hasn't been changed recently. Don't be afraid to ask for a test print of your most difficult page to make sure the blacks are really black and there is no fade-out on any part of the page. There are a few tricks to using quick copy as your printing method.

- Limit or eliminate screens, including tint blocks, which don't print well with this method. If you just have to use a tint block, keep it to 20 or 30 percent and make sure you copy is large enough and heavy enough to read over your screen.

- Don't include any large black areas, such as a banner with a black background or heavy black lettering. They will usually spot or smear, even on the best copiers.

- Don't use type sizes below 10 points. Small letters run together and fill in during quick copy output.

- Don't use very dark paper, heavily textured paper or very heavy paper. Your printer will tell you what papers work best for quick copy.

- Don't place any element any closer than 3/16 inch from the edge of your layout. A half inch is even better. Quick copy, since it's xerography, won't copy within a quarter inch of the edge of your page.

- Don't expect every margin to be an equal distance from the edge of your paper when it is printed. There is no way to register in quick copy, so as paper feeds through the copier it frequently slips and slides.

If you keep your layout clean, uncluttered, and don't include a lot of very dark areas, your quick-copied newsletter should look fine.

Choosing Paper

Paper choice is one of the most important aspects of producing effective newsletters. Your choice of paper may determine whether your newsletter is picked up and read, whether it lasts more than one or two days before it falls apart, or whether it even works well with your chosen type style, graphics, and ink color.

When choosing a paper, there are two major criteria you will need to consider. First, does the paper suit the use to which it will be put? In other words, does it have the right look, feel, color, durability, and so on. And, second, what does it cost?

Suitability

In judging the suitability of your paper choice to your job, you must first determine the nature of your information. Do you want your newsletter to last and be passed from reader to reader? If you do, you'll want to choose a durable stock that will take constant opening, closing, and general handling without tearing. Some pieces are printed on relatively cheap and light-weight stock and are meant to be thrown away soon after reading. Others need to be more permanent. A newsletter outlining company benefits to employees, for example, is one that will probably be kept and used over and over again. It will need to be on a heavier and more durable stock.

Aside from durability, three other factors need to be considered in judging the suitability of your paper: weight, texture, and color.

Weight

Papers come in various weights. Weight is determined by taking 500 sheets of a given type of paper and weighing it. Although a heavier weight usually indicates a thicker stock, it doesn't have to. One 25-pound bond paper may be thicker than another. Likewise, a newsletter printed on one 60-pound stock may be lighter and less durable than another stock. The best way to judge weight versus thickness is to personally handle the paper for each type of stock. Most printers have hundreds of samples of paper stock and can help you select the proper weight and thickness you want for your job.

Texture

Texture is also an important consideration when choosing a paper. Heavily textured paper may impart a feeling of quality or a feeling of roughness, depending on the paper stock and the method of manufacture. Basically, paper breaks down into two broad categories for texture: *matt finish* and *coated finish*. Matt finish ranges from a paper with a rather smooth but nonglossy surface to heavily textured paper. *Coated stock* refers to any paper that is "slick" or "glossy." Again, the range is considerable. Photographs often reproduce better on coated stock, which is what most magazines use. On the other hand, using a matt stock will soften the color and give a photograph an entirely different feeling. Some heavily textured stock may not take ink well but may be perfect for foil stamping or embossing. The best way to tell if your idea will work on a certain texture stock is to ask the printer, look at some choices, and come to an informed decision.

Color

Paper color has to complement all the other graphic elements of your newsletter: typeface, ink color, photographs, and artwork. It will also set the mood of your piece. Color preference is a very personal matter. Remember, however, that you are producing pieces to be read by certain target publics who may or may not like your color choice. Thus, to an extent, color choice is a matter of gauging your intended audience's reaction to it. Research has shown, for instance, that business people will not respond to questionnaires printed on hot-pink paper (not much of a surprise). They will respond to beige and various shades of white, but respond very little to pale blue and green. All colors carry connotations for most people. You need to stay away from outrageous combinations and any color you judge might not get the response you want from your newsletter.

Cost

This may well be the determining factor in your paper choice. Don't despair, though, just because your budget may be limited. Paper comes in thousands of weights, colors, and textures; one of them will fit your cost restrictions. Also remember that a few extra dollars on a good grade paper may well pay off in the long run by impressing your readership.

Choosing Ink

Choosing an ink can be a nightmare for the novice. Even the most experienced designers often have a short list of their favorite inks. Inks come in virtually limitless color combinations. And, each color will be affected by the paper it is printed on. Coated (slick) paper will result in brighter colors while matt finish paper will soften the color. The texture of the paper also affects ink color, as does using colored paper.

There is no easy way to learn which inks to use. The best way for a beginner to choose an ink is to look at other work done using the same ink/paper combination. Also, obtain a copy of the Pantone Color Matching System. It's really just a color sample book,

much like the ones you see when you pick out a house paint, but it is the most commonly used system among printers and designers. You'll be amazed at the variety of colors available to you. Don't be embarrassed, however, to stick to the basic colors to begin with. They are usually the safest to work with. Your printer will usually have a Pantone book you can use while there. Pantone's address is on the sample book. Just write them and ask about obtaining your own copy.

If you don't want any surprises, ask to see samples of work your printer has done using different papers and inks. Most printers take great pride in their work and will be more than happy to share it with you.

Color Printing

Color brings an added dimension to any publication, whether it's as simple as a second color to help accent, unify, or dress out a publication, or as complete as full-color. To use color effectively, you should have a rudimentary understanding of how the different color processes operate.

Spot Color

Spot color is the placement of a second color (black—or whatever the primary inking color—being the *first*) in a publication. (Note that in printing, black is counted as a color.) Unless you're using a multicolor

Exhibit 10.2
Simple spot color separations only require two printing plates—one for the second color (left) and one for the base color, usually black (center). When printed, the second color overlays the first color (right) for a two-color newsletter.

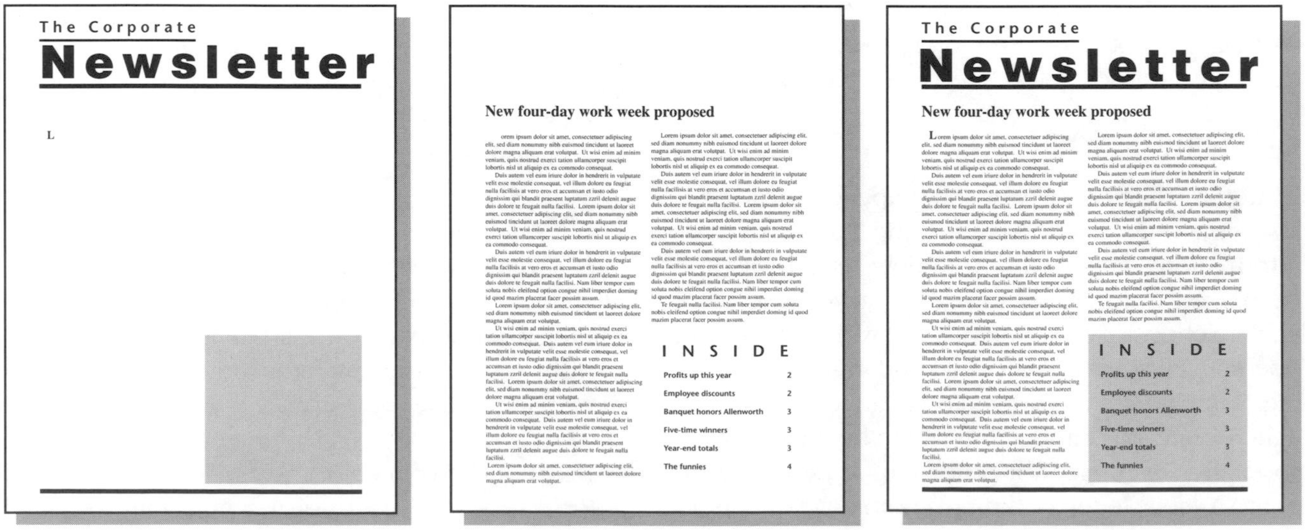

press, applying the second color means an additional press run. That translates to more ink, materials, handling and press time, and money.

In two-color printing, two sets of printing plates are made, one for each color run. Often, a designer will use the second color for the art and graphic highlights—such as dropped-initial letters—and use the black (or other first color) for the type. This also means that you have to create two originals, one for the black plate and one for the second color. This is not an easy process for most people and is usually left to a designer or printer. Check first and see what your printer's needs are regarding two-color printing.

Process Color

Process color or *four color* is used for reproducing full-color artwork or photography. This illusion of full color is accomplished by optically mixing the three primary colors—yellow, red (actually *magenta*), and blue (called *cyan*)—along with black. Four-color plates are shot through a screen to reduce solid areas to printable, graduated dot patterns. Because each color is shot through a slightly different angle screen, the screened halftone of each blends through the overlaid dot patterns.

During printing, each color is applied separately, one plate at a time and one color atop the others. The quality of this four-color overprinting method largely depends upon the quality of the original work, the quality of the cameras, plates and printing press used, and upon the skills and professionalism of those who operate the equipment. Process color is best left to your printer to handle for you. As always, ask in advance.

Proofs

A proof is a finished version of your newsletter, complete with photos, artwork, copy and headlines all in place. Proofs are not actually printed, but they are run right from the negative that your printer will use to make the final plate. They are usually run in a light blue color—which is why they are often called *blue-lines*. It is in your best interest to inspect your proof carefully. Read every word, scan every picture, check every caption. Never assume that a mistake hasn't been made during the time your printer has had your layout. Often, simple errors in handling can result in much greater errors during printing. For example, as part of the process of shooting a negative

from your mechanical from which the printing plate will be made, the negatives are *stripped* (literally taped) into a sort of paper frame. Sometimes (in fact, more often than printers like to admit) that tape shows up on your proof, blocking out some vital word or part of a sentence in the corner of your page.

The point is, don't assume that your newsletter will get through the printing process without a hitch. Always request a proof and always read it cover to cover. Legally, once you've signed off on a proof, any mistake that shows up on your final printed newsletter that was also on the proof you checked is *your* problem—even if it *was* your printer's fault.

Folding

Most newsletters are folded—at least once, perhaps more if they are to be mailed. The number of folds depends on the display size of your newsletter (folded just to the cover), and the size it will be folded down to for mailing. For example, an 11" x 17" newsletter can be folded once to present the normal four-page format, then in half again if your mailer takes up half the back page, or in thirds if your mailer takes up only a third of the back page. The same applies to larger formats, such as tabloid size. Some of the more common folds are shown in **Exhibit 10.3**.

Folding costs extra. How much depends on size, number of copies, and number of folds per copy. Be sure to have your printer estimate the additional cost folding will add to your printing bill. And don't assume you can fold your own. First of all, folding 1,000 newsletters will make you wish you had paid for the printer to do it. Second of all, the post office won't usually take hand-folded newsletters. They claim that only machine-folded newsletters will pass through their machinery properly.

If you're going to have your newsletter folded, also ask about stapling or sealing by some other method. Most people prefer not to staple their newsletters; however, new postal regulations allow for larger bulk-mail discounts for sealing by other methods. See **Chapter 11** on distribution for a complete rundown of these regulations.

Swipe Files Again

Keep a swipe file of samples to show your printer. If you find a piece that you would like to emulate, show it to the printer to get an idea how much it will cost to produce. They can tell you what the type is, whether your copy will fit in that size, what the paper stock is, weight, color ink, and mechanical needs—all of which will affect the price. For the beginner, a sample is worth a ten-thousand word explanation.

Exhibit 10.3

Seen here is a standard newsletter indicating the most common folds: fold once to accomplish the four-page format, and either once more (for a half-page mailer), or twice more (for a one-third mailer). Notice that the indicia (postage) is along the bottom edge, making the mailer upside down to the rest of the newsletter. See **Chapter 11** for more on this new requirement.

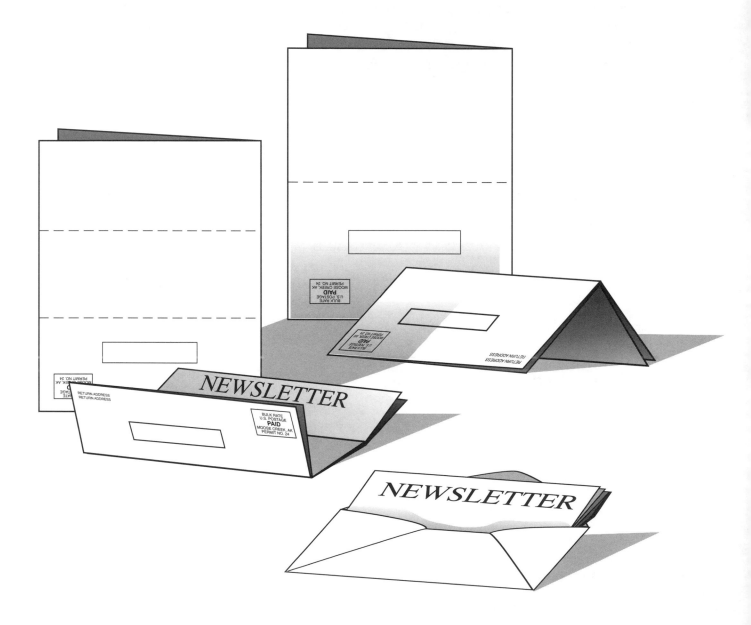

Working with Computer Printing

When computers were new, we were so happy to be working on them instead of typewriters that printing was just gravy. It wasn't long, however, before we began to appreciate the nuances between such terms as *letter quality* and *near-letter quality*. If all we did was churn out correspondence, then either would suffice, so long as the end product didn't look like it had been hand-lettered by someone suffering from a caffeine overdose. Then, along came the desktop publishing revolution, and choosing the right printer became serious business.

Roughly speaking, printers can be broken down into three types:

- ***Daisy-wheel*** printers use a type element that looks like a wheel. Each character is present on the wheel which rotates into place as it is chosen by the computer/printer memory. Daisy-wheel printers provide letter-quality printing but are slow—usually somewhere between 15 and 70 characters per second—and limited as to type size, weight, and style. Bold, for example, is accomplished by simply striking over a letter several times.

- ***Dot-matrix*** printers also form letters by striking an inked ribbon; however, the letters consist of a series of dots rather than a single character. Most dot-matrix printers allow you to run everything from extremely rough drafts to near letter-quality jobs. They are faster than daisy-wheel printers (between 60 and 300 characters per second) and have the added advantage of being able to produce type in different weights, styles and sizes. They can also print graphics— a giant step above daisy-wheel printers.

- ***Laser printers*** are the desktop publisher's answer to typesetting. They are quieter than impact printers (there is no ribbon to strike) and faster, printing lines per minute rather than characters per minute. At upwards of 600 lines per minute, these printers literally assemble entire pages in memory before they print them. The real breakthrough, however, is the laser printer's ability to print documents that are near-typeset quality.

Most laser printers today are based on one of two technologies—the Apple LaserWriter or Hewlett-Packard's LaserJet. The basic difference between the two is that the LaserWriter (and printers based on its technology) uses *PostScript*, a programming language that allows entire pages of both text and graphics to be sent to the printer at one time. Type can be produced at any available size and even extremely complex graphics can be printed out, restricted only by the resolution of the printer. Software/hardware packages that will turn a printer based on LaserJet technology into a printer that accepts *PostScript* are now available, and new LaserJet printers are now coming on the market with built-in *PostScript* capability.

Exhibit 10.4
Although most people can't tell the difference among printers when they read print in 10- or 12-point type, the differences are more readily apparent when you blow up the type to a larger size.

A letter produced on a dot-matrix printer shows the extreme irregularities of line inherent in this technology.

A daisy-wheel printer shows much of the same bleeding as a typewriter would since the technology is essentially the same—a raised letter striking an inked ribbon.

Laser printers use toner cartridges like a photocopier. The result is a cleaner type that still suffers from bleeding when enlarged.

Imagesetters produce type that is absolutely clean, even in the largest sizes, since they can print at greater than 2500 dots per inch.

Keep in mind that, although prices have come down considerably, laser printers can still cost you quite a bit—ranging roughly from $1000 to $5000 depending mostly on the amount of memory the printer comes with.

Some of the newer laser printers—especially those that accept *PostScript*—come with at least 1 megabyte of memory. These can variously be upgraded to as much as 12 megabytes or more, and some accept external hard drives boosting the memory even higher. The greater the memory, the less time it takes to print, the more pages the printer can store at one time, and the more type fonts it can handle. For example, upwards of 30 type fonts now come packaged on some laser printers, and with expanded memory, dozens more can be added. In fact, some font manufacturers sell hundreds of fonts on their own hard drive ready for installation on your system. The difference in printer-memory size can mount up in dollars, however, so be ready to pay for what you get.

Although laser printers are definitely the ideal, you can get along without one. Many quick printers and photocopy stores carry the most common software applications, and can run laser copies right off your disks. If you're in doubt, just call. It pays to at least have a dot matrix printer, however, to run drafts. These won't exactly match your laser output copies, but they will give you some idea of what to expect.

Pre-mechanical Printing

The kind of print job you need depends on where you are in the layout process. Word-processed documents or manuscripts can be proofed from almost any type of printer. If cost per page is a factor, consider drafts run on a dot-matrix printer. With toner cartridges running over $100 each, every copy you run off a laser printer just to edit manuscript pages will cost you more than it's worth.

For the same reason, don't use your laser printer to run multiple copies of multi-paged documents. On the average, toner refills for a photocopier are cheaper than toner cartridges for laser printers. And the wear and tear on a laser printer (which runs hotter than a photocopier) should be taken into consideration. It is much simpler, and cheaper, to take your original laser copy and run multiple copies on a photocopier.

Save the laser printer for drafts that need to be checked for page layout, type alignment, and design

considerations. Here are a few tips for running drafts on a laser printer based on *PostScript.*

- If you've run previous drafts on a dot-matrix printer, don't count on the laser-printed version being the same. Alignment is a good bit different on these two types of printers, as is letter spacing, sizing, and so on. Get your original draft in the best shape you can before you run a copy on the laser printer. Be prepared to make adjustments.

- Prior to running a second laser draft, make as many adjustments to your first draft as you can. For example, don't just adjust the kerning and run another copy when you could have also reset the column width and changed the headline type. Learn to economize and make each copy count.

- Don't expect completely clean copies from your laser printer. These printers are temperamental. Toner quality and distribution vary from cartridge to cartridge, new cartridges take a few copies to "kick in," lightness versus darkness adjustments are tricky, and larger black areas are just not going to print out solid, no matter what you do.

  Some printer manufacturers recommend removing the cartridge and shaking it to spread the toner more evenly. This often works. Don't try it unless you know how to remove the cartridge and put it back. And don't do it in white clothing.

- Read your printer and software manuals' sections on printing. Each program deals a little differently with print specifications. Don't assume that each program will use the same commands or even the same menus. Be aware, for instance, of paper size limitations. Many printers will run letter- and legal-sized documents only. Some allow for different paper trays for each size, while others require hand-feeding anything other than letter-sized paper.

  Some software programs allow you to tile. Tiling breaks larger pages, such as 11"x 17", into four overlapping pieces. You can cut and paste these together for a rough layout. Other programs limit the actual area on a given paper size that will be printed on when using a specific type of printer. For example, *PageMaker* reduces the print area of legal-sized pages to 6.8" x 12" when printing on a LaserWriter;

however, when printing to a Linotronic typesetter, it will run full-sized pages including bleeds and crop marks to indicate trim size (more on this below).

Most laser printers will only print to within a quarter-inch of the paper edge. This limits your ability to use bleeds, or at least to see them on drafts printed on laser printers. But it doesn't restrict your final copy if run on a phototypesetter.

- If you are using bleeds, or if you want to run a tabloid-sized page so you can see it whole—without tiling—try reducing it. Most page-layout programs will allow you to set a reduction value before you print. For instance, an 11" x 17" page can fit onto an 8 1/2" x 11" page at a 70-percent reduction. In most cases, it will still be legible. When reducing, indicate the edges of your document with crop marks, or simply add an unshaded box around the outside edges of your page before you print.

Selecting Paper for Laser Printing

Paper is probably the least thought about part of laser printing. Most of us simply opt for whatever is handy. The fact is, some papers are made specifically for laser printers, and some papers definitely should be avoided. Ask yourself three questions when you pick laser printer paper.

1. Will the laser copy be used as a finished piece or for reproduction?
2. Does the paper say what you want it to say? In other words, what is its look and feel?
3. Does it run well in your printer?

Keeping in mind the paper specifications presented earlier in this chapter, the following rules of thumb should help you select the proper paper for your needs and your printer.

- Brighter paper reproduces well on laser printers. (This doesn't mean *whiter* paper. There are varying degrees of brightness even among white papers.) Brighter papers are also good for reproduction masters. In fact, several paper manufacturers make papers specifically for laser-printer output that will be used for reproduction. Also, since it's hard to predict the degree of darkness of your printer, the brighter the paper, the more contrast you're likely to

have between the print and the paper. In general, avoid colored paper; however, some interesting effects can be obtained with lighter colors such as gray and beige.

- Stay away from heavily textured paper. The heavier the texture, the more broken your type will look because it will be harder for the toner to adhere to the paper's surface. Texture also affects any large, dark areas such as screens and display type. Some texture, like that found in bond paper and linen stock, is fine. The trick here is to experiment.

- Avoid heavy papers like cover stock, generally 90 pounds or more, unless you like removing jammed paper from your printer. On the other hand, extremely light papers, such as onion skin, may stick to the rollers or jam as they feed into the printer. Don't experiment much here. Just settle for a text-weight paper (generally around 60 pounds) and consign covers to your commercial printer.

- Use a fairly opaque paper, especially if your laser-printed copy is to be your final version. If you use a paper with high opacity, be sure it isn't also heavily textured.

- Don't expect heavily textured papers to retain their texture. Unlike offset presses, laser printers flatten the paper as it moves through the printer. In most cases, any texture will be lost.

- By the same token, don't use embossed or engraved papers in your laser printer since they might jam the mechanism and will flatten out anyway.

- Make sure your paper is heat resistant. Since laser printers work in temperatures of around 400 degrees Fahrenheit, certain letterhead inks may melt or stick and any metal or plastic will certainly ruin your printer. Above all, don't use acetate in your laser printer unless it has been specifically designed for your particular printer.

Printing the Finished Newsletter

Printing specifications vary greatly depending on whether you're printing a draft or a final product. Depending on your particular needs, a mechanical might be printed right off your laser printer. For quick-print jobs or "daily tidbits" newsletters, this is probably the cheapest way to go. Remember, though, that a LaserWriter only prints at 300 dots per inch. This is okay for body copy and most display type below 64 points, but for complex gray-scale photos and very large type, you might consider another method.

If you do go with laser-printed originals, the following tips might be helpful.

- Make sure your printer's toner is new or in good shape. If you can't get truly dark originals, try having your laser originals re-copied on a good photocopier. Just remember, each generation of copying deteriorates the image further.

- Use a strong typeface with solid serifs or sans serif. Pick a size that's easily readable (generally 10 or 12 point). And don't work with display type larger than 36 point, since it will tend to show the ragged edges even at 300 dpi.

- Large black areas and wide rules will tend to "gray out" on a laser printer, even one with a new toner cartridge. Try to avoid them.

- If you must use photographs, select those with few heavy black areas and a good contrast level. Remember, they are going to print out at 300 dpi, which will give you only about 33 shades of gray. If possible, work with line art or high contrast photos instead.

- Use a bright, fairly slick paper for your reproduction master.

To get the best possible camera-ready pages, run your mechanical on a computer-compatible phototypesetter or page compositor, such as the Linotronic 300. At 2500 dots per inch, the quality rivals (some say surpasses) traditional typesetting methods. Display type that looked ragged on your laser printer will look crisp and black; shaded areas will look dense and smooth; large black areas will be uniformly black; illustration will be crisp; and photos will appear in a full range of grays. Clearly, there are advantages to using this method, and now that the price of a page of copy on a Linotronic is roughly five dollars, cost is one of the major ones. If you are going to use a Linotronic, here are some tips.

- First, consider whether you need a positive or a negative run. Negatives will save you a step in the printing process, although they can't be checked for accuracy easily. In fact, positives containing photos are best run as negatives since the photos will probably muddy if shot a second time.

- Understand the parameters of your output device before you send anything to be run off. Are you running your pages on a Linotronic 100 with a 1250-dpi capability or a Linotronic 300 with a 2500-dpi capability? If you are using a Linotronic 300, is it actually set for a 2500-dpi default or has it been set down to save running time? In most cases, printing at 1250 dpi produces more than enough resolution and your final product will run in less time than if printed at 2500 dpi. Lower resolution does mean fewer gray levels; however, this usually isn't a problem since most of us can't easily distinguish between 95 levels of gray and 256 levels of gray anyway.

  Also, ask about the default line screen. It can be variously set on many typesetters. If you don't designate a line screen with your software, your gray-scale images will default to the typesetter's settings. If you're running magazine-quality photos, use a 120–133 line screen setting. For newsletters and newspapers, use 85–90.

- Although you can obtain extremely fine reproduction by printing scanned images on a phototypesetter, many images will need further adjustment. In fact, you will often find it cheaper to have halftones shot separately and stripped into your negative.

- Remember, the limitations of print area imposed by your laser printer don't necessarily apply here. The Linotronic 300, for example, can print widths up to seventeen inches and any length. This allows for bleeds and over-sized pages. Don't forget to indicate that you want your pages run with crop marks, however.

- If you're running color separations, be sure to request registration marks—and carefully check your final output for proper registration.

- Make sure you include the type of program you used, copies of the original scanned photos on disks, and anything your printer needs to know to run your pages for you. Printers are likely to charge you even if the pages don't look like you thought they would—especially if it's because of something you didn't tell them.

- If your final product doesn't look like what you laid out, trace the problem to its origin. Computer programs are notoriously fluky, and trading disks between your machine and your printer's machine and thence to the Linotronic allows for many a slip. Among other things, make sure that you are both using the same version of your page-layout program. If you've included any illustrations to be placed by them, make sure they have that program as well. Specify any screens or other vital photographic information. And make sure the typefaces you used are carried by your printer or typesetter. Nothing is more frustrating than having to completely reset your newsletter because your Linotronic operator doesn't have Helvetica Narrow.

Exhibit 10.5

A basic computer-printing configuration below shows a digital scanner for entering photographs and other artwork into a computer-readable format, the computer itself—linked to a laser printer and an imagesetter. The laser printer is capable of printing only to plain paper at approximately 300 dots per inch resolution. The imagesetter can print either to resin-coated paper positives or directly to right-reading film. Printing to film greatly enhances resolution, especially of scanned photographs, since it effectively eliminates one step in the printing process—the shooting of negatives from camera-ready copy. When imagesetting directly to film, always ask for a proof prior to final printing.

Scanner or other peripheral devices

Computer/CPU

Imagesetter

Laser printer

Laser copies on plain paper

Resin-coated (RC) paper positive

Film negative (right-reading)

Distribution

Distributing your newsletter is the costliest part of the production process for most of us. If you're going to be mailing it to your readers, you had better brush up on postal regulations. They seem to be changing constantly, and rates keep climbing.

Awell-designed, well-written newsletter is useless unless you get it to your readers in a timely fashion. Naturally, the perishability of your information will determine, to a great extent, what method you use to distribute your newsletter.

If your information is highly perishable and your audience widely scattered, you will probably want to direct-mail your publication. If your news is highly perishable and your audience is strictly in-house, you might distribute it through internal mail, at selected pick-up points where employees congregate regularly, or mail it to their home addresses.

If your information is not perishable, you might opt for a less-expensive and slower postal delivery method or display it at selected pick-up points.

Depending on which method of distribution you choose, you may or may not need to address your newsletters. Distribution through pick-up points and interoffice mail doesn't usually require addressing. Of course, any distribution handled by the post office will require addressing. Your options for mailing are varied; however your options for addressing are fairly limited. Basically, they are two: you can make up your own mailing labels or you can hire an outside mail house to do it for you.

If you opt to mail your own newsletter , there is much you have to learn about postal regulations.

Postal Regulations

Part of the problem of dealing with the United States Postal Service (USPS) is that their regulations are constantly changing. At this writing, postal rates have just gone up and the requirements for bulk-mailed items, such as newsletters, have also changed due primarily to new automated processing equipment. There is a silver lining, however. If you are able to take advantage of the new automated processing guidelines, the USPS now allows some considerable discounts—but more on this later.

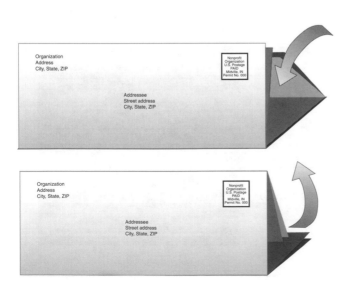

Exhibit 11.1
The latest postal information recommends that you place your mailing information so that when you fold your newsletter, the open side is up. If you place it on the outside edge of your folded newsletter (the bottom), instead of one-third or halfway up, your mailing information will be upside down to the rest of your newsletter.

First of all, you have to decide where on your newsletter you will want to reserve space for the mailer—the area on which you will affix your address label, return address, and indicia. Indicia are the postage permit designations that appear in the spot where you would place a stamp on a personal letter.

Generally, the area that you designate as your mailer should be blank except for the mailing information. That means, if you are using half of the back page of an 8½" x 11" newsletter, nothing can appear below the halfway mark on the page but mailing information. If you choose to fold your newsletter in thirds, the post office prefers that nothing appear in the lower third of the page used for a mailer. This includes a standard newsletter folded in half. However, larger than letter-size newsletters (commonly called *flats*) can use a mailing space as small as 4½" x 2½".

Letter size, according to USPS guidelines, is a minimum of 3½" x 5" and a maximum of 6⅛" x 11½". Neither the minimum nor the maximum size can exceed ¼" thickness. The distinction between letter size and non-letter size is extremely important since the price of postage varies considerably between the two designations.

On letter-size documents, including newsletters folded to letter size, the indicia and return address must be aligned parallel to the longest dimension of the piece. The latest USPS guidelines suggest that you place your return address and indicia so that if you are holding the mailer so that you can read it, the open edge of the folded newsletter is at the top (See **Exhibit 11.1**).

The words in an indicia can be centered, flush left, or flush right, and may be enclosed in a ruled box. Never use a ZIP code in an indicia. All mailed items should include the complete mailing address of the *permit holder*, and a ZIP code.

Classes of Mail

You have three basic choices and several nuances within those choices.

First-class mail is used primarily by for-profit newsletters that need to arrive in a timely fashion and with the prestige first-class postage imparts. Generally, first-class mail takes two to three days to reach almost anywhere in the country. Naturally, it is the most expensive way to mail a newsletter.

Second-class mail takes about the same amount of time to deliver as first-class, and it's cheaper. Why, then, would someone use first-class mail instead? Most of the reason has to do with qualifying for a second-class mailing permit. Second-class mail has a number of restrictions as to editorial content, amount of advertising, weight, number of times a year it's published (four), etc. However, before you send

Exhibit 11.2

The USPS has developed a special discount for mailings specially prepared for automated processing. The requirements include using a nine-digit ZIP code, pre-barcoding, sealing of self-mailers with adhesive tabs or tape, and providing a clear area for optical scanning. Requirements for placement of mailing information are shown below. Note that the right and left 1-inch margins will increase to 1½ inches after February, 1992.

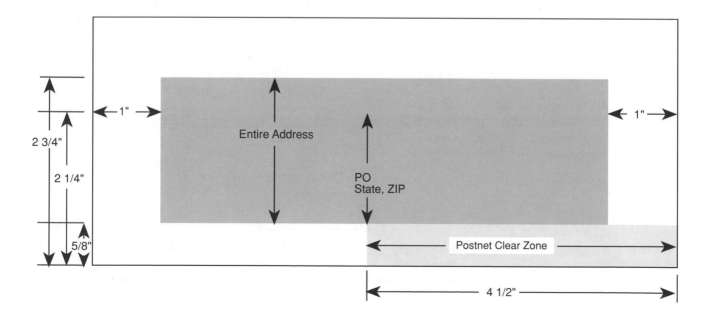

COMPARATIVE POSTAGE RATES		
First-class Regular Rates	**Bulk Third-class Regular Rates**	**Bulk Third-class Non-profit Rates**
Letter- and Non-letter size	**Letter-size**	**Letter-size**
Base Rate $0.29 per oz.	Base Rate $0.198	Base Rate $0.111
additional ounces are $0.23	**Non-letter size**	**Non-letter size**
	Base Rate $0.233	Base Rate $0.125

Exhibit 11.3

Considerable savings can be earned by using third-class mail, especially if you qualify for a non-profit discount. Stay tuned, though, the Postmaster General has recently asked for additional increases which would, among other things, raise the base rate for third-class non-profit from 11.1 to 13.5 cents.

anything first class, check to see if you qualify, or can adjust your newsletter in order to qualify for second-class.

Most newsletters are mailed third class because it's cheaper—about half as expensive as first-class. Third-class mail requires that you have at least 200 pieces, all identical. There are basically two types of third-class mail—*bulk* and *non-profit*. There is quite a bit of difference in price between the two, so if you qualify for non-profit, it is in your best interest to use it. You qualify by applying to the USPS, and the process is complex, naturally. However, the discounts are usually worth it. (See **Exhibit 11.3**).

Third-class mail moves much slower than first- or second-class mail. You can count on it taking about a week to arrive at its destination, sometimes longer. While first- and second-class mail usually leaves each station (or post office) it passes through within one day, third-class can sit (according to USPS rules) up to 48 hours at each station.

Discounts

The post office will also reward you with additional discounts for meeting new guidelines for automated processing equipment and certain bulk-mail requirements. These new guidelines have been effective since February 1991, but will change again after February 2, 1992.

One example is the new guideline affecting how folded self-mailers are sealed. If you don't want a discount, you can still send a folded newsletter with no fastener. In fact, the post office would just as soon you didn't use *staples* to seal a self-mailer. They tend to come off in their equipment. However, you can receive substantial discounts for using other methods to keep your mailer closed during automated processing, such as tabs or an adhesive applied to the corners of the open end of your folded newsletter. But, even as the discounts are increasing, the requirements you must meet to receive them are changing as well. While you can receive the discount for sealing your self-mailer by affixing one tab in the middle of the horizontal open side, after February 2, 1992, you will have to use two tabs. This only applies to newsletter printed on 20-pound paper. Heavier paper requires only one tab, both now, and after the next postal regulation change in 1992. (See **Exhibit 11.4**).

You can also receive discounts for presorting your mail. Presorted first-class mail gets a relatively small discount and requires a fairly large mailing to qualify (check with your post office for exact details). Second-and third-class mailings require presorting, but still carry discounts. Presorting itself has a number of requirements as to sorting, labeling, and bundling. Don't attempt it if you are unfamiliar with these guidelines.

Many print shops will handle your bulk-mail needs and will charge you accordingly for taking on your headaches. In addition, there are numerous mail houses whose sole business is handling bulk mail. They usually have the ability to computerize your mailing list (some can even develop one for you), print out labels, presort and bundle your bulk mailing, and mail it for you. Their charges vary, but once you've used one, you'll probably never consider doing it yourself again.

Designing for Direct Mail

In addition to deciding on where to place your mailer, there are several other considerations in designing for direct mail. Obviously, size is a major factor. The post office is very picky about the size of your mail, and its thickness when folded down. Smaller mail is generally cheaper mail. However, weight plays an important part as well. Lighter mail is also cheaper mail. For example, right now, anything that weighs between 1 and 3.3 ounces goes at the same rate. From 3.3 to 15.9 ounces, the rate not only increases, but it is charged by a different method—what is known as pound rate.

Is your newsletter a self-mailer or will it be mailed in an envelope? Usually, putting a newsletter in an envelope is a waste of money; however, some smaller newsletters are often placed in paychecks or billings. Obviously, you want to pick a very light weight stock for inclusion with other information as it will effect the postage of your original mailing; however, USPS regulations also cover paper weight. For example, a folded self-mailer such as a newsletter must be at least 20-pound paper stock if you want to receive an automation discount. That's about the weight of typing paper.

Whatever method of mailing you use, don't decide without a thorough look at USPS regulations, a comparison of costs versus advantages, and an honest appraisal of the trade-offs. It may ultimately be worth it for you to go ahead with that heavier paper and higher mailing costs, especially if your image depends on it. The choices are up to you.

ELIGIBILITY REQUIREMENTS FOR AUTOMATION DISCOUNTS

Mail not meeting these criteria for automated processing are not eligible for discounts.

Weights	**Sealing, folding & tabbing**
Before February 2, 1992	*After February 2, 1992*
Folded self-mailer sealed with 1 tab multiple or single sheets 20 lbs	Folded self-mailer (multiple or single sheets) with fold on bottom or top must have one tab in middle
Weights effective February 2, 1992	*After February 2, 1992*
Folded self-mailer sealed with 2 tabs 20 lbs	Folded self-mailers with fold on bottom (multiple or single sheets) and 20-lb weight must have 2 tabs.
Folded self-mailer sealed with 1 tab multiple sheets 24 lbs	Folded self-mailers with fold on bottom (multiple sheets) and 24 lb weight must have 1 tab in middle
Folded self-mailer sealed with 1 tab single sheet 28 lbs	Folded self-mailers with fold on bottom (single sheet) and 28 lb weight must have 1 tab

Exhibit 11.4
The addition of tabs to folded self-mailers allows them to pass through automated processing equipment without jamming. For the same reason, staples are discouraged as they tend to clog the machinery.

Evaluation

The success of a newsletter has to be based on solid evidence of reader satisfaction. Evaluation must be done periodically to keep your newsletter on the right track and doing the job it was designed to do—serving its readers.

The term *evaluation* is something of a misnomer. Most people think it means to look at your results after something has been done to see if it worked the way you had hoped. This is true. However, evaluation also means that you have to take a hard look at what you plan to do *before* you do it. Evaluation is really just a part of the overall research process that involved targeting your audiences and designing your messages to reach them.

In order to conduct a complete evaluation, you'll need to test your messages and their success (or potential for success) on several levels.

First, and before you even commit to put messages in your newsletter, you have to ask yourself whether they reflect your original objectives as set during the planning process? You should ask yourself why each message has been developed. If the answer relates to accomplishing one of your objectives, then the message has succeeded at that level.

The adequacy of your selected format and message strategy for your target audience can be tested at the same time. The best approach is to test your message and your format on members of your target audience.

Methods of Evaluation

Focus Group Testing

Focus group testing has become a fairly common practice for those in advertising, marketing, and public relations. It can be used for testing both the content and the look of your newsletter. The technique requires that you assemble a small group (usually not more than ten or so) from your target audience, present them with the newsletter (or a mock-up of the newsletter), and ask for their reactions. Your approach can be fairly formal (a written questionnaire to be filled out following the presentation), or informal (open-ended questions asked in an open discussion among the participants). The key is to design your questions in advance and to cover all the areas you need to analyze. Be sure to explore whether your message's language is appropriate to your audience. Is it difficult to follow, or have too much jargon, or too many technical terms? Does your audience understand the message? Does the message speak to them, or do they feel it is meant for someone else? Is the newsletter-look appropriate? Would your readers take time to read the message if it came to them in the mail? As an insert in their paychecks? If they saw it on a rack? Answers to these questions should give you a fair idea of how your larger audience will react to your message.

The best way to set up a focus group is to hire a moderator who is experienced in asking these questions and interpreting the responses properly. Don't assume that because you are the writer, and the closest to the project, that you can interpret audience feedback clearly. In most cases, you are not the one best suited to act as the focus group's moderator.

Readability Formulas

Readability formulas analyze everything from the level of education needed to understand your mes-

How to conduct a focus group

1. Specify what you are trying to find out before you conduct the focus group. Don't go into a focus group without a clear idea of your objective. In fact, as with any other MBO-oriented program, you should develop a list of objectives for your focus group study. Make up a list containing exactly what you hope to discover from this meeting. Are you trying to find out whether your target audience will read stories about other employees? Do they react differently to different colors? Which color or combination of colors do they react most favorably to? In effect, what you are trying to do is get your group to react to various stimuli that you are going to present to them.

2. Decide on a moderator. It is best to hire someone who has done this before. Focus group moderators are experienced people with special skills in leading others into answering questions and reacting to stimuli without letting on what they are looking for. Moderators literally moderate—that is, they lead the discussion, call on different respondents, and keep the discussion going without allowing a free-for-all to occur. If cost is a factor (and good moderators can cost a bit), you might consider conducting the focus group yourself. However, if you have never conducted a focus group or seen one conducted, you should attend a session or two before you attempt it yourself.

3. Schedule according to your participants' needs, not yours. If members of your target audience are busiest during certain hours of the day or days of the week, don't hold your focus group during those times. Make the meeting convenient for them. This courtesy will help put them in a cooperative frame of mind. Know your audience and their special needs when you schedule. For example, if day care is an issue, perhaps you can arrange for it. If lunch is the only time you can hold your meeting, provide lunch.

4. Select your participants properly. Develop a valid method for picking members of your target audience. In most cases, you only need a representative cross-section of your audience. For example, if 60 percent of your readers are women aged 25–35, make sure that 60 percent of your focus group are women with those demographics. Holding a focus group with non-representative participants is self-defeating. If you are in doubt about who to select, develop a screening questionnaire that will tell you whether the respondents are really part of your target audience or not.

5. Provide for payment. Nearly all focus groups are paid. Most people won't participate for the fun of it (although some like having their opinions counted). Base what you pay on who you are interviewing. Professionals, such as physicians and attorneys, should receive around $100, while others may be happy with $20–$50 for the session. Make sure your participants know they will be paid. The screening questionnaire is a good place to mention it.

6. Like the airlines, always over-book. If you need ten people, book 15 or 20. Some will invariably not show up. If everyone does, just take them as they arrive, and turn away the rest once you've reached the number you need. But pay everyone, including those you don't use.

7. Meet with your moderator and set up guidelines for the study. It is best to use your objectives as a starting point, and develop a set of procedures from them for the actual focus group interview. Lay out these procedures step by step so that if you conduct more than one focus group, you will be able to follow exactly the same procedures in each session.

8. If possible, and your moderator doesn't think it will be obtrusive, you might want to sit in on the focus group as an observer. Always allow yourself to be introduced and don't interrupt or talk during the session.

9. Provide refreshments, even if it's just coffee or juice. Most people expect some amenities in addition to the payment they receive. And it helps to put them in a better frame of mind.

10. The day of the focus group, check to make sure everything you will need for the meeting is ready and on hand. You'd be surprised how many rooms get cross-booked and you show up to find that someone else is using your room; or you counted on someone else to bring the overhead projector, and they forgot. Or you find you needed to have pencils on hand, or paper, or waste baskets, or any number of small items that can make or break a

(continued.)

focus group meeting. As with everything else, it is best to make up a list of everything you will need to do or bring prior to the actual meeting. Then, arrive an hour early and check off your items one at a time.

11. Hold the focus group. Whether you are the moderator, or someone else, the following guidelines apply equally.

- It is a good idea to audio- or video-tape a focus group. Many nuances of expression and voice aren't captured by simply taking notes or relying on written responses. If you use audio tape, make sure you have enough tape for the entire session, that it is good quality tape, and that your recorder will actually pick up everyone in the room. Don't rely on that tiny recorder you use to tape reminders to yourself. If you video tape, you'll need to hire a camera operator. Just positioning a stationary camera and turning it on won't do since you'll never be able to cover everyone in the room at once. And, if you do decide to tape, let your participants know in advance and remind them again when they are seated and ready to start. Don't rely completely on the tape, however. Use it as a backup and always take complete notes. If the tape fails, for whatever reason, notes may be all you have to go on. Plus, note taking makes the participants feel that you are doing your part as well.

- Always put your group at ease by telling them something about yourself, why you are conducting this study and the fact that it is entirely informal and open. Have everyone introduce themselves. Make sure they understand that you expect each one of them to play a part and that everyone's opinion counts equally. Stress that there are no right or wrong answers.

- A warm-up question that is easy to handle is a good way to get started—something fun, yet thought-provoking. For example, if part of your study is to gauge reactions to the new look of your newsletter, you might begin by asking each participant what his or her favorite color is.

- Remember a moderator moderates. Don't lose control of the group discussion. To ensure that everyone gets an opportunity to speak, try going around the table allowing each member of the group to answer each question, and don't ask a new question until everyone has answered the question on the floor. However, don't be afraid to veer from the point if an interesting side issue is raised. Just make sure everyone has a chance to respond to each issue in turn. If you find that one or two people tend to dominate the answers, focus on the quiet ones for a while, draw them out, and encourage their participation. Remind the group that everyone's opinion counts.

12. There is no set length for a focus group study. However, an hour to an hour and a half should be enough time to get what you need without tiring your participants. If you do go 90 minutes or longer, take a break midway through. When the meeting is over, thank everyone personally for their help and make sure they are paid before they leave.

13. Immediately after the focus group study is over, sit down with your notes and begin answering the questions you couched as objectives when you began this whole process. This is only the beginning, however. Don't draw hasty conclusions until you've had a chance to look at everything in context (including any tape you might have made of the meeting). Once you have a handle on the big picture, assemble all the evidence in the form of answers to your questions. Be sure to note if anything was incomplete. Perhaps you should have asked something else about reader interest in a particular area. Maybe you didn't probe deeply enough as to color preferences. Make note of these shortcomings so that if you conduct another focus

sage to the number of personal pronouns used (a measure of the level of friendliness in the tone of your message). Two of the most common readability formulas are described below in the box.

This sort of evaluation is known as preparation evaluation. Obviously, it can only tell you if the message and the way it's packaged and presented are acceptable to your target audience. What it won't tell you is whether or not your audience will respond to your message. You'll have to wait for that.

Surveys

There are a number of survey methods for judging the effectiveness of your communication once it is dis-tributed, ranging from expensive to relatively inexpensive, and from complex to simple. Let's take the simplest first: *readership surveys.*

Readership surveys are simple questionnaires, usually included with your newsletter, that seek to find out whether anyone out there is paying attention. A few, plainly put questions—about what interests your readers the most, the least, what they would change if they could, what they would include or leave out—will tell you a lot. Most commercial publications run an occasional readership survey just to make sure they're operating on the same wave-length as their readers.

The Gunning Fog Index

1. Select a sample of 100 words from the middle of your message.
2. Count the number of sentences and divide that number into 100 to find an average sentence length (ASL).
3. Count the number of words consisting of three syllables or more in the 100 words. Do not include proper nouns, compound words like *typesetting,* or words that end in *ed* or *es.*
4. Add the totals from steps 2 and 3 and multiply by 0.4.

The resulting score approximates the number of years of schooling required to read the piece. College graduates usually can read at about a score of 16 while most best sellers are written at 7-8. Obviously, if your piece is intended for vertical distribution, such as a company magazine, you will need to reach an "average" audience. Newspapers, for instance, are written at about the sixth-grade level.

The Flesch Formula

1. Select a sample of 100 words from the middle of your piece.
2. Count the number of sentences; divide that into 100 to find the average sentence length (ASL).
3. Count the number of syllables in the sample and divide this figure by 100 for the average word length (AWL).
4. Plug the resulting figures from steps 2 and 3 into the following formula:
   Readability = 206.835 – (84.6 x AWL) – (1.015 x ASL)
5. Interpret the scores based on the following scale:

70–80 = very easy (romance novels)
60–65 = standard (newspapers, *Readers Digest*)
50–55 = "intellectual" magazines (*Harpers, The Atlantic*)
30 and below = scholarly journals, technical papers

This formula is based on ease of reading determined, to a large extent, by the length of words. This assumes that polysyllabic words slow down and often confuse the reader. Other formulas gauge the degree of familiarity by noting personal pronouns, for instance.

How To Develop a Readership Survey

Readership surveys should not be done immediately after your first issue. Instead, you should wait for several issues until your readers have had a chance to absorb your informational approach and develop some reactions to it. A few guidelines will help you develop a readership survey.

1. Keep questions simple, short, and clear. Include only one idea per question. More than one idea will get you more than one answer. For example:

    Wrong
    Do you read the entire newsletter or only part of it?
    　　Yes　　No

    Right
    Do you read the entire newsletter?
    　　Yes　　No

    If not, which part(s) do you typically read? (check all that apply)

    　　Feature story　　　　　Editor's column　　　　Personal　　　Calendar

2. Use words whose meanings will be understandable to your readers. Check to make sure both the denotative and connotative meanings of your words are clear. Avoid jargon. For example:

    Wrong
    How do you rate the overall grid of our newsletter?

    　　Good　　　　Fair　　Poor

(Are your readers going to know what a grid is?)

    Right
    Do you think the three-column format of our newsletter is

    Easy to read　　　　Fairly easy to read　　　　Fairly difficult to read　　　　Difficult to read

3. Don't lead your readers' answers by implying a bias. For example:

    Wrong
    Our newsletter recently won "Outstanding Newsletter Design" from IABC. What do you think about the new design?

    　　Good　　　　Fair　　　　Poor

    Right
    How would you rate the overall design of our newsletter?

    　　Good　　　　Fair　　　　Poor

    Wrong
    Do you like our bright, new banner style?

    　　Yes　　No
    (Words like *bright* and *new* imply that your readers *should* like your banner.)

    Right
    Do you like our banner style?

    　　Yes　　No

    If you don't like it, please explain why.

Wrong
Do you think we should increase the amount of personal news?

> Yes   No

(This question implies that the current amount of personal news is the only point of comparison.)

Right
Do you think the amount of personal news should

> be increased?   be decreased?   remain the same?

4. In general, if you ask a question that can be answered *yes* or *no*, you might need a follow-up question to plumb the reasons why a reader would answer *no*. This is especially important if you want more than just one-dimensional answers. For example:

Do you read the personals column?

> Yes   No

If *no*, why not?

(This will give you a better idea of how to improve the column to enhance readership, or let you know whether you should drop it altogether.)

5. Try to get the most precision possible from each response. For example, the question above could have been stated this way.

How often do you read the personals column?

> Every time   Sometimes   Not often   Never

6. Decide exactly what information will be most valuable to you and construct your questions and choices of answers to get that information. For example:

On a scale of 1-5 (1 being the lowest rating and 5 the highest), how would you rate the overall design of the newsletter?

> 1   2   3   4   5

(This scaled response allows you to rate your newsletter's design numerically.)

How would you rate the overall design of the newsletter?

> Excellent   Good   Fair   Poor

(This scaled response calls for a connotative rating.)

Do you think the overall design of the newsletter

> Is fine the way it is?
> Could use some improvement?
> Could use a lot of improvement?
> Should be totally redesigned?

(This method limits options but most respondents like something to choose from that is concrete and not abstract.)

7. The following areas are basic topics to cover in readership surveys.

- Reader demographics such as age, gender, income, occupation, etc. This information will tell you if your readers are really who you think they are according to your original audience analysis.

  Please check the applicable ranges.

Age	Income	Occupation
25–30	$10k–$20k	(include a list appropriate to
31–40	$21k–$30k	your audience analysis, leaving
41–50	$31k–$40k	a space for *other*.)
51–60	$41k +	

- Reader reaction to content of articles (usually rated on a scale ranging from *very important* to *not important*).

  How important do you think a personals column is to this newsletter?

  Very important   Important   Not very important   Not important

  Do you find the general topics of the articles

  Very interesting   Interesting   Not very interesting   Not interesting

- Reader reaction to design elements, listed one element at a time for clarity.

  Do you think the number of photographs included in the newsletter is

  Just right?   Not enough?   Too many?

- Reader reaction to appropriateness of language, use of jargon, etc.

  Do you find the level of technical language used in the articles

  Appropriate   Somewhat appropriate   Inappropriate

- Reader recommendations for improvement (usually open-ended questions and last on your survey).

  Please list, in order of importance, what you would change about the current newsletter.

8. Always thank your readers for their time. If possible, offer them some incentive to respond, such as coupons or free passes. And make it easy for them to send their surveys back to you. *Never* make them pay postage. If possible, use a self-mailer with postage paid.

On the more expensive level are formal, statistical surveys measuring everything from whether your readers are actually receiving your message to whether or not they're changing their attitudes or behaviors because of it. These surveys are best left to highly qualified specialists who will ask the right questions and properly interpret the answers. The results can be invaluable, particularly with persuasive messages. Remember, behavioral change can often be easily measured in increased sales of your new widget, attendance at the company picnic (remember to factor in the free beer as a contributing variable), more votes for your candidate, or a decrease in the number of complaint letters you receive on an issue. Attitude change, on the other hand, is more difficult to measure but, nonetheless, equally important.

Modern survey techniques, contrary to what critics say, can accurately define attitudes and measure shifts in them. Because of the complexity of the operation, however (and the need to perform both a pre- and a post-survey in order to have something to compare), you will have to pay the price. Good research isn't cheap.

Evaluating Your Production Schedule

In addition to evaluating the success of your publication with its target audiences, you're probably going to want to take a close look at your publication schedule. The first time you produce your newsletter, you are going to have precious little time to reflect on how it's going during the publication process. However, after the dust has settled, you need to get together with your staff (if you have one) and your supervisor or publisher (unless you're doing it all yourself). Regardless of how many people are involved, or even if you're the only one involved, you should look at every aspect of your publication schedule to see where problems occurred and to make recommendations for streamlining the process for the next issue.

Among modern business management strategies for maximizing efficiency, there is a fairly complex strategic planning method known as PERT analysis. PERT analysis is used to allocate resources based on how much time it takes to accomplish the *most time-consuming activity* in a given project. The assumption is that you can't get a job done any sooner than it takes to do the most time-consuming part of it. The trick, then, is to locate activities that don't take as long

to accomplish and see if the people who worked on those jobs can help speed up the slowest activity. A simplified version of PERT analysis can be used to determine ways in which your own newsletter production schedule can be streamlined.

The first step is to develop what is known as a GANTT chart. A GANTT chart is a quick, visual representation of the order in which various parts of a job occur and how long it takes for each part. You will need to take your original schedule and construct a GANTT chart based on various jobs listed on it. (See **Exhibit 12.1**.)

Once you've got a GANTT chart made, the rest of the process goes something like this.

1. Look at your schedule. Go over it item by item.

2. Locate the blockages as well as the places where things went faster or smoother than you had expected.

3. Calculate an average time for each item on your schedule. List the times by each of the scheduled items on the GANTT chart.

4. Locate the most time-consuming activity.

5. Locate the least time-consuming activity.

6. Ask yourself if any resources allocated to the least time-consuming activity can be transferred to the most time-consuming activity in order to speed it up.

7. If the answer is no, locate another activity that took less time than the longest activity, and ask the same question.

8. Continue this way until you are able to reallocate some of your resources to help shorten the longest part of your schedule.

You will notice that activities usually break down into two basic categories: those handled in-house (such as interviewing and writing) and those jobbed out (such as photography and illustration). The only way to speed up activities you have done outside by free-lancers is to set tighter deadlines or contract faster free-lancers. However, at the points at which you become involved (selection and sizing of photos and artwork, for instance) you may find ways to cut down on the time. Otherwise, your best bets for streamlining are in-house activities—those that involve people under your direct control, including you.

Let's say that after looking at your schedule, you discover that the job that took the longest in-house time was obtaining critiques of the first and second drafts of your articles. Perhaps you have a long list of supervisors who must sign off on each draft, and the copy tends to spend too much time in interoffice mail. You might try hand-carrying the copy through the approvals chain, set stricter deadlines, try to reduce the number of approvals needed, or back-time the deadline for receipt of the first and second drafts to accommodate the delay at the approval's end.

Or, perhaps the most time-consuming activity turns out to be gathering information and writing the stories. You might be able to assign an extra writer to the job, or handle the feature story yourself each issue to ease the load on the other writers, or set stricter deadlines.

If there are areas in which others can help, pinpoint these activities and seek in-house support. For instance, your secretary might be able to help you edit the copy or set in on the computer. If you have writing help (lucky you), they could develop their own headlines, captions, and pull quotes.

The real key is making yourself delegate part of *your* job to others who can help you out. If you're like most newsletter editors, you probably hate to relinquish any part of your control to others. You're afraid that they won't take the same care that you do. Don't worry. Tell them exactly what you want, how to do it, and when you want it. You will still be the editor, and as such, you retain ultimate control over your newsletter. Remember, an editor edits. He or she doesn't have to create everything from scratch.

Exhibit 12.1

The GANTT chart below is based on the production schedule shown in Chapter 3. A chart such as this can be designed to reflect as small or as large a time increment as you need for accuracy.

Activity	Mon.	Tues.	Wed.	Thurs.	Fri.	Mon.	Tues.	Wed.	Thurs.	Fri.
Decide on basic content for current issue	▓									
Determine number and type and approximate length of stories	▓									
Make up dummy layout for current issue	▓									
Gather information and/or interview appropriate sources		▓	▓							
Write first draft			▓	▓						
Obtain critiques and edit first draft					▓					
Create graphics for each story (photos taken, illustrations created or obtained, charts/graphs created, etc.)		▓	▓	▓						
Write final draft						▓	▓			
Obtain critiques, edit final draft and copyfit to dummy							▓	▓		
Write headlines, captions, pull quotes, etc., and copyfit to dummy					▓	▓				
Send all copy out for typesetting if needed								▓	▓	
Select graphics (photos sized, cropped and printed, artwork sized) and fit to dummy						▓	▓	▓		
Send all graphics out for screening or PMTs								▓		
Create mechanical									▓	
Proof mechanical									▓	
Send to printer									▓	
Check proofs										▓

Basic Newsletter Templates

Within this chapter are three basic templates for newsletter design: a standard 8½" x 11" format, an 11" x 17" tabloid, and a half-page 5½" x 8½" format. At the end of this chapter are sample grids for you to photocopy for your own use. If you are new to newsletter publication, you may want to follow the directions exactly as to size, margins, column widths, etc. Or, you may want to deviate slightly from the basic design and, thus, increase your flexibility. Whichever method you choose, remember—experimentation is the key to creativity.

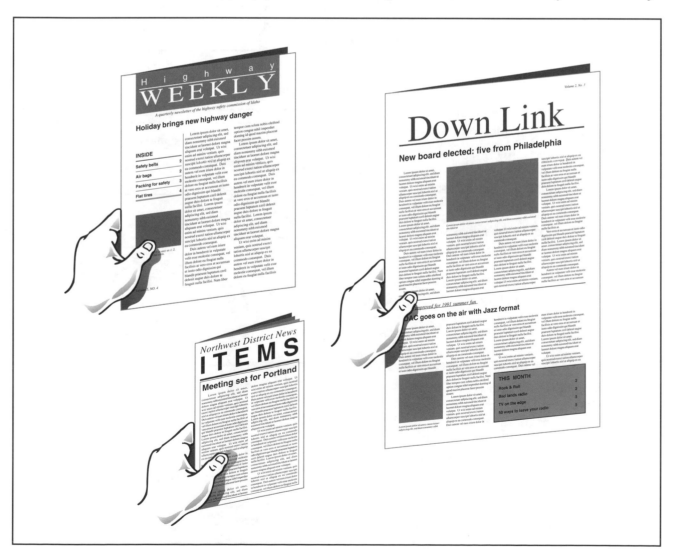

Getting Started

Because printers and typesetters typically work in picas, the directions that follow will be in that measure. It is in your best interest to invest in a pica ruler if you plan to do any amount of work with a printer. Remember that there are six picas in an inch and twelve points in a pica. The way to indicate fractions of a pica is somewhat different from inches. For example, four and one-half picas would be written as 4p6 (four picas and six points). For each newsletter, develop a template of plain, white paper that you will use as a layout grid for your paste up. Proceed as follows.

- Begin by selecting a paper size that is slightly larger than your final layout.

- Align and tape the paper to your drawing surface, then measure and draw with a pencil the outside perimeters of your newsletter double-page layout.

- Locate the center of your double-page layout and mark it at the top and bottom edges with tick marks. Use these tic marks to line up your ruler, then draw a pencil line down the center of your layout, dividing it into two pages. Use this tic-mark technique for all subsequent lines.

- With your pica ruler, lay out the outside margins of your pages by measuring in from the outside edge of the newsletter perimeter you have just drawn.

- Line up your ruler with the two tic marks you have made for the first margin, and join the marks with a pencil line. Alternatively, you can line up your ruler or T-square horizontally, place your triangle along this horizontal guide, aligning it with the top tic mark, and draw your vertical line, moving the T-square downward as you go. Horizontal lines use the same tic-mark method and either your T-square as the drawing edge, or your pica ruler.

    For vertical lines, make tic marks at the top and bottom of your page. For horizontal lines, place tic marks on the right and left edges of your page. If you don't have a T-square or ruler long enough to reach across your entire page, measure and place several tic marks horizontally across your page and move your ruler as you go, making sure to align with the tic marks each time.

- Once you have penciled in all of the necessary lines, go over them with black ink—again using your ruler for a straight edge.

When your template is finished, tape down your newsletter paste-up paper over it, carefully aligning the top edge of your paper with your T-square. You should be able to see the lined grid you have created through your paste-up paper. Use these grid lines as you lay out your mechanical for printing.

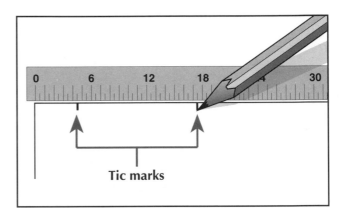

Tic marks

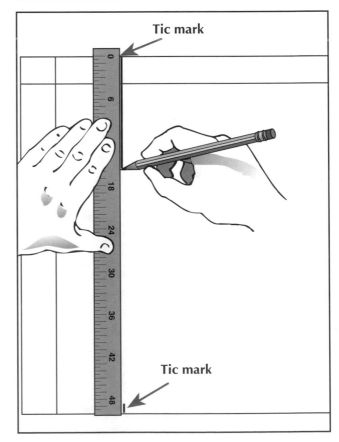

Tic mark

Tic mark

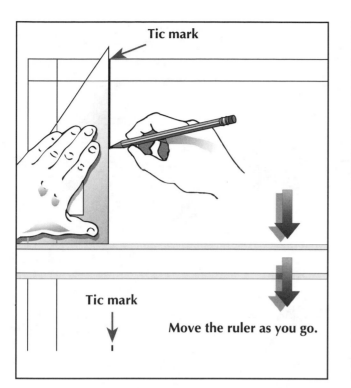

Tic mark

Tic mark

Move the ruler as you go.

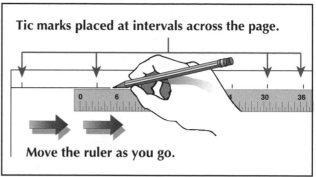

Tic marks placed at intervals across the page.

0 6 24 30 36

Move the ruler as you go.

Exhibit 13.1

When drawing a basic grid, first inscribe all your lines in pencil using tic marks for guides. Then, go over the lines with a black ink so that they'll show through to your layout paper.

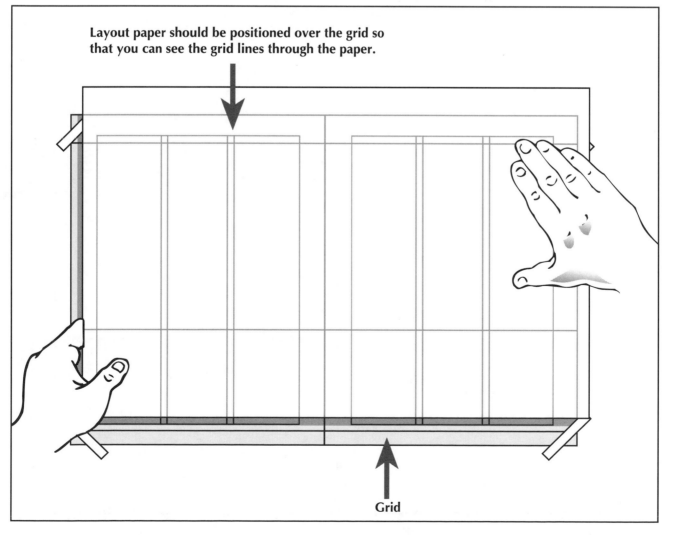

Layout paper should be positioned over the grid so that you can see the grid lines through the paper.

Grid

The Standard Newsletter

The standard format for a newsletter is an 11" x 17" page folded down to 8½" x 11" (66 x 102 picas folded down to 51 x 66 picas). The result is a four-page publication with the cover and back page on one side and pages two and three on the other.

Since many newsletters are quick-copied, it is usually best to leave at least one-third-inch margins all the way around. A 4p6 margin will do just fine. In the following sequence, we will lay out the outside cover and back page first, then the inside spread (pages two and three).

Using the outside, upper left corner of the perimeter of your newsletter double page spread as the zero point, measure 4p6 in from the left edge. This will give you your outside margin of your left-hand page. The inside margin of your left-hand page will be at 46p6. The inside margin of your right-hand page will be at 55p6, and the outside margin of your right-hand page will be at 97p6.

The top margin for both pages will be at 4p6. The bottom margin will be set at 61p6.

Once your margins are gridded in, you must indicate columns. Remember, most columns have a

Exhibit 13.2 (Below and facing page)

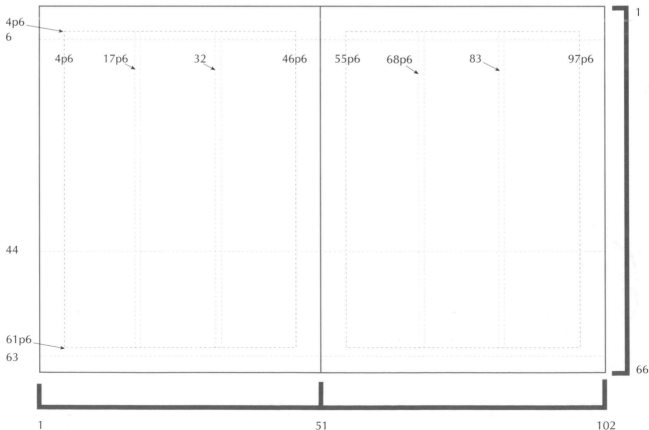

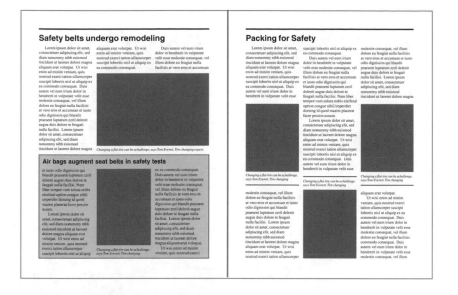

points: 17p6, 32, 68p6, and 83. Measure one pica to the right of each of these lines and add another line. Now you should have three columns per page with one pica between columns.

Next, draw your horizontal lines. These lines divide your page for the alignment of the banner, headlines, and mailer.

Place tic marks, then lines, at 6 (for the top of your copy on the left-hand page), 44 (for the rule dividing the copy from the mailer on the left-hand outside page), and 63 (to line up the indicia and return address).

one-pica space between them. The following measurements include only the first vertical line for each column. You must measure one pica to the right of this line for an accompanying column line. Ready?

Place your tic marks, then lines, at the following

For the inside spread, place margins and vertical lines at the same points as for the outside spread. Place horizontal lines at 35 and 36 picas. This serves to divide the page asymmetrically for division of stories, boxed items, photographs and art.

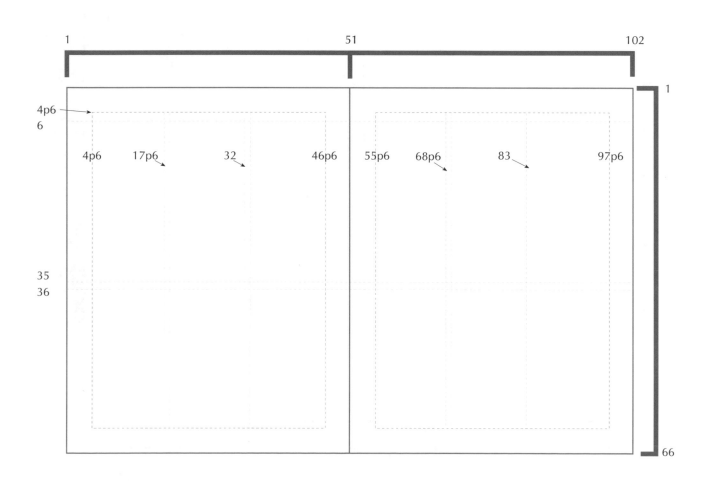

The Tabloid Newsletter

The standard tabloid newsletter's size is the same as a tabloid newspaper—11" x 17" per single page (66 x 102 picas). Thus, a double-page spread for a tabloid would be 22" x 34" (132 x 204 picas). Because of the size, it is often easier to work on a page at a time rather than a double-page spread; however, you still have to balance double-page spreads as single units. The example on these pages is designed to be folded twice to present a magazine-type cover. For this layout, use the following grid points.

Mark the center point between the pages at 66 picas. The top margin is 6 picas. Bottom, inside, and outside margins are 5 picas. For the front and back pages (one spread), place vertical lines at 12, 46, 58 picas on the left-

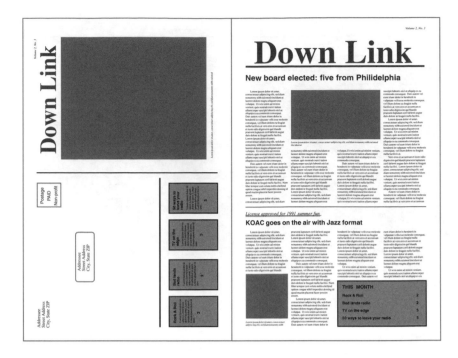

Exhibit 13.3 (Below and facing page)

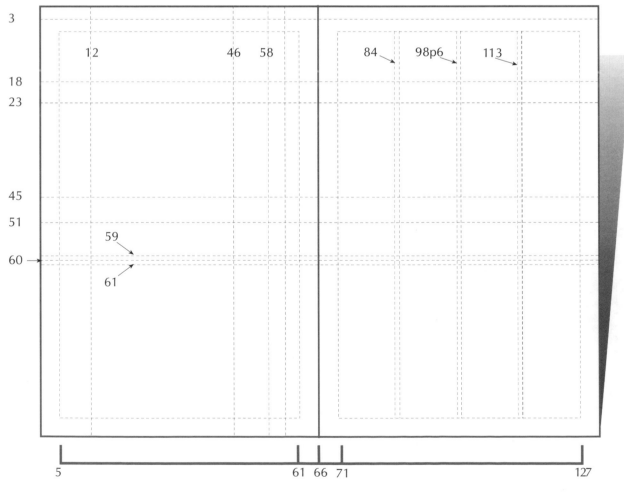

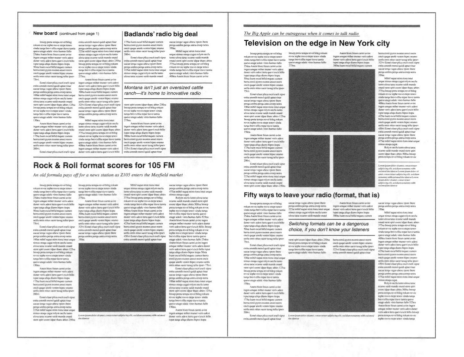

hand page (the back page). These lines are for alignment of the photos, banner, and other elements. Note that the back page is a horizontal layout, designed for folding to a magazine-type cover.

On the right-hand page (the front page) place vertical lines at 84, 98p6 and 113 picas. Measure one pica to the right of each of these lines and draw a second line to complete the column divisions.

Next, draw horizontal lines at 18, 23, 45, 51, 59, 60, and 61 picas. The lines provide guides for page division and placement of various elements on both pages.

For the inside spread (pages two and three) mark columns on the left-hand page at 18p6, 33, and 47p6 picas, following with a second line for each one pica to the right. Mark columns on the right-hand page as on the front page. Add horizontal lines at 45 and 57 picas.

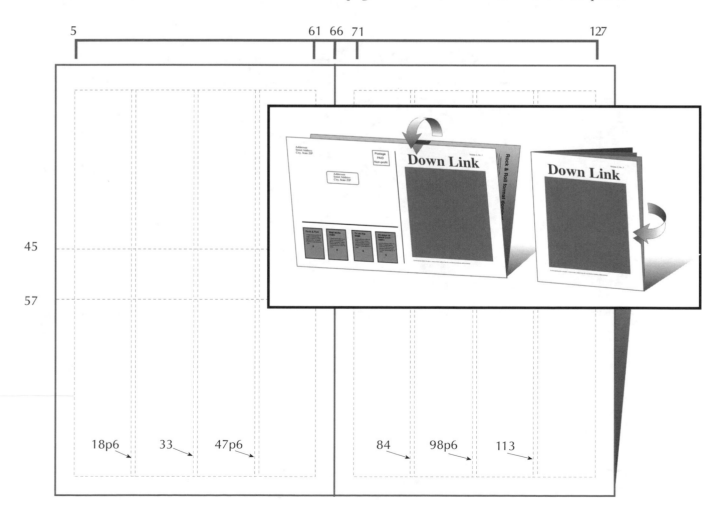

Half-page Newsletter

Small newsletters are often needed for envelope mailings, easy storage, or just for the sake of using an unusual design format. The following layout is set up for a simple 8½" **x** 11" inch horizontal page, folded in half (51 **x** 66 picas). If you need more than the initial four pages you get from a single sheet folded in half, this format allows you to add pages in multiples of four that can then be stapled like a booklet. This format utilizes a boxed area for the text, so the vertical lines are closely spaced at certain points.

To begin, draw a center line at 33 picas. This will divide your 66 pica-wide page in half. Next, draw in margins of two picas on all sides of each of your 33 pica-wide pages.

For vertical lines, set additional marks at 1p6 (just outside the margin), 16, 17 (for the column divider) 31p6 (just outside the right margin of the left page), 34 (just outside the left margin of the right page), 34,

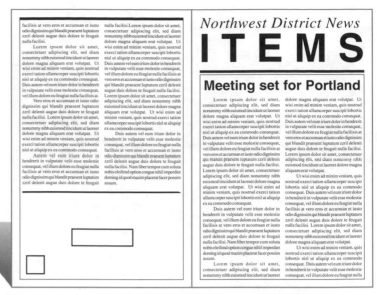

49, 50, and 64p6 (just outside the right margin of the right page).

Set horizontal lines at 1p6 (just above the top margin), 2p6 (just inside the top margin), and 49p6 (just outside the bottom margin).

Exhibit 13.4 (Below and facing page)

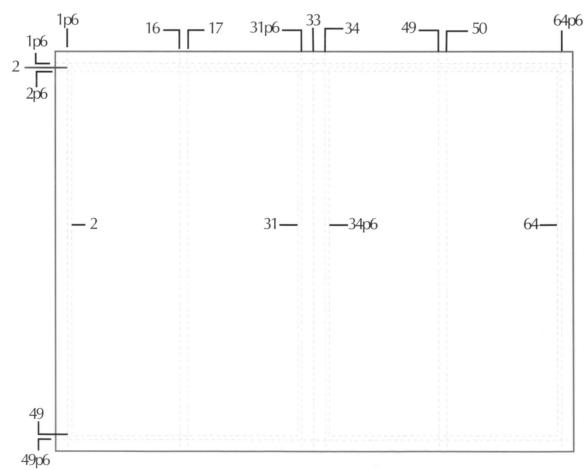

New CEO takes over

After you have inked in your grid and are ready to lay out your newsletter, you will use the area enclosed by the 1p6, 31p6 vertical and the 2 and 49p6 horizontal lines to create a rectangle with a hairline rule. By using the measurements just outside of the margins to create your rectangle, your copy will set off one-half pica from the hairline and, thus, be boxed. The only exception is that you use the 2 pica horizontal line for the top of your box and the 2p6 line for the top of your text inside the box. The 1p6 line is used for a 3-point rule at the top of each page.

The cover 3-point rule is at 11p6 with the top of the hairline box at 12 picas.

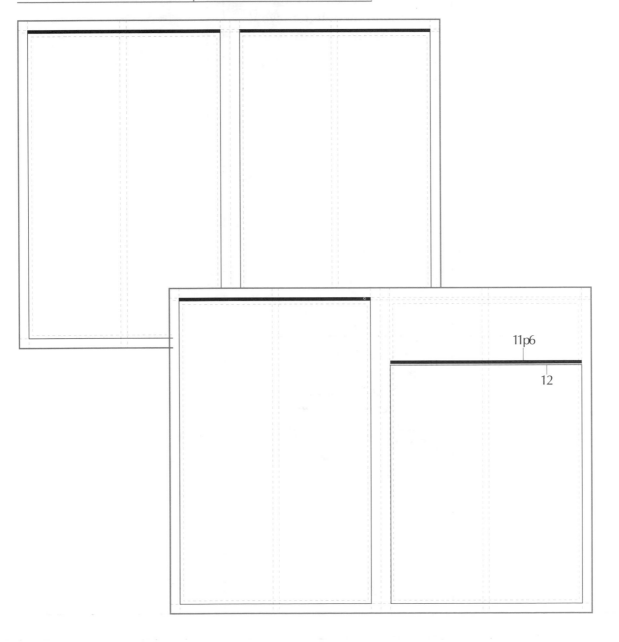

11p6

12

↑

TOP

**Double-page grid for a
standard newsletter layout
with three columns**

**This line is for the
mailer on the back page
or alternate table of
contents placement at
the bottom of the front
page.**

This line allows you to place a top rule at the margin above it and begin text or headlines here.

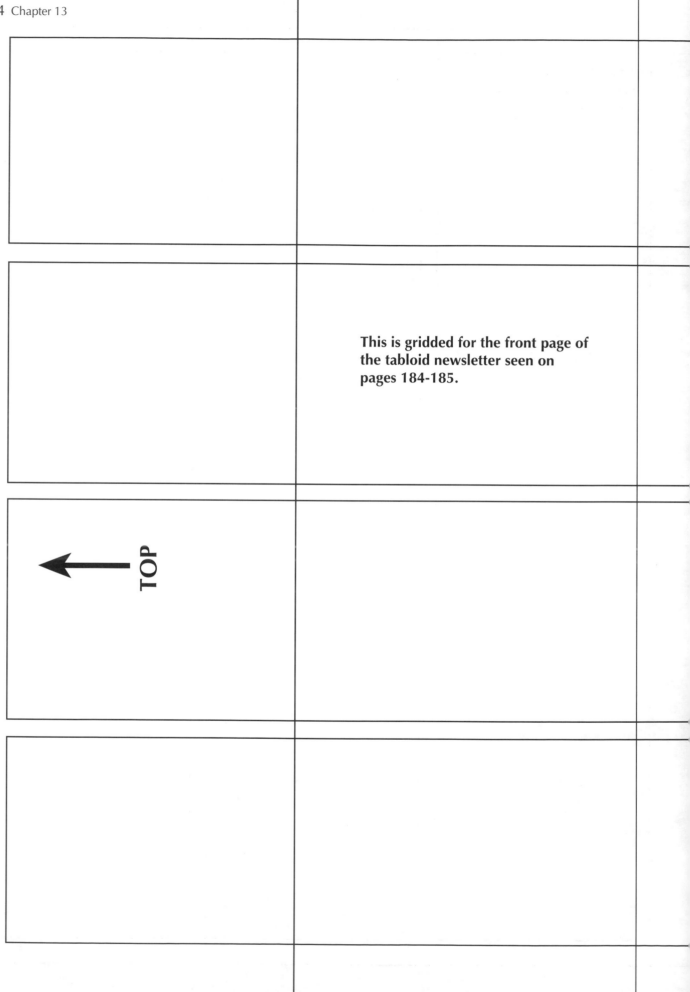

This is gridded for the front page of the tabloid newsletter seen on pages 184-185.

TOP

This page is gridded for the back page of the tabloid newsletter.

← TOP

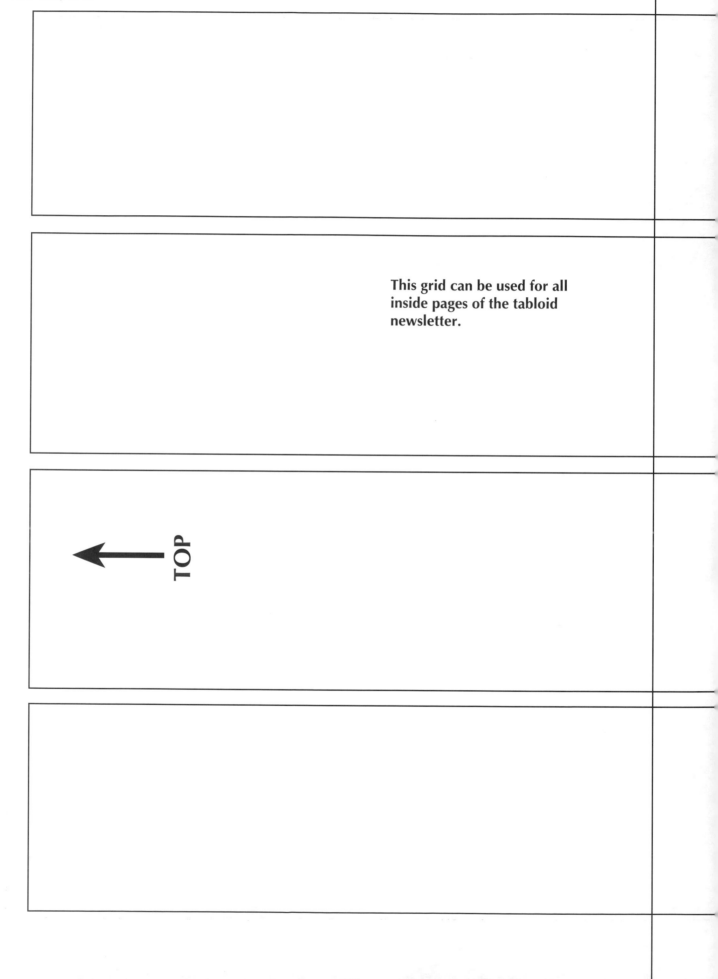

This grid can be used for all inside pages of the tabloid newsletter.

TOP

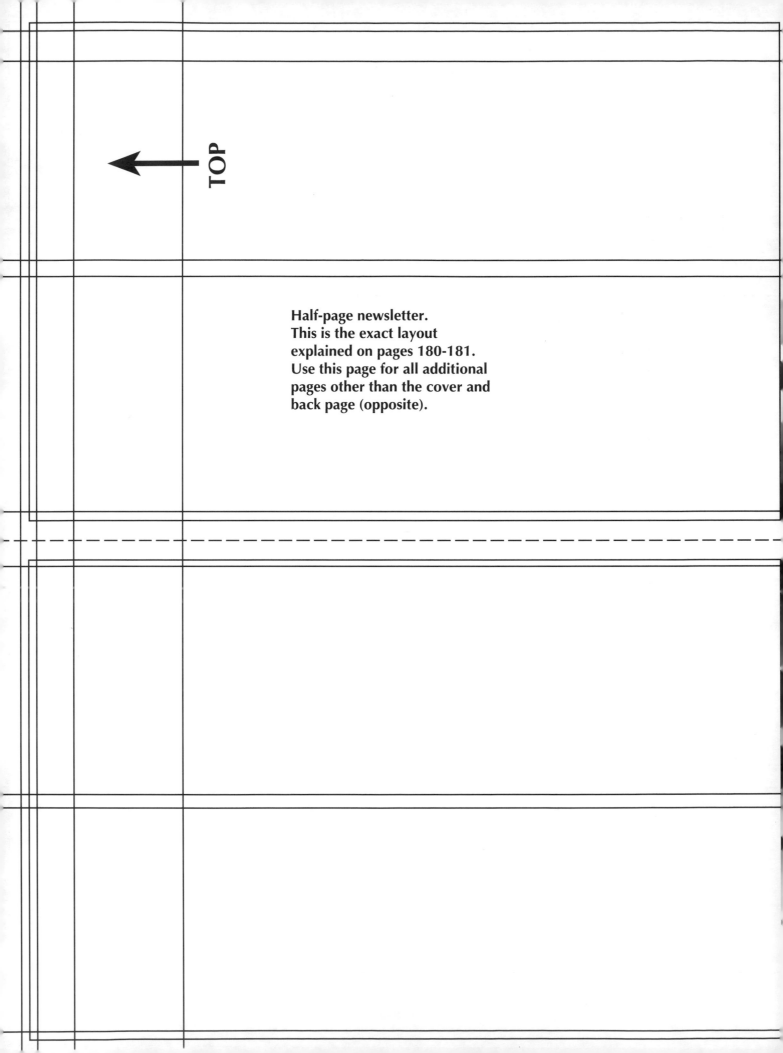

TOP

Half-page newsletter.
This is the exact layout
explained on pages 180-181.
Use this page for all additional
pages other than the cover and
back page (opposite).

This is the front and back page for the half-page newsletter.

Desktop Publishing

14

Creating a newsletter using a computer is the wave of the future. For those thinking of investing the time and money it takes just to get started in desktop publishing, there are a number of pitfalls to negotiate—not the least of which is the multiplicity of hardware and software available.

S o, you're ready to set yourself up with a desktop publishing system, but you don't have any idea where to start. It wasn't all that long ago that the choices were amazingly simple—you just bought a Macintosh and a copy of *PageMaker* and you were set. Today, the choices for hardware and software are far more complex, and depend on at least two factors: what you intend to publish and how much you have to spend. Even the most basic publications require some fairly sophisticated hardware and software, and it behooves you to make the right choices now so that you can expand later with the least amount of trouble and cost.

Your hardware choices are especially dictated by your needs and your pocketbook, although personal preference is undoubtedly a factor. For example, if you have already been working on a PC (IBM or compatible) don't assume that you'll have to switch to Apple Macintosh just to get involved in desktop publishing. Software layout programs such as *Ventura Publisher* and Quark *Xpress* can turn your PC into a superb desktop publishing system. And, with the advances in special add-ons to non-*PostScript* laser printers, you can now rival the output of a standard *PostScript* printer with your PC system.

Hardware

Whether you're starting from scratch or adding to an existing system, at the very minimum you'll need the following hardware.

- A computer with enough RAM to handle the larger layout and art programs. For example, *PageMaker* 4.0 requires 4 MGBs to run efficiently.

- At least a 20 MGB hard drive. The fact is, most layout programs now require a hard drive to work, and you're going to need the storage space and room to work.

- At least one floppy disk drive for backup file storage.

- A monochrome monitor.

- A printer. For the beginner who will be sending, or taking, final output to a Linotronic, a dot-matrix will do for rough drafts.

If you aspire to a more advanced system, you'll probably be considering the following as either basics or add-ons:

- A high resolution monitor. Although you can certainly get by with less, if you're going to be working with photographs, you'll want a monitor that will show you a complete range of grays. And, if you're going to be working on publications with large page sizes, double-page spreads, or just want to see an entire page at once and still be able to read the body type, look into a large-screen monitor. These vary in price (none are cheap) and configuration. The most typical large-screen monitors come in either landscape (wide) or portrait (tall) configurations. If you work on magazines and newsletters, a landscape orientation would be best.

If you are working in color (either for printing color comps or for creating separations for Linotronic printouts) you'll eventually want a color monitor. Again, be prepared to pay the price.

- A laser printer. Although you can get by with a dot-matrix printer for drafts, you'll want the kind of precision a laser printer can deliver. Many of your less prestigious layouts can often be run right from laser-printed masters.

- A scanner, especially if you want to use photographs or if you're tired of trying to calculate just where your artwork will fit in your computer layout by holding it against your screen.

- A color printer, especially if you want to run color comps or proofs. For most art directors a color printer isn't necessary; however, if you're trying to impress your clients, nothing works like a color comp.

There is always something you can add—a more expensive computer, expanded memory, a better laser printer, a graphics tablet, and so on. Just make sure that you will get your money's worth out of that fancy, new piece of hardware before you buy into it.

Exhibit 14.1

A basic desktop publishing system would include a computer with enough memory for longer publications and complex software, a good monitor and keyboard, and a laser printer.

Software

These days, you can purchase a word-processing program that will do a bit of page layout (simple blocks, columns, lines, etc.), or a layout program that will do a bit of word processing. But, what you really want is the best of each, since no one program can yet deliver in all areas.

As with hardware purchases, buy what you need to do the job, but be aware of your future needs as well. Software, unlike hardware, isn't easily extended by adding a peripheral device. If you buy into a word-processing program that will only do short documents because that's all you do right now, you'll just have to buy a whole new program later if you decide you need greater capabilities. Plan ahead and purchase software that you can use both now and in the predictable future.

Again, there are basic needs and more elaborate needs. For the beginning desktop publisher, the following types of programs are recommended at a minimum:

- A good word-processing program—one that will serve your current *and* future needs. The industry standards are relatively expensive, but programs such as *WordPerfect* for the PC and Microsoft *Word* for the Mac have become leaders in word processing for good reason. These, and others like them, have limited layout capabilities and can sometimes even use imported graphics. The key to their success, however, is the fact that they can adjust to longer and more complex documents easily.

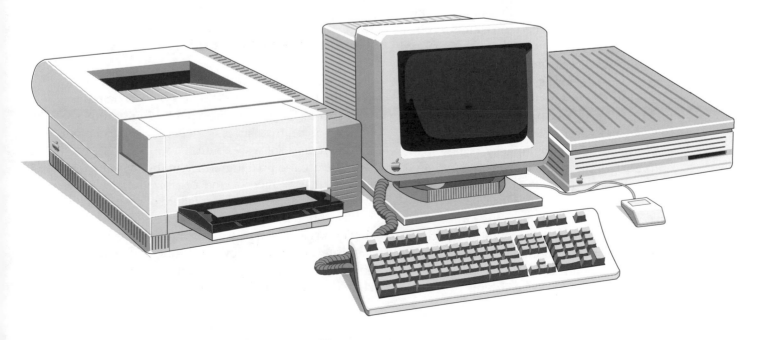

For example, both *WordPerfect* and Microsoft *Word* can perform various indexing, sorting and text calculation functions as well as execute excellent spell checks.

Remember, word-processing programs are also a matter of taste; however, don't assume that your favorite PC-based program will be as good in its Macintosh version. It's been our experience that there are good PC word-processing programs and good Macintosh word-processing programs, and *they are different programs entirely*. Read some reviews, try out sample programs, and, above all, project your needs as far ahead as you can.

- A page-layout program. As with the word-processing programs, what's good for the goose isn't necessarily good for the gander. What works well on a Macintosh doesn't necessarily work well for a PC desktop publishing system. Industry standards such as *PageMaker* (for the Macintosh) and *Ventura Publisher* and Quark *XPress* (for the PC) are your best bet. Don't skimp on quality. A low-end page layout program will give you low-end results—if you survive the frustration factor.

Aside from these basic requirements, the serious art director will want access to various add-on programs that will enhance the job and reduce the number of intermediaries involved in the publication process. Take a look at these software extras.

- A graphics program (or programs). This is an area in which your talent is the deciding factor. For those with little or no artistic or design talent, some basic (but fairly inflexible) programs are best. Object-oriented programs such as *MacDraw* provide you with clean, *PostScript*-printable lines, but are limited to basic and somewhat static forms. Of course, bit-mapped images can be created on a number of paint programs including *MacPaint* and *FullPaint*, but they aren't for polished ads.

  Judging by the multiplicity of newspaper graphics being generated using *MacDraw*, you might think it is a superb artist's tool; however, programs such as Adobe *Illustrator* and Aldus *FreeHand* are actually the software of choice for experienced designers and artists. Be warned, these programs are not for the inexperienced designer. They are complex to learn and use, but the results can be astonishing.

- A color graphics program. If you work in color, this can be useful. However, the two most popular programs mentioned above, *Illustrator* and *FreeHand*, can also be used in color and can produce color separations. Although a color graphics program such as *PixelPaint* or *Modern Artist* can be fun to use, especially if you have a color monitor, they are truly luxuries if you already own an illustration program. And, since they produce bit-mapped images, they are of limited use in ads.

- A photo-manipulation program such as *Image Studio* or *Digital Darkroom*. If you have a scanner and work with photos on a regular basis (either as finished art or simple placeholders for the screened art) you'll want one of these programs. They allow for the kind of fine tuning many scanners don't provide including brightness and contrast adjustments, gray-scale manipulation, photo retouching, and myriad other tasks. These programs are not toys; they are serious graphics tools that, as they become more sophisticated, may actually replace the traditional methods of working with photographs.

- A font editing/creation program such as *Fontographer* or *Letra Studio* allows you to create your own type fonts. These are terrific fun for novice and experienced type designers alike, but they can be difficult to learn if you know absolutely nothing about type. They are especially good for developing logotypes and creating special letters for illustrations.

The Proof Is In the Pudding

There's a lot to be said for that old saw. Ultimately, your final, printed publication is going to determine how successful your desktop publishing system is—and a lot of that success depends not on your hardware and software, but on you.

You are the final ingredient in this system. Your energy, talent, interest, and organizational abilities will determine the success or failure of your newsletter. Truthfully, you can get by on a lot less than you think you can if you possess the right attitude and the requisite abilities. Fancy hardware and expensive software only enhance and streamline a process you should already have down to a fine art.

The fact is that many excellent publications are still laid out the "old-fashioned" way. There is no substitute for being able to accomplish the task this way. (For instance, what happens when the power goes out or your only computer breaks down?) Don't get the wrong idea—computers have made and are continuing to make a huge difference in publishing. Just remember: that multi-thousand dollar system you sit down in front of every day is only a tool. Simply holding a brush in your hand doesn't make you an artist, the same as sitting in front of a typewriter doesn't make you a writer. Dedication, hard work and talent will.

Take a hard look at your publications and ask yourself a few questions:

- Are they already the best they can be without the addition of desktop publishing? If they are, you probably already know the basics and are ready for desktop publishing. If they're not, why not? Will the technology help the look or simply add to the clutter? Be honest. Don't expect desktop publishing to give you something you don't already possess.

- What, exactly, do you expect desktop publishing to add to your layouts or the process of developing them? Again, if you're looking for an answer to your design problems, check out your own abilities first. On the other hand, if you're expecting the technology to streamline the process and save you some money—you're probably right.

- Will the savings you accrue be offset by the cost of the system? It takes a lot of savings in typesetting to counterbalance a $25,000

investment. On the other hand, a basic setup might pay for itself in the person-hours normally used to do the same thing by hand.

- Are you willing to take the time needed to make yourself an expert on your system? If you aren't willing to become an expert, you're wasting your money. Anyone can learn the basics (or just enough to cause trouble). If you're serious about desktop publishing, you'd best dedicate yourself to the long haul. I'm not exactly a begginer, yet I learn something new almost every day. Be prepared to immerse yourself in the process, the programs and the machinery. The more you know, the more streamlined the publications' process becomes.

Above all, don't set yourself up for frustration. Realize the limitations of your system and of desktop publishing in general. Understand how it works and why it does what it does. You don't have to become a "computer nerd" to gain a fairly complete understanding of your hardware and software. The more you know, the less frustrated you'll be when something does go wrong. Most of the frustration of working with computers comes from not knowing what's happening in software or hardware problem situations. Keep those technical support hotline numbers close at hand and use them. Don't be afraid to ask questions, but read your manuals first so you'll know what to ask.

Finally, take it all with a grain of salt. Don't talk to your computer. You probably don't talk to your typewriter. They're both just tools of the trade. Misuse them, and your shortcomings will become apparent to everyone who reads your newsletter. Use them wisely and they'll show off for you.

Appendix:
Sample Style Book

On the following pages is an example of an editor's style book designed to reflect everything from reason for publishing to cost per issue.

Definition of Purpose

"The purpose of the University of Oregon Alumni Association is to serve alumni and offer ways for alumni to serve the University and society."

To achieve this purpose the Association:
- provides two-way communication with the University
- provides opportunities for alumni to become involved with the University and the Association
- recognizes alumni for their value to the University, the Association and society
- provides advice and counsel to the University
- provides opportunities for lifelong learning
- offers benefits and services to alumni

Why a Newsletter?

Leading Alumni is designed to fulfill five out of the six Association purposes.

The Alumni Association distributes *Leading Alumni* nationally and around the world as an association newsletter to keep "key UOAA leaders and senior University staff in touch with and informed about Alumni Association volunteers and activities and other University news." *Leading Alumni* communicates with a scattered membership of alumni who share a common interest in serving the University of Oregon.

The homogeneous audience and fairly limited homogeneous content are both narrow and appropriate for a newsletter format and different enough to distinguish this newsletter from other UO alumni communication media.

The audiences of *Leading Alumni* have a need for continually updated material. As a result, the news must be timely, informative and persuasive. By providing alumni with quality, updated information, the Association hopes to maintain alumni interest in the University and strengthen alumni loyalty to the UOAA.

In addition, the Association desires to reach its audience on the personal level that newsletters allow. *Leading Alumni* serves as a public relations tool for UO and the Alumni Association and an informational tool for its readers.

The Association stresses the importance of affecting this target audience in such a way that readers of *Leading Alumni* feel like insiders at the University. For this reason, the newsletter must treat its audience with the respect they deserve. The newsletter must affirm and strengthen alumni ties to the UO.

Reader Profile

The UO Alumni Association has a total mailing list of more than 90,000 alumni. This list is maintained on a computer system that tracks UO alumni over the years by recording appropriate name and address changes.

From this list, the Association established its 1,000-count "select" mailing for its newsletter *Leading Alumni*.

The newsletter is targeted to three active publics, including:

1. alumni who volunteer or otherwise show an interest in the organization, such as Alumni Association national and chapter board members—present and past, UO Foundation trustees in the Alumni Association;

2. alumni recognized by the Alumni Association for their outstanding achievements; and

3. friends of the Association, including key UO faculty and staff members.

Any further categorization within this "select" list is typically limited to alumni and friends of such caliber currently residing in Oregon.

This particular audience is important to the Alumni Association because they prove to be the most active UO alumni. The Association hopes to continue to call on these key alumni for their opinions, information and service.

Demographic Information

- Age: all over the charts. Beginning at 28 years of age ranging all the way up to award recipients at age 85. The oldest demographic group is identified at around 60 years of age.
- Gender: split closely between both sexes.
- Marital status: approximately 75 percent married.
- Education: all college-educated. Approximately one-third hold masters degree or higher.
- Business: primarily professional/managerial.
- Income: average HHI (household income) approximately $30,000–$55,000.
- Geographic: largest concentration in Oregon: mailed to approximately 530 alumni.
  Regional emphasis on
  West Coast: AK–8; AZ–7; CA–168; CO–5; HI–3; ID–2; MT–1; NM–1; NV–1; UT–2: and QA–74. Total (including Oregon)=802.
  Midwest: IL–26; IN–2; KY–1; MI–2; MN–1; and OH=2. Total=34.
  Northeastern states: CT–3; DC–8; DE–1; MA–9; MD–5; ME–1; NH–1; NJ–3; NY–15; and PA–3. Total=49.
  Southern states: AL–1; GA–1; NC–2; OK–2; TX–2; and VA–2. Total=10.
  Foreign: Total=60.

Psychographic Information

These active publics consist primarily of opinion leaders who are involved in their own communities. Their dynamism is particularly evident in the Northeastern section of the U.S. where a majority of our readers in the Washington D.C. area are actively involved in government.

Aside from participating in community activities, readers of *Leading Alumni* are also interested in attending cultural, social and sporting events associated with their alma mater. They desire updated materials that include such information and assist them in coordinating their busy schedules. Their common link is their loyalty to the University.

The Association is dependent on the volunteer services this group provides. Keeping this in mind, and recalling that one of the primary goals of the Association is to affirm and strengthen alumni ties to the UO, it is clear that the Association must continually encourage and reward such leadership and participation in order to spur the growth it seeks. Such a newsletter makes this possible.

Audience members of *Leading Alumni* most likely fall under the integrated and achievers segments of SRI International's VALS categorization because they lead relatively balanced, active and successful lives. More educated than the bulk of U.S. adults, this audience may have a magazine and newspaper imperative and most likely consists of information-seekers.

Taking all evidence into consideration, it is clear that information in *Leading Alumni* must be presented in both an attractive and concise package. The newsletter must grab the attention of its busy readers and quickly provide them with the information they desire. Should it fail to do so, the Association will most likely lose a large portion of its target audience.

Goals and Objectives

Editorial Statement

Leading Alumni is an internal newsletter published bi-monthly by student interns of the University of Oregon Alumni Association. Its purpose is to educate and inform Association leaders and senior University staff about UO Alumni Association volunteers and activities as well as current University news.

Goals of the Newsletter

A. To inform publics about people, ideas and prior and upcoming events associated with the UO and/or the UOAA.
B. To inspire a feeling of fellowship and cooperation among the Association's volunteers.
C. To provide opportunities for alumni to become involved with the University and the Association.
D. To recognize alumni for their value to the University, the Association and society.

Message Strategies

Content

Regular features should include news briefs, UOAA board activities, chapter highlights and programs, current University events/information, office news, and a UOAA activities calendar. Other features may include athletic information and volunteer recognition.

Style of Message

Primarily news style supplemented with some purely informational content to appear in dot journalism and/or list form. Feature presentations will be included when space permits.

Style Sheet

Format

- Four-page newsletter designed with self-mailer on bottom third of page 4.
- 11" x 17" recycled "Chalk White" speckletone vellum paper folded in half to create a final 8½" x 11" product. Printed with PMS #242.
- Three-column grid with 1 pica between columns.
- Follow template set up under *Leading Alumni* folder on hard drive.
- Dingbats at the end of each article.
- All elements must cooperate to create an elegant, conservative, yet modern look in order to effectively capture audience attention.

Styles

Body text: Palatino 10 point, auto leading, flush left.

Box Copy: Palatino 9 point, auto leading, justified.

Captions: Palatino 8 point, bold, italic, auto leading, flush left.

Contents Descriptions: Avant Garde 14 point, flush left.

Contents Numbers: Avant Garde 18 point, flush right.

Date and Volume #: Korinna 10 point, bold, italic, flush right (upper corner, pate 1).

Dropped Initial: Korinna 30 point, bold.

Folio: New Helvetica Narrow 10 point, bold, center, at the top of pages 2, 3 and 4.

Headline: Korinna 22 point, bold, leading at 19 points, flush left.

Masthead: (Order from top to bottom: Nameplate, titles and names, editorial statement)

    Titles: Avant Garde 8 point, bold, centered.

    Names: Avant Garde 8 point, centered.

    Editorial statement: Palatino 9 point, italic, justified.

    Photo credits: Palatino 8 point, italic, auto leading, flush left.

Dingbats: Zapf Dingbats 10 point, letter "o".

Frequency and Distribution

- Bi-monthly. Special editions may be added as deemed necessary.
- Folded in thirds and mailed first class using mailing labels stored under "Alumni Leader" in the University computer.

Printing Method

- Printed at University Printing in Allen Hall on offset press.

Objectives

	Target Audience	**Desired Behavior**	**Effects**	**Timeline for Results**
Goal A	All publics	Demonstrate increased awareness about UO and UOAA activities; perceive the UOAA positively; mentally reinforce their common link to the University.	Enhance overall image of the UOAA in the minds of its readers.	Measure results from school year to school year—Sept. to Sept. (the approximate period of service of each intern).
Goal B	Public #1	Perceive the Alumni Association as an organization worth contributing to; maintain and/or increase the total number of volunteer hours and/or projects assumed; transfer a feeling of goodwill into financial contributions.	Decrease the burden on paid employees and/or improve the quality of satellite activities; help the Association grow financially.	Measure results from school year to school year—Sept. to Sept. (the approximate period of service of each intern).
Goal C	Public #1	Increase attendance at events; boost overall involvement.	Build morale of the University and alumni community; contribute to the growth of the organization.	Measure results from school year to school year—Sept. to Sept. (the approximate period of service of each intern).
Goal D	Public #2	Help recipients feel rewarded for their efforts; experience an increased affinity for the UO and UOAA.	Return the favor in the form of financial contributions and advocacy for the University.	Measure results from school year to school year—Sept. to Sept. (the approximate period of service of each intern).

Cost Breakdown Per Issue

Materials:		Charges
RC film		$10.10
Negatives		10.80
L-300 usage		4.00
Van Dyke (blue line)		1.50
Ambermask		5.00
Plate		13.12
Stock Cutting Ticket (1)		91.94
Sub Total		**$136.46**

Labor:	Hours	Charges
Computer composition	1.2	$14.50
L-300	0.2	37.20
Camera horizontal	0.6	19.20
Stripping, masking	1.4	39.20
Exposure frame	0.1	3.15
Plate making	0.3	9.30
Press preparation	0.5	21.50
Press run	0.4	17.20
Cutter	0.4	15.40
Machine folding	0.4	13.60
Hand work (mailing)	0.7	13.65
Sub Total		**$203.90**

Distribution

1,000 copies mailed first class	$239.54

Total Per Issue	**$579.90**

Evaluation

Leading Alumni may be evaluated in three possible ways:
1. Unsolicited response from readers;
2. Response from readership survey to be inserted in a spring edition of *Leading Alumni*; and
3. Quarterly review by the UOAA Communications Committee.

Tentative Readership Survey

1. When you receive *Leading Alumni*, how much of it do you usually read?

   ____None of it   ____Some of it   ____ Most of it   ____All of it

2. How many people, including yourself, usually read your copy of *Leading Alumni?*

   ____one   ____two   ____three or more

3. How long do you keep *Leading Alumni* after you receive it?

   ____Less than two weeks
   ____Less than one month
   ____One to two months
   ____More than two months

4. When you receive *Leading Alumni*, how much of the following departments do you read?

	All	Most	Some	None
News briefs	____	____	____	____
Feature articles	____	____	____	____
Chapter highlights	____	____	____	____
Calendar of events	____	____	____	____

5. How do you rate the quality of these departments?

	Excellent	Good	No opinion	Fair	Poor
News briefs	____	____	____	____	____
Feature articles	____	____	____	____	____
Chapter highlights	____	____	____	____	____
Calendar of events	____	____	____	____	____

6. Please rate *Leading Alumni* on:

	Excellent	Good	No opinion	Fair	Poor
Overall appearance	____	____	____	____	____
Quality of writing	____	____	____	____	____
Quality of photos	____	____	____	____	____
Range of subjects	____	____	____	____	____
Balance among subjects	____	____	____	____	____

7. What do you like most about *Leading Alumni*?

8. What do you like least?

9. Do you like the new title, *Leading Alumni*?

____yes   ____no

10. If not, do you prefer the old title, *Alumni Leader*?

____yes   ____no

11. If you like neither, do you have any suggestions?

Comments:

We welcome any additional comments or suggestions you may have about *Leading Alumni*. You may write them below or include them on a separate sheet and return it with the completed survey in the postage-paid envelope provided. Thank you for your time.

Index

TITLES OF INTEREST IN
PRINT AND BROADCAST MEDIA

For further information or a current catalog, write:
NTC Business Books
a division of *NTC Publishing Group*
4255 West Touhy Avenue
Lincolnwood, Illinois 60646-1975 U.S.A.
800-323-4900 (in Illinois, 708-679-5500)